Archaeology
of Bronze Age Mongolia

Archaeology of Bronze Age Mongolia

A Deer Stone Diary by William W. Fitzhugh

A co-publication of
Arctic Studies Center,
Smithsonian Institution
&
IPI Press

ISBN 978-1-7366902-8-4

International Polar Institute Press
Post Office Box 212
Hanover, New Hampshire 03755

Arctic Studies Center
Smithsonian Institution
National Museum of Natural History
Washington, D.C.

Distributed in North America by Casemate Publishers
and worldwide by Oxbow Books

Excavating horse head features at Bor Khujiriin Gol-1.

Contents

1. Preface and Introduction *13*

2. Research Problem and Rationale *19*
Ancient Mongolia and the Arctic. Searching for Influences on Early Eskimo Art. Mongolian Deer Stones: Meaning, Function, and Chronology.

3. Project History and Setting *29*
The Deer Stone Project. Bronze Age Ritual Landscapes. A Land Filled with Spirits.

4. Darkhad: Setting the Stage *37*
Deer Stones at Ulaan Tolgoi. Quarrying Deer Stones. The Erkhel Lake Granite Quarry. Volkov's Deer Stone Types. Early Dating Ideas. Dating Deer Stones at Ulaan Tolgoi. Stone Circles: Altars or Hearths?

5. Learning From Dukha: Reindeer, Ritual, and Religion *54*
Menge Bulag 2001-2004. Enroute to Minge Bulag. Dukha/Tsaatan—Mongolian Tuvans. Dukha Traditional Knowledge. Ovoo Worship Sites. Oliin Davaa. The Sailag Davaa Ovoo. Deer Stones, Dukha, and Shamans. Mongolia and Circumpolar Shamanism. A Shishged Sky Burial.

6. Deer Stone Ancestors *69*
Söyö: a Neolithic and Medieval Site. The Khogorgo Gol-3 Burial.

7.Defining Deer Stone-Khirigsuur Culture *76*
A Deer Stone at Tsatstain Khushuu. Ulaan Tolgoi II: Dating Deer Stones. Dating Horse Heads and Deer Stones: Post- or Pre-Scythian/Saka? Herodotus on Scythian Royal Burials. Deer Stones and Horse Ritual. Ulaan Tolgoi Khirigsuurs. Conservators Rescue Mound B Horse Head. Khirigsuur Form and Function. Herodotus Describes a Pontic Scyth Burial. Khirigsuurs as Chariots for the Dead. DSK Cultures, East and West: Steppe vs. Altai. Khirigsuur Size and Symbolism. Building the Deer Stone Story. Scanning Deer Stones: Science, Conservation, Documentation, and Preservation. Modeling Uushigiin Uvör Deer Stone 14. Laser Scanning Experiments. Looting: A Scourge on Heritage.

8. Chasing Deer Stones: Initial Surveys *115*

Transport Transitions. Gunj (Khairkhan). Square/Slab Burials and Repurposed Deer Stones: Sakhalt Khairkhan (Burdnii Ekh). Evdei-1: A Turkic Slab Memorial. Evdei-2: A Buddhist Enclosure Site. Evdei-3: Deer Stones. Erkhel Lake North. Khushuugiin Devseg. Khanuy Valley Excursions. Naadam Day Races. Urt Bulagiin. Gol Mod-2: A Royal Xiongnu Cemetery. Jargalant Am.

9. Following the Volkov Trail: The Darkhad Valley *143*

Shishged Surveys. The Darkhad Mongols. Ikh Davaa. Avt Mod. Shishged Rock Art Panel. Shishged-Khogorgo Rock Art. Kholboo Tolgoi-1. Kholboo Tolgoi-2. The Power of Smoke: Fragrance, Medicine, and Ritual. Zeerdegchingiin Khushuu. Targan Nuur. Sortiin Denj. Khort Azuur. Zuun Shuregtei. Tomst. Khyadag East. Herders Arrive. Khyadag West. Tugsoo Site.

10. On the Volkov Trail: The Northern Steppe *176*

Uushigiin Uvör. Bor Khujiriin Gol-1. Officials Arrive. Bor Khujiriin. Gol-2. Bor Khujiriin-3. Bor Khujiriin-4. Khushuugiin Gol-1. Khushuugiin Gol-2 and 3. Buyant Gol. Deer Stone Project 2009. Badrakhin Ovoo. Mongolia's Achilles Heel: Summer Water.

11. Following the Volkov Trail: Arkhangai *195*

Zunii Gol. Surprise Visit. Khushuugiin Am. Galt Surveys. Khuurain Bulangiin Tarkhi (Dry Corner). Khirigsuur Surveys. Nukhtiin Am-1. Nukhtiin Am-2. Nukhtiin Am-3. Khorkhog Feast. Teeliin Am. Shin Ider: Family Visit and Town Meeting. Tsokhiotiin Ovoo. A Freezing Summer. Duruljiin Am. Urd Khurain. Ikh Tamir. Tsatsiin Ereg 1, 2, 3. Shuvuutiin Am. 2009 Project Summary.

12 Intersecting Worlds: Eclipse of the Deer God *245*

Postscript *247*

A note on Mongolia, Nomadic Art, and Eskimo Connections.

Acknowledgments *253*

Appendix *263*

1. Radiocarbon Date List.
2. Smithsonian Museum Conservation Institute Slag Report for Finds from the 2008 Deer Stone Project Field Season.

References *271*

Prying Zunii Gol DS10 from its pit.

An ovoo at Salag Davaa pass in the mountain tundra west of the Darkhad valley. Dukha visit these remote worship sites every year to rebuilt the altars and make offerings that renew their ties to the spirits of such places. (photo: P. DePriest)

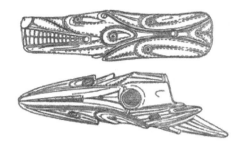

Scythian-Saka deer-feline image; Alaska Ipiutak walrus carving; Alaskan Old Bering Sea engraved hat ornament and harpoon head carved as a hunter's bird spirit helper.

1. Preface & Introduction

My connection with Mongolia and its deer stones began when I met Ed Nef at a cultural event at the Embassy of Canada in Washington, D.C. in the winter of 2001. Ed had served as the cultural affairs office at the U.S. Embassy in Ottawa but grew tired of political duties and the bureaucracy of State Department service. He was an activist and itched to see more progress than was possible or permissible as a mid-level diplomat. So he bailed out, and when the Soviet Union fell and Mongolia declared independence and opened relationships with the United States and other Western countries, he answered a US Government RFP requesting proposals for creating an English language school in Ulaanbaatar. He had already established a school in Washington that was teaching foreign languages to government and military people headed for overseas posts. "Why not add Mongolian to our list," he

thought. His proposal was accepted, and off he went to Mongolia to get the lay of the land and find English-speaking Mongolians who could teach in Arlington, Va. and in a new school in Ulaanbaatar.

The problem was that Mongolians, after several decades of Soviet domination, spoke Russian, not English, and the United States wanted Mongolians to learn English. On one of Ed's exploratory forays into the Mongolian countryside he traveled into the northern region known as the Darkhad Valley, a subarctic grassland west of Lake Khuvsgul that was underlain by permafrost left over from the last Ice Age. There he was introduced to a small band of reindeer herders known as Dukha, a branch of the Tuvan people living in Russia south and west of Lake Baikal. After spending a few days at their summer reindeer-herding camps in the Sayan Mountains west of the town of Tsaaganuur and Lake Khuvs-gul, seeing the Dukha struggling to shift from a socialist system to a Western capitalist without a social safety net, he offered to provide the group with twenty horses bought from ethnic Mongolian pastoralists in the nearby Darkhad Valley. Until then, Dukha had only their reindeer for transporting goods and people between their mountain camps and Tsaaganuur. Horses would make their lives easier, safer, and hopefully would enable them to continue their nomadic reindeer-herding way of life.

Ed had heard about my search for the origins of ancient Eskimo art in expeditions across northern Russia in the mid-1990s. "I think you should see the Bronze Age Mongolian deer stones," he told me. "You might be surprised. There is something strange about the art on those monuments. No one seems to know where they came from or what they mean. They are something like the pictures you showed me from the ancient Eskimo cultures." After seeing a few of Ed's pictures showing Scythian-like figures of Mongolian stags, I was hooked and agreed to join the expedition he was planning for the coming summer, 2001. "You'll see lots of deer stones, ride horses into the mountains to meet the Dukha (known in Mongolia as "Tsaatan", meaning reindeer people) herders—and their 95-year of shaman, Suyun." I had just completed a search for early Eskimo traces in Northern Siberia and had spent time with Nenets reindeer herders in Yamal where I met their shamans who had recently emerged from decades of persecution or death during the Soviet regime. Scholars had never figured out how reindeer became domesticated. Sevyan I. Vainstein (1980, 1981) believed it began in northern Mongolia or southern Russia among Tuvan forest peoples who were interacting regularly with Mongolian sheep and cattle herders in the grassy steppe to the south. There seemed to be lots to learn about the cultures and history of this former Soviet satellite—more than just its dinosaurs eggs discovered in the Gobi

Desert by Roy Chapman Andrews in the 1920s.

I had lots of reasons to say "yes" to Ed and within a couple of months I was on a plane to Ulaanbaatar along with Steven Young, an Arctic ecologist and ancient landscape expert. We joined Ed's team and the twenty horses he purchased from Mongolian herders and rode out from our camp at Söyö (translated as 'fang' because of the hill's conical shape) on the Khug (Melody) River with Dukha guides into the taiga, the mountain forests west of the Darkhad valley. I had never ridden a horse, but here I was, on a beast I could not control, swallowed up by the Siberian forest, venturing into the unknown searching for deer stones and ancient Eskimo connections.

In the pages that follow I lay out the rationale that led me, my Mongolian partners, and our students to thirteen years of deer stone research in northern and western Mongolia between 2001-2013. Deer stones had been studied previously for their beauty and mystery beginning as early as the mid-19th century by Mongolian and Russian scholars who tried to decipher their art and symbolism but never found a way to date them accurately or to determine their meaning or cultural affiliation. Deer stones stood as 'silent stone warriors' throughout the Mongolian countryside, devoid of any known cultural context, and their origins were as mysterious as ancient Eskimo art. "They are our old stone men," a herder's ten-year old daughter told me, "and have been here forever." I was determined to find answers that explained why they reminded me of the famous art of Iron Age Scythian warriors and the Old Bering Sea Eskimos. There had to be connections. I aimed to find out.

Perhaps it was fortunate that deer stone studies had fallen out of favor after the Russian scientist V.V. Volkov (1981 [2002]) published his monograph *Oleni Kamnii Mongolei (Deer Stones of Mongolia)* on his decade of studies in the 1970s. Volkov had catalogued the sites and published sketches of the art but was not able to solve the mystery of their age or relationships.

Unable to find large caches of archaeological treasure known from burials of later cultures, Soviet archaeologists turned to those cultures with huge cemeteries and glamorous artifacts. By 2001 it was time for new ideas and the application of new techniques like radiocarbon dating, laser scanning, environmental archaeology, and ethnographic analogy. We arrived in Mongolia at the right time, finding a cadre of young Mongolian students and professionals eager to learn Western research methods and anthropological theory.

the National Museum of Mongolia (NMM) to be a robust partner and worked closely with that institution for many years. My original archaeology field partner was the museum's curator, Ochirhuyag Tseveendorj, but after 2002 he decided to leave the field of archaeology to began a career in business. That summer he introduced me to his replacement, a young archaeologist named Jamsranjav Bayarsaikhan. "He's smart. You'll like him!" Ochirhuyag told me. We became fast friends and research colleagues.

The National Museum of Mongolia and some of our 2004 partners, (l-r) Paula DePriest, Ts. Ayush, Carolyn Thome, Paul Rhymer, Dr. Ayudain Ochir (NMM Director), and Bill Fitzhugh, standing in front of the Smithsonian gift, a replica of Uushigiin Uvör Deer Stone 14, created by Thome and Rhymer.

I turned to the National Museum of Mongolia to find a partner for the Deer Stone Project. Most western teams that began working in Mongolia after 2000 chose to work with the Mongolia Academy of Science's Institute of Archaeology, which had been created, like most Mongolian university and science institutions, following the scholarly structure of the Soviet Union, whose western science tradition, in turn, was a legacy of Peter the Great. I chose the National Museum because I wanted a partner that shared our interest in combining scholarly research with public education, exhibition, and collection care. I found

Over the years Bayaraa developed into one of the most productive archaeologists in Mongolia and a research partner to many archaeologists attracted to Mongolia because of its favorable research climate, open society, and research potential. Mongolia soon became known for having established a previously unknown pathway to civilization: the nomadic pastoral empire.

Bayarsaikhan spent his early years developing his career as a museum archaeologist, conducting field research as my Deer Stone Project partner, but also teaming up with a score of other archaeologists beginning to work in Mongolia, who, like me, found the museum a strong and reliable partner. In addition to our Bronze Age deer stone studies, Bayaraa researched other cultural periods ranging from the Paleolithic to historical times. Besides establishing a fine publication record in English and Mongolian, he mastered museum curatorial duties, developed exhibitions, and worked to establish sound cultural and archaeological policies for the Mongolian government. A few years after joining the NMM, he enrolled in the PhD program at the Mongolia National University under the guidance of Professor Erdenebat Ulambayar and Ts. Turbat, and after completing his training began working on a PhD thesis synthesizing knowledge on the Late Bronze Age deer stone culture, building his dissertation from the data we spent a decade collecting from central and northern Mongolia. All our data, jointly collected and published in articles and in the Smithsonian Arctic Studies Center's annual Deer Stone Project Field Reports (Mongolia Field Reports (si.edu)), as well as data Bayaraa developed on his own became grist for his deer stone thesis.

Bayarsaikhan's thesis was published in Mongolian in 2017 and appeared in English translation as *Deer Stones of Northern Mongolia*, published by the Arctic Studies Center as the first of a two-part synthesis of the Deer Stone Project, of which the present book is Part II. His monograph is the most detailed, most analytical, and most interpretive study of the deer stone art since the pioneering studies of Volkov and his research partner E. A. Novgorodova. Bayarsaikhan's monograph introduces us to that flamboyant, classical era of Late Bronze Age Mongolia by dissecting deer stone art, analyzing its motifs and elements and searching for its meanings and purposes. He does not include detailed studies of the flip-side of DSK ceremony and ritual—the archaeological context of deer stones and the khirigsuur (burial mound) part of the mortuary-ceremonial system. That task, as well as further analysis of the deer stone phenomena, is the purpose of the current volume.

What has been missing, and still remains missing, is information on the utilitarian, non-ritual, non-mortuary side of what Bayaraa and I have called the 'Deer Stone-Khirigsuur Complex', in other words, its foodways, clothing, domestic artifacts, dwellings, metallurgy, herding equipment, trade, military, and political life. These aspects of LBA Mongolia are still mostly unknown, other than the certainty that the economy was based on nomadic pastoralism of sheep, goats, horses, camels, and bovids. LBA technology is known mostly from finds looted from mounds, and from the few domestic sites that have been

Jamsranjav Bayarsaikhan recording rock art at Khoton Nuur in the Mongolian Altai; Richard Kortum at the Biluut site; and Paula DePriest mastering the art of camel-riding.

discovered and excavated. The ephemeral, elusive nature of the whole culture of which the DSK is a part can be attributed to the nomadic lifestyle of its people and the lack of permanent settlement and architecture that has hindered archaeological discovery. As a result, what we know comes mostly from deer stone and khirigsuur ceremonial sites. Only recently has more detailed information on Late Bronze Age domestic activities begun to appear at traditional winter camps where herders returned to the same sheltered locations year after year (Houle et al. 2022).

Because Bayarsaikhan's thesis is a synthetic study based largely on deer stone art and symbolism, much of the field data collected during our expeditions is not included. It seemed useful, therefore, to prepare a parallel work that provides site descriptions, information on excavations and finds, environmental data, and field observations that add to the corpus available for contextualizing Bayarsaikhan's more deer stone-focused study. Some of this primary data has been included in journal publications, but it is most comprehensively reported in the Arctic Studies Center's annual field reports (https://repository.si.edu/handle/10088/105380/recent-submissions). These reports include a narrative diary of each expedition season from 2001 to 2012, including information on the events, weather, landscapes, travels, and people met during each project. They also include archaeological fieldnotes, GPS locations, collection lists, excavation maps and profiles, technical studies, radiocarbon date lists, and results of expedition projects in botany, ethnography, rock art, mound surveys and many others. Although published on-line through the Smithsonian Library, they are not easily accessed, and many site reports span several reporting years. Therefore, I have abstracted salient data from these reports to build composite site descriptions and preliminary results for each site. Interspersed with these descriptive notes I have added, in italics, sections dealing with thematic issues such as ethnographic descriptions, shamanism, land-scapes, interviews with herders, commentaries on controversial ideas or interpretations, personalities, and other topics that paint a broader picture and give flavor to our experiences as we conducted our studies from year to year.

The need to consolidate work done at some sites over several years has complicated the task of building this story into a single report or trajectory. Each year we would travel from UB to the Darkhad valley, visiting sites along the way before beginning our excavations, generally starting in the north and proceeding south, eventually reaching UB at the end of the season. In the early years we visited the Dukha reindeer people soon after arriving in the north, but after discovering that deer stones and khirigsuurs are restricted to the steppe zone and are not present in the taiga forest, we had to say goodbye to our Dukha friends and worked thereafter in the open steppe lands home to ethnic Mongolian herders. Nevertheless, we found our ethnographic experiences with the Dukha so important for understanding DSK culture and deer stones that I have included these experiences and the archaeological finds from the taiga in the first section of this report. In addition, because of the multi-year nature of our site visits, I have condensed the results of multi-year work at sites like Avtiin, Khort Azuur, Ulaan Tolgoi, Khushuutiin Devseg, Khushuugiin Am, and others into single descriptions to avoid confusion and to make the reporting as comprehensive as possible.

More problematic has been the task of integrating fieldwork done be American and Mongolian members of our combined team working in different parts of the same sites, which often resulted in two sets of notes and maps in Mongolian and English language. Inevitably this has led to discrepancies in the numbering of deer stones, khirigsuurs, and their respective features. I have tried to resolve these problems by relying on Volkov's and Bayarsaikhan's deer stone number designations. However, it is likely that some discrepancies have been carried into this report,

A blind Dukha woman presenting a gift to Ed Nef on behalf of the West Taiga Dukha people for his donation of horses to the community, and her Minge Bulag camp relatives in 2001. Ed has written about his interesting life in an auto-biography titled Life Out Loud: a Memoir of Countless Adventures and No Regrets *(Nef 2020)*

so future researchers should be forewarned. Designations given in the field and present in field notes, have been changed in this report to conform as best as possible to identifications used by Volkov and Bayarsaikhan. For these reasons, it has not been possible to fully integrate both sets of data, Smithsonian and Mongolian. Apologies are in order, but funds and language barriers routinely result in such problems.

Despite incongruities, we believe these two parallel treatises, my *Mongolian Deer Stone Diary* and Bayarsaikhan's *Deer Stones of Northern Mongolia*, like deer stones and khirigsuurs themselves, add up to more than their separate parts. For non-Mongolian readers, it is important to understand something of the culture and environmental context of Mongolia—for instance, the continuing importance of horses and nomadic life; Mongolian attitudes about khorhag; traditional beliefs about the medicinal qualities of certain organ meats and plants; why Mongols and Dukha (also known locally in Mongolian language as 'Tsaatan' or reindeer people) continue to build and ritualize ovoos; and more. These

and other descriptions covered in the overview volume, while not integral to Bayarsaikhan's analyses, provide the reader of his archaeological interpretations a basis for understanding his interpretation of shamanic connections, mythology, and traditional Mongolian culture. In the end, I believe both studies support and augment each other and can be considered like a pair of geese crossing a quiet lake or flying together more comfortably than either would be traveling alone.

There is still much to learn, but we hope to have 'moved the needle' to a new interim place, farther down the path than Volkov ventured, ready for another new synthesis at some future time.

Thank you, Ed Nef, for bringing us together and the inspiration to make our work possible.

Author's Note: Unless otherwise credited, illustrations and graphics are the author's, the Smithsonian's, or open access. For frequently credited illustrations I use JB for Jamsranjav Bayarsaikhan, PDP for Paula DePriest, HFB for Harriet (Rae) Beaubien, BF for Bruno Frohlich, JC for Julia Clark, BB for Barbare Betz, and KR for Richard Kortum. Captions follow the same sequence of the illustrations they describe.

2. Research Problem & Rationale

19th century southwest Alaska Yup'ik ceremonial mask from the Lower Yukon River. (Smithsonian Institution)

Ancient Mongolia and the Arctic

Most people do not see Mongolia as an Arctic or even a northern nation. Its eastern and southern (Gobi) regions are deserts, hot in summer and cold in winter. Yet, with much of its land at elevations above 4000 feet, Mongolia has many characteristics that can be considered Arctic. Mongolia's elevation has contributed to human biological and cultural adaptations that are similar to those of more northern regions—a nomadic life and settlement pattern, light mobile housing, reliance on hunting and gathering, minimalist technology, flexible social organization, and shamanist religion. The most compelling evidence for northern connections comes from their physical resemblance to Eskimo peoples of Alaska and across Arctic North America (Szathmary 1984). These features include shovel-shaped incisors, broad faces with high cheek bones, short stature with robust musculature, cold-adapted circulatory system, and a short leg-torso ratio. Recent genomic studies provide more specific biological evidence of Northeast Asian-Eskimo ancestry (Flegontov et al. 2019; Sikora et al. 2019). Less easily quantified are psychological characteristics that those familiar with Eskimo and Inuit peoples see in Mongolian and Korean people. For these reasons, the Deer Stone Project explored the possibility that Mongolian Bronze Age peoples may have been involved in the spread of cultural materials and ideas that contributed to the foundation of early Bering Sea Eskimo cultures, as outlined in one of our early Deer Stone Project reports:

One of the principal goals of the Deer Stone Project is to explore Mongolia's cultural, historical, and environmental relationships to northern Eurasia and the North Pacific. Therefore, at the outset it may be helpful to explain why Mongolia—a sparsely populated, nation of 2.5 million people located nearly 2000 km south of the Arctic Circle—might have some bearing on Arctic issues like reindeer breeding, the diffusion of metal and other technologies, and the spread of peoples, ideas, and art around the northern world. In particular, as in the case of the peopling of the New World, the development of early Eskimo cultures in the Bering Sea has been profoundly influenced by the appearance of metal, shamanistic concepts, and new artistic traditions emanating from northern and northeastern Asia. However, one highly significant element of Eurasian Arctic culture did not cross the Bering Strait and enter Alaska: reindeer breeding. Although the spread of this technology resulted in a profound transformation of almost all Eurasian arctic hunters into herders and pastoralists, North America's Arctic and Subarctic peoples remained isolated from this powerful agent of change although they were subject to many other Siberian and East Asian influences. Bronze Age Mongolians may have had a role in these innovations and transmissions.

For more than 100 years archaeologists have searched without success for the cultural influences that contributed to Eskimo culture in Arctic regions, in the Bering Sea, and along the coast of northeast Asia from Japan to Chukotka. Although physical similarities between Eskimos and Mongolians suggests historical connections, Mongolia's remoteness and mid-20th century political isolation discouraged investigation of a possible role in North Pacific history. Today, with Mongolia accessible to Westerners for the first time since the 1920s, it has become possible to explore such questions as: Did Mongolia play a role as a center of population dispersal into Northeast Asia and Alaska? Was Mongolia involved in the development of reindeer domestication? And could its early cultures have been sources or transmitters of cultural information from Central Asia into the North Pacific region? (Fitzhugh 2003:4)

Mongolia's relations to the Arctic regions of Eurasia and potentially to North America during the past 15,000 years make it an important area for a wide range of environmental archaeology and cultural studies whose relevance range beyond Mongolia and its Eurasian Arctic connections to such topics as the peopling of the New World, origins of ancient Eskimo art, and the development of reindeer domestication. The fact that climate is warming in ways that may threaten Dukha/Tsaatan economic and cultural survival makes documentation of their reindeer husbandly system an urgent task. The effort led by Clyde Goulden of the Philadelphia Academy of Natural Sciences to document Khuvsgul's biotic and physical ecosystem, which he led to support its proposed designation as a World Heritage site, concentrated on biological rather than on cultural and historical studies. For that reason, our initial cultural studies in the Darkhad Valley in 2001-2006 contributed to a broader understanding of the Khuvsgul region, today and in the past.

Nayambayar, one of our Mongolian drivers, could pass for an Alaska Eskimo tourist in Mongolia! A frost-heaved pingo mound with a perennial ice core, an Arctic feature indicating subsurface permafrost, 2004.

Searching for Influences on Early Eskimo Art

Since the 1930s, archaeologists investigating the development of Eskimo cultures that developed about 2000 years ago in the North Pacific and Bering Sea region have suspected that key features including shamanic ritual, art, and religious concepts probably originated in Eastern Asia (Jenness 1933; Collins 1937, 1951; Schuster 1951; Schuster and Carpenter 1986). In particular, bone and ivory implements of the Okvik and Old Bering Sea (OBS) cultures, dating ca. A.D. 0-800, carry elaborate decoration illustrating hunting magic and animal-human transformation beliefs. While Okvik and early OBS engravings were carved with stone tools, OBS II and III, as well as the later Punuk culture (A.D. 700-1000), utilized metal engraving tools of Asian origin (Fitzhugh et al. 2009; Fitzhugh 2014b). While the East Asian sources of the art styles and motifs outlined initially by Henry Collins (1937, 1951, 1971) were prescient, few exact parallels are known outside the Bering Sea region. Among the more distinctive features are artifacts found in OBS burials like ivory chains and open-work carvings that were inspired by Asian bronze castings (Arutiunov and Sergeev 1975; Arutiunov and Fitzhugh 1988). Asian contacts are even more explicit in finds from the Ipiutak site in Point Hope, Alaska, where Larsen and Rainey (1948) found ivory composite death masks similar to Chinese Zhou composite masks of jade and nephrite (Collins 1971; Childs-Johnson 1998), and ivory and bone ornaments that were identical to metal ornaments used by Siberian shamans to decorate and empower their ritual costumes. Larsen and Rainey attributed many of the exotic forms to the introduction of a Siberian shamanistic complex and linked specific artifact types to the Permian Bronze and Iron Age of West Siberia. A few years later, Carl Schuster noted that these and other forms of early Eskimo art were instead probably related to the Eurasiatic animal-style art complex (Schuster 1951). Lacking a broader base of archaeological materials, dated finds, and contextual information from Siberia and the Far East, these theories were impossible to test and remained as alluring hypotheticals in circumpolar culture history (Fitzhugh 1998; 2002). Renewed interest in ancient Asian connections of Eskimo art has been stimulated by recent publications on ritual and iconographic evidence from Neolithic cultures of Northeast China dating to third and fourth millennium BC (Qu 2013, 2014, 2015, 2017, 2021). Similar elements in deer stone art—particularly animal transformation imagery—suggested that cultures of Bronze and Iron Age Mongolia may have played a role in the eastern spread of peoples and ideas.

The opening of Russia to Western scientists produced an opportunity for the author to collaborate with Russian archaeologists investigating Neolithic, Bronze, and Iron Age sites in the lower Ob River and Yamal Peninsula of Western Siberia during 1995-96. I had previously concluded that convergent development rather than trans-Atlantic contact was responsible for similarities between Scandinavia Younger Stone Age cultures and 4000-year-old Maritime Archaic cultures of Northeastern North America, and that neither had anything to do with Eskimo origins (Fitzhugh 1974, 1975). But Chernetsov's discovery of an early 'Eskimo-like' arctic maritime culture on the shores of the Kara Sea (Chernetsov 1935; Chernetsov and Mozhinskaya 1974) – the same find that prompted Larsen and Rainey to propose West Siberia connections at Ipiutak in the 1940s – needed re-evaluation. Chernetsov's 1930s claim was less suspicious when Larsen and Rainey published Ipiutak in 1948 than it is today, because it was then still believed that Eskimo culture might have developed from European Paleolithic cultures that moved into the Arctic via Scandinavia at the end of the Ice Age. Despite the fact that this idea was discredited in the 1950s and that no Eskimo traces were known from the intervening 3000 miles from Chuktoka to Yamal (Chard 1958, 1974; Fitzhugh 2002), no field studies had been done to confirm the absence of Eskimos from the remote central Russian arctic coast. Four years of field and museum studies with Russian Arctic colleagues Andrei Golovnev, Natalia Fedorova, and Vladimir Pitul'ko convinced me that Chernetsov's 'early arctic maritime culture' of Yamal was neither maritime nor proto-Eskimo (Fitzhugh 1998; Fedorova, Kosintsev, and Fitzhugh 1998; Pitulko 1991). Further, our studies of Permian Bronze and Iron Age artifacts demonstrated that their putative similarities to early Eskimo art were untenable based on stylistics, chronology, geography, and ritual. Subsequent research in Taimyr, along the Laptev Sea coast, and at an 8000-year old Mesolithic site on Zhokhov Island in the northeastern Laptev Sea (Pitulko 1991, 2003; Pitulko et al. 2004, 2012), have so far continued to bring negative results with regard to Russian Arctic coast origins of early Eskimo culture and art.

Deer Stone 4 from Ulaan Tolgoi site in Khuvsgul Aimag illustrating the iconic 'Mongolian Deer', a stag with the head and bill of a bird. (graphic: J. Bayarsaikhan)

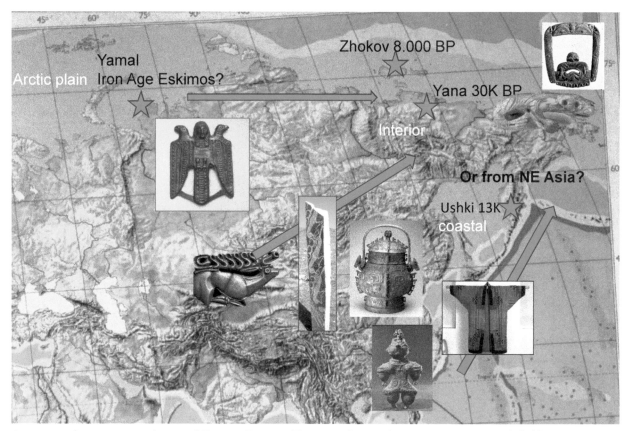

Ancient and recent art traditions of Eastern Eurasia. Tan coastal areas show Ice Age continental shelf areas.

In the meantime, research in the Bering Sea and western North Pacific (Powers and Jordan 1990; Dumond and Bland 1996) had identified Asian prototypes for a number of archaeological complexes and culture elements known in Alaska, including the likely origins of 4000 B.P. Arctic Small Tool tradition ceramics and lithic assemblages. However, work on such cultures as Tar'insk (Lebedintsev 1990), Lakhtina (Orekhov 1987), and Old Koryak (Dikov 1979), which are still relatively little known, has not revealed much that can be closely related to Old Bering Sea art and religion, even though many aspects of early sea mammal hunting cultures have been discovered. Neither, so far, have studies further south, around the mouth of the Amur, in Sakhalin, northern Japan, or Korea revealed prototype material related to Early Bering Sea art. Many of these East and Northeast Asian complexes do not have preserved organic remains, and without this crucial material, evaluating similarities remains extremely difficult. Added to the problem is that the early shorelines of Northeast Asia and Chukotka have been submerged by rising sea levels, making most ancient sites inaccessible.

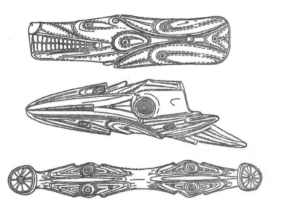

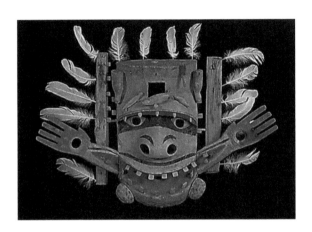

Liangzhou Neolithic ritual vessel 3400-2250 BCE. (Liangzhou Chinese Palace Collection); Old Bering Sea hunting ritual art on a hat ornament, harpoon head, and a pail handle. (Collins 1959); 19th c. Yupik Eskimo ceremonial mask; Old Bering Sea harpoon counterweight from the Chukotka site of Ekven; and composite burial mask from Ipiutak, Alaska (AMNH).

The one bright spot in this picture is information on the mask-like images of the Chinese Neolithic Liangzhu culture mentioned above (Qu 2014). Another relevant source of data is from Chinese rock art, especially face masks thought to date ca. 3000-1000 B.P. in the Lower Amur region and northern China (Okladnikov 1981; Song 1992, 1998), documenting a long tradition of body decoration, masking, and labret use. These practices, known also from Old Bering Sea and later Beringian cultures, are perhaps the most likely medium for links between Eastern Asia and the North Pacific-Bering Sea region. Another possible Asian technology connection may lie in the introduction of ground slate artifacts, which appear in Old Bering Sea, Northeast Asian, and Korean cultures about 2-3000 years ago, coincident with and possibly stimulated by the introduction of metal from Central Asian and Siberian sources. This introduction seems to have been independent from the earlier 6-4,000 year old Ocean Bay slate-grinding tradition of Southern Alaska and Kodiak Island. It seems likely that the Bering Strait cultures developed their ground slate tools as a substitute for prestige metal goods (knives, spear points, arrow points), as was the case with ceramic vessels and Old Bering Sea ivory chains, both styled after Siberian prototypes.

The decoration of ethnographic clothing from such groups as the Ainu, Nanai, Nivkh, and other Lower Amur River peoples, as well as those of Alaska and the Northwest Coast, may eventually be shown to be a legacy of earlier traditions of highly ornate clothing and body decoration of early East Asian and Pacific peoples (Fitzhugh 1988). Given the widespread evidence of body painting and tattooing, these artistic traditions of the northeast Asian maritime region are probably related to the decorative arts of Central Asia, especially as seen in the Scythian tombs of the Altai (Rudenko 1970; Gryaznov 1984; Polosmak 2000). Mongolia's deer stone monuments, which represent an early form of animal style art applied to a monumental human-form plinth attracted my interest because they occur geographically along a natural path of communication between Central Asia and the North Pacific coast, and because the Mongolian and South Russian Late Bronze and Early Iron Ages Pazyryk cultures date 1000 years earlier than Okvik and Old Bering Sea Eskimo and have similar shamanic, spiritual, and artistic traditions.

I do not propose a specific historical connection between Mongolia and the North Pacific peoples, but in 2001 it seemed useful to investigate the possibility that elements of Asian art, culture, and religion may have infiltrated the indigenous cultures of the North Pacific. This possibility is strengthened by genomic studies that suggest human biological affinities between Northeast Asians and Alaskan Eskimo peoples (Flegontov et al. 2019; Sikora et al. 2019). The specific artistic forms – whether they be Scythian, proto-Scythian, early Korean, Jomon, or others – as well as their dating, need investigation, as do the cultural complexes and functional categories in which they occur, such as death ritual, hunting magic, representations of deities and animal spirits, shamanism, and mythology. What strikes me as most similar in comparing deer stone art with early Eskimo art is the transformational nature of the deer stone images, which combine features of Asian elk – the most magnificent and powerful cervid of central Eurasia – with bills of water birds, much in the way that Alaskan Eskimo have long represented transformation figures combining features of the wolf and the killer whale, or seal and water bird, whose spirits were believed capable of changing physical forms while crossing barriers between land and water, water and air, or land and air. It is quite possible that ultimately these features may have roots in the Paleolithic cultures of Asia. However, the hypothesis I wished to test in Mongolia is more specific and relates to relationships and forms of the late Neolithic, Bronze, and early Iron Age. The existence of mythology and art representing these transformation concepts in modern ethnological traditions argues strongly for their presence in remote prehistoric times, as Carl Schuster, Edmund Carpenter, and others theorized and researched.

We clearly have much to learn about the meaning and connections of images and iconography in both Eskimo and Siberian-Mongolian contexts. Esther Jacobson and her Russian colleagues have brought us a considerable way toward that goal (Jacobson 1993, 2002; Jacobson-Tepfer 2001). As we will demonstrate below, it seems likely that deer stone carvings may faithfully represent the body art on specific DSK individuals that protected them both during their lifetimes and ensured an honored leader's safe passage into the afterlife in the upper world.

Presumably this function is the same or similar to the body art preserved in the frozen graves of Rudenko's, Gryaznov's, and Polosmak's Pazyryk Altai warriors. It seems likely that similar forms of body decoration may have been present on Old Bering Sea Eskimos and probably functioned in a similar fashion, protecting them from spiritual dangers as was the case among early peoples of eastern Asia and the North Pacific for the past 3-4000 years. Could an archaeological investigation of deer stones and Mongolian Late Bronze Age culture reveal an archaeological connection between Mongolia and the North Pacific? We explore this idea by presenting the results of a decade of field research and return to this question at the end of this exploration.

Pazyryk deer and Scythian antlered feline, and a golden Scythian deer whose antler styles appears hundreds of years earlier on Mongolian deer stones (Wikipedia Commons).

Mongolian Deer Stones: Meaning, Function and Chronology

The second goal of our investigation was to develop an understanding of the deer stone and its place in Mongolian Bronze Age society. Speculated upon since the mid-19th century, and researched by archaeologists since the 1930s, deer stones held a place in the Mongolian past somewhat like the concept of Mongolia held by most western peoples until 1990. Deer stones were equally mysterious as the Mongolia citself—a land of horses, throat-singers, and the homeland of Genghis Khan, a near mythological reality of hoof-beats and throat-singers only briefly brought to Western attention by the swashbuckling exploits of Roy Chapman Andrews. The real function of deer stones was almost as little known to Mongolians as Mongolia's people and lands were to the outside world.

The advent of professional archaeology, instituted in Mongolia by Russians in the 1950s, did little to reveal the essence of deer stones despite the fact that they occurred throughout the Mongolian landscape and were like old friends—"our old stone men" as a young Murun herder girl informed me. Russians and their Mongolian archaeological partners agreed on the general timeframe when deer stones existed because the tools hanging on the belts shown on the stones were similar to weapons known from Late Bronze Age burials in southern Russia, suggesting dates between 1500 to 500 BCE. Beyond that, all was mystery. There was no consensus as to what culture they belonged to and what their function was. Even their identity was unclear: were they chiefs? ancestor figures? gods? mythological beings? No one had answers.

We decided to try and find out—not by conducting an art historical study of deer stone images, like Volkov and Novgorodova, and more extensively recently by Bayarsiakhan (2017/2022), but through excavation of deer stone site contexts, the spatial relationship between deer stones and the archaeological features and structures associated with them. Deer stones were almost always surrounded by groups of stones—some seen as small stone circles, some as small stone mounds, but almost always seen as a scattering of cobble-size rocks with no obvious pattern from surface indications. Russians and Mongolians had dug a few of the circles and found them empty, and the stone mounds sometimes contained a horse skull. But there was no understanding of what these features were or why they existed. We thought that taking a broader view might provide answers. What could be learned from these rock distributions? Could we obtain charcoal or bones from deer stone foundation pits? And what was their relationship to the large—sometimes huge—rock mounds that often occurred in the vicinity of deer stones? We knew from Russian excavations that they were burial mounds that Mongolians identified as "khirigsuurs'—a term based on a Khirgiz word for a type of burial beneath a stone mound. In southern Russia these mounds were called kurgans. Excavations of khirigsuurs rarely turned up artifacts or grave goods, and often no human skeletons, so even their cultural identity was not known. Were khirigsuurs related to deer stones? Were they part of the same unnamed culture? Or were they intrusions from different cultures or chronological periods? Given all these uncertainties, we needed to begin building our deer stone study from the ground up, starting in the earth, not relying on speculation based on deer stone imagery alone, or reanalysis of earlier archaeological work.

So these were our twin scientific goals: (1) understanding deer stone function and chronology, and (2) relating our finds and deer stone art to the culture history of central Asia and seeking clues about its possible influence on the development of North Pacific cultures and specifically ancient Eskimo art.

We also had a third goal, about process: (3) We wanted our project to help bring Mongolian archaeology into the mainstream of modern archaeological and conservation science, to educate students, and to build museum collections and provide materials to educate the public through museum exhibitions and other media. Above all, we wanted to bring deer stones out of their shadowy past and have them become recognized as public monuments of an illustrious, ancient Mongolian cultural heritage. Doing so would bring tangible benefits besides knowledge and education; it would provide Mongolia with an iconic heritage object as powerful and pervasive as the image of Chinggis Khan—a symbol of a 2000-year historical past that could help build Mongolia's economy by attracting world attention, bringing tourists, fostering regional economic development, and creating new knowledge.

Jargalant deer stone.

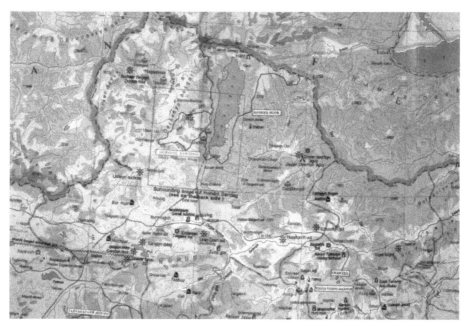

Map of Khuvsgul and Arkhangai Aimags (provinces) in northern Mongolia with Lake Khuvsgul and Lake Baikal in Russia at upper right.

3. Project History & Setting

Geographically remote and without a pre-Soviet scientific tradition, when the Deer Stone Project began in 2001 Mongolia was one of the least-known archaeological regions of Central Asia. Soviet archaeologists had worked in Mongolia sporadically since the mid-19th century, and more intensively from the 1950-70s. However, during the 1990s, when Mongolia emerged from Soviet-imposed isolation, it rapidly became a focus of scholarly interest and international collaboration as knowledge of Mongolian contributions to Central Asian history and the culture pastoral societies began to accumulate. Unlike its better-known relations with China and silk route connections, Mongolia's role in cultural development, population movements, and regional interactions with southern Siberia, the Far East, and Northeast Asia was largely unknown. While Mongolian, Soviet, Korean, and Chinese research sheds light on these subjects, much remained to be learned (see Honeychurch 2015 for a Mongolia-wide archaeological synthesis, and Fitzhugh et al. 2013 for a full culture-historical overview).

Drama is no stranger to Mongolian landscape and eminences such as this one were often chosen as burial sites.

During June of 2001-2002 the Smithsonian's Arctic Studies Center conducted brief reconnaissance projects in Khuvsgul Aimag between Murun and the Darkhad Valley, and in the mountains between the West Darkhad and the Russian (Tuva) border. In 2003-9 we returned yearly for several weeks of ethnological, archaeological, and botanical investigations. As noted above, the project began initially through collaboration with a humanitarian effort organized by Ed Nef, founder of the Santis English Language School in Ulanbaatar, to provide educational, medical, and financial assistance to a small group of reindeer-herders living in the West Darkhad taiga between Lake Khuvsgul and the Tuva border, a people known in Mongolia as 'Tsaatan' and to anthropological circles as 'Dukha' (Vainstein 1980; Wheeler 2000; Plumley and Battulag 2000). Our initial purpose was to explore the potential for archaeological, anthropological, and environmental studies that might illuminate the growing challenges for Tsaatan survival resulting from global warming, environmental change, transition to a capitalist economy, and political and geographic isolation from other Tuva-speaking peoples in the closure of the Mongolia-Russian border in 1991 (Cultural Survival 24(2); Milnius 2003). Following our discovery that the Late Bronze Age deer stones that brought us to Mongolia in the first place (later to be defined as the Deer Stone-Khirigsuur or DSK Complex) did not extend into the taiga forests north of the grassy Mongolian steppe, we shifted our research to the steppe regions of the Darkhad Valley and regions of north-central Mongolia and Arkhangai.

The geographic setting of the Khuvsgul-Darkhad region was the northernmost territory occupied by the DSK culture complex other than its extension into Russia south of Lake Baikal. Lying north of the 50° parallel that roughly defines the northern boundary of present-day Mongolia, Khuvsgul Aimag–dominated by Lake Khuvsgul, the Darkhad Valley, and the eastern extension of the Sayan mountains–is geographically transitional between the Mongolian steppe and the Siberian taiga (forest). Its basin-and-range topography, high elevation, colder climate, greater rainfall and forest cover, and its northern Yenisei- and Lena-bound drainage—all contribute to making the region more 'Siberian' than the lower, more open steppe that dominates central Mongolia south of the Selinge River. Separated from the Murun steppe by a barrier of high hills and plateaus rising to 2300 meters, known as Toomin Davaa and Oliin Davaa, the Darkhad has retained an ecological, cultural, and historical character distinct from the Mongolian steppe to the south and has a different ethnic and historical character. In the Darkhad, Mongolian herders and Siberian hunters and reindeer-herders have coexisted, and to some extent blended for hundreds if not thousands of years. This environmental and cultural divide was evident historically as far back as the 13th century when Chinggis Khan's forces entered the Darkhad Valley to subjugate the Darkhad and south Siberian Tuva and Buryat tribes.

2003 Mongolian and American team departing from Gobi Hotel in Murun for Tsaatan country with Mongolian drivers, Ayush, Kevin Robinson, Adiyabold, Scott Stark, Ochirhuyag, Bayarsaikhan, and Sanjmyatav.

Yaks and landscape in Darkhad Valley north of Ulaan Uul with the Khoridol Saridag Range lying along the west side of Lake Khuvsgul in the distance. Views to east.

Camels in the Darkhad Valley in 2004, and a June camel shedding winter dress. (photo b: PDP)

Uushigiin Uvör deer stone site west of Murun.

Uushigiin Uvör DS2 reset by a Japanese-Mongolian excavation, seen re-erected showing salt encrustation from centuries of partial burial; Uushigiin Uvör DS9 lost its top, probably from a lightning strike; and Julia Clark at Uushigiin Uvör DS4 showing damage from animal rubbing, frost, and sun.

The Deer Stone Project

Following my investigations searching for early Eskimo traces in the Russian Arctic and northern Japan where I studied Ainu culture and its Jomon predecessors, the opportunity to explore Mongolia connections with Scythian animal style art was an exciting challenge. Ed Nef's reports of stone monuments bearing images reminiscent of Scythian forms intrigued me because it was the only place where Bronze or Early Iron Age art looking similar to early Eskimo art was known from Inner Asia. Interior regions of Siberia were a 'black hole'; almost nothing was known or published from this time period that had preserved organic remains due to the corrosive acidic soils of the Siberian taiga forest. The chance of finding ancient art, which would usually be found as sculpture or carvings on bone or other organic materials, was exceedingly slim. For this reason,

Nef's report of stone monuments with elaborate carvings dating to the millennia before the appearance of Old Bering Sea Eskimo art caught my attention.

Deer stone site distribution. (after Volkov 2002)

The Deer Stone Project took shape as a multi-facetted exploration of Northern Mongolia when the country was emerging from the cloak of decades of Soviet stewardship. Nothing about its prehistory was known outside the Soviet archaeological community. Since the time of Chinggis and Kubilai Khan, Mongolia had been hidden behind Chinese or Soviet borders with the exception of a brief period in the 1920s when the dinosaur expeditions of Roy Chapman Andrews sponsored by the American Museum of Natural History created a surge of interest in Mongolia's dinosaurs and the fabulous discovery of dinosaur eggs and nests. Publications by Soviet archaeologists working in Mongolia were not generally available outside Russia and were not available in English translation. However, I soon discovered they could be accessed partly through the prolific writings of Esther Jacobson (1993, 2001) an art historian from the University of Oregon who had a passion for Central Asian and South Russian rock art and archaeological iconography, knew Russian language and literature, and had been working for years with Russian archaeologists. Among the key reports documenting several generations of Russian and Mongolian research are A. P. Okladnikov (1954), N. N. Dikov (1958), N. L. Chlenova (1984), V. V. Volkov (1981), Volkov and A. E. Novgorodova (1975), V. D. Kubarov (1979), Yu. C. Khudiakov (1987), D. G. Savinov (1994), T. Sanjmyatav (1995), A. D. Tsybiktarov (1998, 2003, 2006, 2011), and Tseveendorj et al. (1999). Although the pace of Russian research in Mongolia slowed after 1990, some researchers continued excavations and reporting (e.g. Kovalev et al. 2016), while researchers from other nations joined the effort, such as Allard and Erdenebaatar (2005); Allard et al. (2007), Takahama et al. (2006), Wright (2007, 2014, 2015, 2017), Mcgail (2008, 2015), Houle (2016), and of course many Mongolian researchers like D. Erdenebaatar, Ts. Sanjmyatav, J. Bayarsaikhan, and others who worked independently or collaboratively with international scholars like

Francis Allard, Jean-Luc Houle, Joshua Wright, Julia Kate Clark, and others. Much of this history is summarized by Bayarsaikhan (2022: 17-23).

In addition to studying deer stones, I was also interested in meeting Dukha reindeer herders, the southernmost reindeer people in the world and who maintained and still practiced a nomadic life herding reindeer. Russian ethnologist V.V. Vainshtein studied the Dukha extensively and believed their ancestors may have been the first people in Eurasia to domesticate reindeer some 2000 years ago. Having briefly lived among and researched the tundra reindeer herders in Yamal, Arctic Russia, I was curious to compare Nenets practices with the forest herders of northern Mongolia and, with luck, find early sites with reindeer bones that might shed light on their domestication history.

The Darkhad Valley offered a perfect geographic locus for studying deer stones and finding archaeological sites dating back potentially to the end of the Ice Age. At that time, the Darkhad Valley was a pro-glacial lake before the late glacial ice dams and moraines burst, allowing waters to drain north into the Arctic Ocean via the Yenesei and Lena rivers and leaving behind a fertile plain for ruminants and hunters. Located at the edge of the steppe-taiga transition, the Darkhad offered opportunities for geological and paleoecological studies, for assessing the effects of modern climate warming on landscapes and people, and investigating ethnology and shamanism that could be relevant for deer stone interpretation. There was also its 8000 years of archaeological history that included early hunters and foragers, the transition to pastoral economies represented by the modern Darkhad Mongols, and the beginnings of social complexity as represented by deer stones and mortuary ceremonialism. I decided to let others like Daniel Rogers and Bill Honeychurch investigate the last 2000 years when northern Mongolia progressed through a series of empire eras, including the Xiangnu, Turk, Khitan, Mongol, and Jurchen, leading to the modern day (Rogers 2019; Honeychurch 2015). Our initial tasks were wide-ranging, and our results were published in annual Arctic Studies Center field reports that can be accessed through the Smithsonian Institution's digital library resources. Our first projects began with ethnographic observations as they apply to understanding and reconstructing deer stone culture, its surrounding physical and social environment, and its archaeological predecessors and descendants.

Bronze Age Ritual Landscapes

Our early visits to the Dukha reindeer herders and the Darkhad Mongol pastoralists provided context that, as the project developed, made important contributions to the way we conducted our deer stone research and interpreted its results, especially with regard to the contemporary subsistence systems we encountered: nomadic pastoralism, hunting/gathering, and reindeer herding. Also important was gaining an understanding of the contemporary role of landscape ritual as expressed in various types of 'ovoo' constructions and devotional behavior, and modern interactions of herders with khirigsuur burial mounds, which included placing ritual deposits of animal bones and artifacts at these ancient sites, and at deer stones, which also receive contemporary deposits of bones, artifacts, and khadags (prayer flags). Practices related to these features will be described in the pages that follow. Observations on contemporary ritual contributed to our understanding of Bronze Age monuments. Although we quickly realized that deer stones and khirigsuurs are not present in the taiga forest zone and are restricted to the open steppe or steppe-forest zones, our experiences with Dukha and Darkhad Mongolians brought awareness of the critical importance of landscape ritual, the central role of shamanism, and the pervasive belief in spirits—the unseen but ever-present forces that are still believed to guide or control human life and destiny among many peoples today, as also in the deep past. Deer stones, khirigsuurs, and their associated features were our sign-posts into this ancient world, and we were fortunate that deer stone art and iconography, and the architecture of deer stone and khirigsuur installations, provided clues for deciphering these ancient beliefs.

Ulaan Tolgoi deer stone and khirigsuur site with DS4,3,2,1 left to right. View southeast.

A Land Filled with Spirits

Standing out in the landscape as anomalous uprights or dark mounds against the rolling green hills of the steppe, deer stones and khirigsuurs are often the only human marks one sees in an otherwise natural landscape, and it has been so for three thousand years. These became the first human constructions to permanently humanize the Mongolian landscape and, as such, were constant reminders to all who followed of a time that must have been seen and remembered as a classical era, perhaps even one when gods came to earth and left their messages and imprint on the land.

The impact of the DSK ritual and landscape on later peoples and cultures can be seen also in 2000-year old Xiongnu cemeteries when mounded burials with ramps and east-side human graves (vice DSK horses) return to mark the land with a new cultural history built upon ritual landscape traditions established during the DSK period. But Xiongnu sites are few and hidden away, almost never seen. More visible are monuments from the Turkic period ca. AD 700-800 when more realistically carved human mortuary figures reappear together with ceremonial fences and east-ranging bal-bal alignments of small vertical slabs—memorials for a new set of steppe post-DSK leaders. Even today, travelers crossing the open steppe, cresting a pass between two valleys, find their eyes caught instantly by the dark shadows of khirigsuur mounds and the glint of light from deer stones orthogonally breaking the undulating sweep of the rolling grasslands. The DSK has provided the Mongolian steppe with a magical presence that persists today in the eyes of all who behold it. The sense of timelessness and mystery is further enhanced by

Mongolian horseman herding sheep against the backdrop of their felt ger tents venting plumes of aromatic dung-smoke. More than just a romantic image, deer stones and khirigsuurs have become an integral part of the foundation on which Mongolian culture and its deep nomadic heritage is seen, valued, and persist today.

This near surreal view was brought home to our crew dramatically one dark night in 2006 when Rae Beaubien and her crew, including both American and Mongolian members, were scanning deer stones after midnight at the Uushigiin Uvör site using laser scanning gear that required pitch black conditions to create a sharp image. In the midst of their work a pulsing disc of light appeared over the site, hovered, and then moved rapidly away. All present agreed they had witnessed a supernatural phenomenon for which they had no scientific or meteorological explanation.

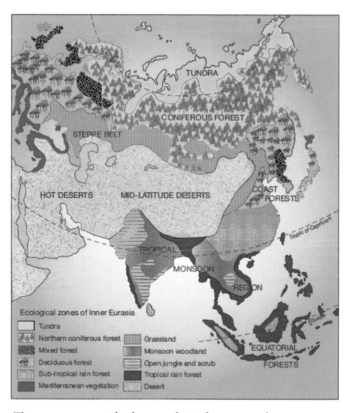

The grassy steppe is both an ecological region and a transport corridor through the mid-latitude heart of Eurasia.

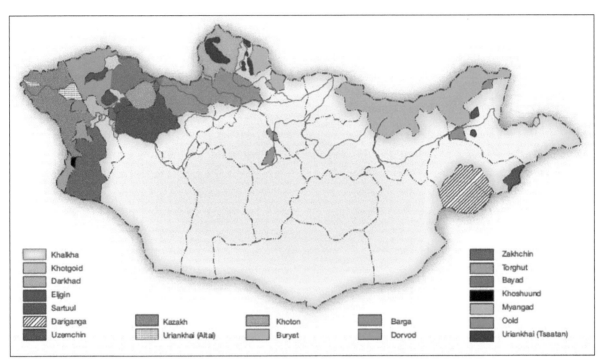

Map of ethno-linguistic groups of Mongolia. Khalk Mongols dominate.

Deer stone and khirigsuur monuments date to a period when steppe societies had been transformed by major economic, social, and religious change resulting from domestication of the horse and the beginnings of horseback riding, resulting in a dramatic expansion of pastoral economy and military technology (Sandra Olson 2006; Taylor et al. 2017). Geographically, these monuments are found in the steppe grasslands between the Gobi Desert and the Russian taiga forest, an environment well-suited for sheep, goats, horses, camels, and bovids. In the northern parts of the steppe the south-facing hills are covered with grass while their northern slopes, shielded from the summer sun, hold more moisture and are forested with Siberian larch that host reindeer, elk, wolves, snow leopards, wolves, and small furbearers. Plant and fish resources are also important to both herding and hunting peoples for food, medicinal products, and ritual. The legacy of this cultural geography continues today in the relationship between the minority Dukha reindeer-herders dwelling in the taiga and the politically dominant Darhkhad and Khalkh Mongols of the steppes to the south. Exploring the complex history of Khuvsgul-Darkhad cultures, peoples, ritual, and changing environments for the past 4-6000 years became a scientific challenge that also could have practical benefits by advancing tourism, education, sustainable development, cultural survival, and international recognition.

With these introductory comments, we can begin our explorations.

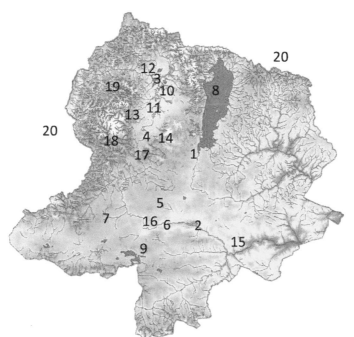

Geography of Khuvsgul aimag with locations mentioned in the text. 1 Khatgal, 2 Murun, 3 Tsagaanuur. 4 Ulaan Uul, 5 Arbulag, 6 Burantoktok, 7 Tsagaan Uul, 8 Lake Khuvsgul, 9 Sangiin Dalai L., 10 Rinchinlhumbe, 11 Darkhad Valley, 12 Shishged R., 13 Khug R., 14 Khoridol Saridag Mts., 15 Selinge R., 16 Delger Murun R., 17 Oliin Davaa, 18 Sayan Mts., 19 Minge Bulag, 20 Russia. (map: J. Bayarsaikhan)

4. Darkhad: Setting the Stage

Following our arrival in Mongolia on June 19, 2001, and a week of orientation in Ulaanbaatar that included meetings with officials, scientists, and logistics preparation, the Nef Khuvsgul Expedition flew to Murun, the capital of Khuvsgul Aimag (District), on 25 June. Here we spent a day organizing food, arranging jeep rentals, hiring a cook, and meeting Governor Damdinsuren to obtain permission for access to the western Darkhad Valley and the remote mountainous region between Darkhad and the Tuva (Russian) border. A visit to the Uushigiin Uvör site a few kilometers west of the Murun airport acquainted us with one of the most important Late Bronze Age sites in northern Mongolia, exhibiting large khirigsuur mounds and one of the largest concentrations of deer stones in Mongolia. We left Murun on the afternoon of 25 June in a caravan of four jeeps and a van and made a brief visit to the Ulaan Tolgoi deer stone site west of Lake Erkhel. Named for a prominent

conical hill at this location. Ulaan Tolgoi has several khirigsuurs, square burials, and five deer stones, including one extremely large, extraordinary specimen, making this site an excellent target for beginning our investigations. (25 June 2001)

Deer Stones at Ulaan Tolgoi

My introduction to deer stones began eight km west of Lake Erkhel, about 30 km north of the regional center town of Murun. Ulaan Tolgoi, located at 49°55.907' N 99°48.250'E in Alag Erdene soum in Khuvsgul Aimag, is a large Late Bronze Age mortuary complex combining deer stones and khirigsuur boulder mounds. The site also has several square burials—also known as slab burials because they are outlined with standing slab rocks—dating to the Square Burial culture that immediately followed the deer stone period. Khirigsuurs have a distinctive architectural form: a central mound of rocks enclosed within a square or round boulder fence of small rocks placed side-by-side. Outside the eastern part of the fence one finds small external 'satellite' mounds, and beyond the fence on the west side, small circular or oval rock rings. The deer stones and khirigsuurs are located on the southeast side of a prominent hill named Ulaan Tolgoi which rises in the center of a wide plain west of Erkhel Lake. Deer Stone 2 is one of the largest and most beautifully carved deer stones in Mongolia. This great granite slab stands 3.2 m above ground, the second from the southern end of a north-south alignment of four other deer stones, all of different sizes, cross-sections, and degrees of decoration. An erosion scar

angling across the top half of Deer Stone 2 indicates it had fallen in antiquity and lay partly buried for hundreds if not thousands of years. The site was not known when Volkov did his field surveys in the 1970s and was found in 1988 by our field partner, senior archaeologist T. Sanjmyatav. Although most of the Ulaan Tolgoi deer stones had been re-erected, no excavations were conducted at the site until our team arrived in 2002. Thermal erosion and wind-borne sand blasting had reduced the intricate above-ground carvings on DS2 to a faint tracery that could be seen only with difficulty when low-angle sun rays raked across its flat sides. The portion of the stone that had been buried retained most of its original clarity.

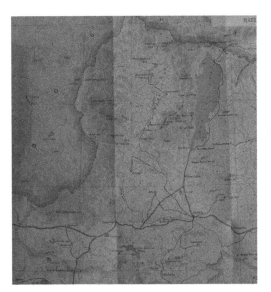

Satellite View of Khuvsgul aimag showing Darkhad Valley and major geographic features north of Murun; Khuvsgul Province and the Darkhad Valley—Transport routes; Darkhad Valley and Khug River with Saridal Khoridal mountains in the background. View south.

East and south (left to right) faces and graphic of Deer Stone 2 at Ulaan Tolgoi, west of Erkhel Lake. Much art has been lost to erosion. (photos: WF, HFB; graphic: JB)

The carvings on DS2 display the characteristic art that defines the deer stone style. The central motif are three or four right-ascending stags stacked one on top of the other, whose bodies and antlers wrap around the four sides of the stone. The carvings are excavated only a few millimeters below the dressed surface of the stone and their interior surfaces had been smoothed and polished. Scrolling down the backs of the deer, all of which have a sharply pointed ears and shoulder withers, are racks of wave-like antlers, two tines of which spread forward over the head. While the scrolling antlers are a characteristic of the Siberian elk *(Cervus elaphus sibiricus)*, the two front antlers do not occur on the elk but may reference brow tines of reindeer *(Rangifer tarandus)*. Reindeer were wild during deer stone times and did not begin to be domesticated in Asia until the Late Iron Age, ca. 2000 years ago. While the body and antlers are those of a stag, the long pointed ears have no cervid parallel, and the head (sometimes appearing squared) and beak represent a bird with a large round eye and an elongated beak and bulbous open tip. A line of closely-spaced shallow pits encircling the top

of the stone represents a necklace that was partly obscured during our visits by a coating of bird droppings. Above the necklace, two round circles on opposite sides of the stone represent earrings, known because a few deer stones show actual ears with this type of round earring ornament, often with dangling pendant. No pendants are seen dangling from the DS2 rings. Instead, a smaller engraved circle above and to the left of the large ring may be a second earring. However, some scholars also interpret these large and small rings as sun and moon, and on some deer stones they are circled by an array of grooves representing rays, so this feature may have a dual function. At the top of the east-facing side there is a blank area for a human face. This is known because real human faces are seen in this position on other deer stones, as on Uushigiin Uvör DS14. The lower part of the stone has a belt ornamented with a geometric pattern of nested diamond-shaped patterns, and on the side opposite the face there is a pentagonal shield-like emblem with 12 or 13 chevron bars and a round disc in the upper part of the shield. Below the belt one sees the eroded deer images.

In addition to these basic features—deer, necklace, earrings, belt, and weapons—deer stones have a specific geotaxic (compass direction) setting. All deer stones were meant to be set facing east/southeast, probably so the individual being represented faced and greeted the rising sun, which must have been a major deity to deer stone people, as it was to many other cultures. The east-facing side of the stone always has a 'face,' but the face rarely takes actual human form. More commonly it is shown symbolically by two or three forward (//, ///) or backward (\\, \\\) slashes, the meaning of which is unknown. In many cases this area appears only as a blank space, as it does on DS2. It is highly likely—although not yet proven yet by pigment analysis (but see Esin et al. 2017)—that this and some other deer stones may have carried a painted portrait in this space. The west side opposite the face often carries the pentagonal shield-like image described above with a series of V-shaped chevron bars. The round disc within the pentagon on DS2 is usually interpreted as a bronze mirror, an artifact used by shamans for curing and forecasting. Such round discs are usually seen on the front (east) side of deer stones. The shield and its chevron bars may be insignias of rank; they have also been compared to thoracic skeletal designs seen on shamanic robes. In many cultures, skeletal images refer to the seat of one's personal spirit. Earrings are always found on the north and south sides of the stone. Most people who re-erected fallen deer stones did not understand the orientation rule and set them facing the wrong direction. This error turns out to be useful for alerting researchers that the stone is not in its original setting.

Attempts at understanding the meaning of deer stone art leads us into a labyrinth of graphic and symbolic interpretation which has been explored in great depth by Bayarsaikhan (2017/2022). At the most basic level, deer stones are anthropomorphic and might have been called 'man-stones' or 'person-stones' if the dramatic representation of deer had not ensured preservation of 19th century Russian *(olenni kameni)* 'deer stone' nomenclature. The overall presentation is not just that of a human, but of a high-ranking warrior, leader, shaman, or some combination of all three. Sometimes it is possible to interpret which of these individuals is represented, as in the case of the shamanic DS14 at Uushigiin Uvör, identified as such by the stone's open mouth, meant to indicate singing or chanting. Gender can be inferred only indirectly by warrior dress and weaponry. We must consider that some of those warriors, shamans, or leaders might have been female, but there are no certain indications of gender on deer stones, or for that matter on the images of deer except in a few unique rock art images illustrated below.

  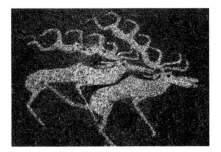

Rock art images of the Mongolian deer from western Mongolia, including rare instances of gendered Mongolian deer and possible copulation. (photos: RK)

Beyond its basic human form, deer stones are cloaked in ambiguity. As noted above, the deer is not a real deer but rather a creature combining the body of an antlered deer with the head of a bird with a round bird's eye and a long bulbous-tipped beak. Combining elements of both earth and sky, these deer are usually shown in an upward pose as though leaping into the firmament. Other features reinforce the transformative cosmological nature of deer stone composition including the division of the stone into three sections: sky or upper world (above the necklace, with its solar and lunar rings), an earthly torso section with deer figures and tool belts, and an under-world below the belt, undecorated and buried in the earth.

make of the myriad belt patterns researched by Novgorodova (1989; Bayarsaikhan 2022:149)? Is their diversity a clue to the deer stone's personal identity—an early form of dog-tag function? Is the round sunken disc truly a shaman's bronze mirror known so well in historical ethnography? Our research has confirmed the suspicions of early Russian scholars like Nikolai Dikov and most modern scholars that deer stones represent warriors-leaders. The recovery of frozen bodies of Pazyryk warriors dating to ca. 2500-2800 BCE (Rudenko 1970; Gryaznov 1980) carrying elaborate animal designs of Scytho-Siberian animal style art suggest that deer stone carvings may replicate the tattooed designs on the bodies of DSK warriors (Jettmar 1994; Fitzhugh 2009).

The south side of Ulaan Tolgoi DS 5; DS5 carvings (graphic: JB); and laser scan (HFB et al.)

Many questions arose as we considered the carvings on Ulaan Tolgoi deer stones. What is the significance of the pentagonal shield-like emblem and enigmatic face slashes? Could there be connection with similar-shaped bronze arm guards found on Xinjiang warrior burials dating to the Scythian period which also include predator-prey motifs and deer with DSK type antlers (Miniaev 2013; Bayarsaikhan 2022:159). What can we

These initial studies raised many questions that inspired us to delve deeper into the Bronze Age world of deer stone ritual and iconography and how it relates to khirigsuurs and the lives and beliefs of the earliest Mongolian monument-builders.

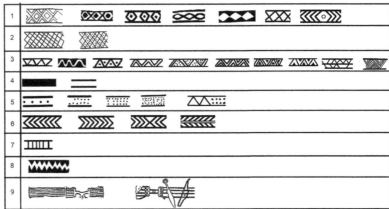

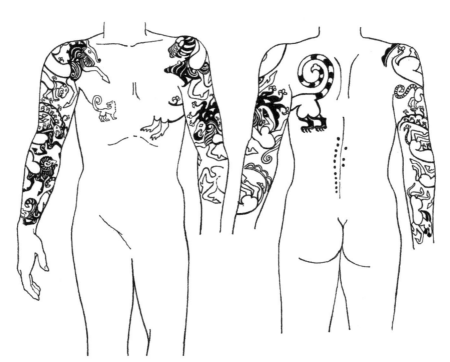

Deer stone belt patterns compiled by Novgorodova (1989); and grouped by type (JB 2022:149); Tattoos on the frozen warrior from a Pazyryk tomb in the Russian Altai, by Sergei Rudenko (1970)

Quarrying Deer Stones

Deer stones were created in a variety of sizes and quadrilateral shapes based on the condition of the original block extracted from a quarry. Most deer stones in northern Mongolia are made of granite, although some are basalt or greenstone schist. Granite and basalt have a tendency for right-angle cleavage, and naturally fractured blocks in granite outcrops often have square or rectangular cross-sections. This physical quality enabled deer stone producers to select naturally fractured blocks that required less effort to modify into a desired size and shape. Deer stones were not carved to standardized sizes but were conditioned by the size and shape of the available stone and by the economic cost of production—essentially how long it took an artisan to make it—and all of these factors depended on the status of the individual represented. Unlike khirigsuur burials which seem to have been available to most if not all people, illustrated deer stones were made only for high-status individuals who could compel the months of artisanal work and the cost of rare metal tools. In Mongolia, khiriguurs—large and small—exist in the hundreds of thousands, whereas deer stones number between one and two thousand. Over time many have fallen; some have been re-erected during the Russian research period, but many still remain buried and unknown.

In most cases, some portion of the stone had to be broken from bedrock. 'Plug and feather' fracture (produced by inserting hardwood pegs into a line of drilled holes and filling the holes with water, causing the pegs to expand and split the rock) was not available to Bronze Age workers, who probably used large boulder hammers, levers, and fire. The rectangular surfaces of the resulting blocks were then shaped by pecking and grinding with abrasive rocks. Fine-grained granite and basalt were preferred because their fracture planes required less finishing than coarse-grained rock. Both the rectangular cross-section and smooth, level surfaces were the key to producing the shadow-effect that allowed even lightly-incised carvings to be seen in raking sunlight. Standing vertically, the images were highlighted on each flat face as the sun swung around the horizon during the course of the day. The smoother the surface finish, the less deep the carving needed to be, allowing for more intricate art. Today many deer stone carvings are difficult to see, especially in broad daylight, because their surfaces have suffered from thermal erosion (cycles of frost and solar warming) and animals using them as rubbing stones. Stones of coarse-grained granite are most susceptible to surface attrition. Stones with polished surfaces provide fewer entries for water infiltration and frost damage. More traumatic are lightning strikes and modern graffiti or defacement. In some cases, deer stones appear to have been actively defaced, toppled, or purposefully broken in antiquity for political, ideological, or other reasons. Eroded carvings that cannot be deciphered in daylight or raking sunshine can often be observed with side illumination at night. But shadow effects were probably not the only means for enhancing visibility. Traces of red pigment have been found on a few deer stones (Esin et al. 2017), making it likely that the carvings may have been fully painted as has been discovered on Greek and Persian sculpture dating only a few centuries later than deer stones.

The granite quarry on the south shore of Erkhel Lake where Ulaan Tolgoi deer stones most likely originated, 2006.

The Erkhel Lake Granite Quarry

On the north side of the hill rising along the south shore of Erkhel Lake, only a few kilometers east of Ulaan Tolgoi, we found high-quality granite outcrops that had been quarried in recent decades for architectural building stone. Modern extraction used the plug-and-feather technique, and in one instance a single huge rectangular block 15m long and 3m high had been cleanly split off from bedrock. Evidence of prehistoric quarrying is not present, but we found naturally occurring blocks with dimensions similar to deer stones. Some of these blocks had red-colored cleavage surfaces like those on Uushigiin Uvör Deer Stone 9. Apparently, slabs like this were selected for deer stones because of the contrast shown when carvers cut through the iron-stained surface into the uncolored granite beneath. In this case the 'readability' of the art depended on color contrast rather than shadow effect. The Erkhel Lake quarry must have been the principal source for the Ulaan Tolgoi deer stones. (July 2003)

Volkov's Deer Stone Types

The most highly ornamented deer stones are found in north-central Mongolia around the northern fringes of the Arkhangai Mountains where the steppe is well-watered compared to the more arid Gobi and eastern deserts or the mountainous Altai region of western Mongolia. Paradoxically, while their distribution coincides with Mongolia's prime horse country and is part of a culture already dependent on horse riding and transport (Taylor 2017), deer rather than horses are the animal featured on deer stones. More will be said about this dichotomy later in this report.

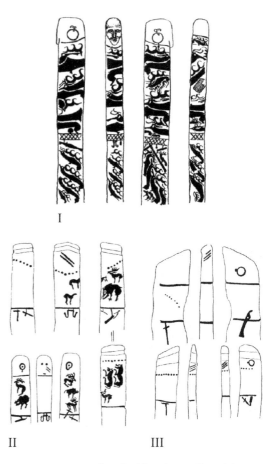

Deer stone types as classified by V.V. Volkov: Type I Classic Mongolian; Type II Sayan-Atai; Type III Eurasian. (WF and JB 2021:fig. 3)

Deer stones from this area are usually described as Type 1 Mongolian or Classic deer stones when they appear in the form described above for Ulaan Tolgoi DS2. Volkov (1981, 1995) recognized two other deer stone types which he saw as geographically distinct: Type II Sayan-Altai" and "Eurasian". Although its range overlaps the classic type, the Sayan-Altai deer stone is found in northern and western Mongolia in the foothills of the Sayan and Altai Mountains. It is a much-simplified version of the Mongolian type and is smaller and less well-finished, has a single-groove belt, and shows a necklace, ring grooves for ears, and sometimes slash marks for the face. On these stones the iconic Mongolian deer image often appears alone or with animals rarely seen on the classic stones, like moose, horses, and sometimes felines or pigs. Animals and weapons often "float" on the stone without being packed together or attached to the belt. There is little formal organization on Sayan-Altai stones beyond the separation of torso and head by a belt, necklace, and earrings. Few are carved on all four sides, and the stones tend to be small and roughly finished. Type III, the Eurasian deer stone, is found primarily in western Mongolia, eastern Kazakhstan, and Russian South Siberia, but occasionally occurs further west, even to the Black Sea shores and Ukraine (Volkov 1995). This stone is simpler still and is usually identified only by a belt and earring grooves, with few other markings. There is sense to Volkov's classification, which was a major break-through in its day; but as we shall see, this largely geographic-based classification has now become complicated by geographic overlapping of the types. In addition, Bayarsaikhan (2022:80) proposes a slightly different classification: 1) deer stones with styled images; 2) deer stones with realistic animal images; 3) deer stones with mixed animal images; and 4) deer stones without animal images. The present volume uses the simpler Volkov scheme.

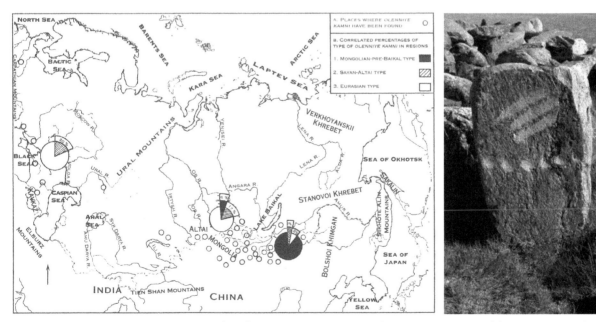

Deer Stone types I, II, III across Central and Western Asia. (Novgorodova 1989: 181), and b, Eurasian DS from Mongolian Altai.

Early Dating Ideas

Dating has been a major concern for deer stone researchers ever since they were first described by Radlov in the 19th century and Okladnikov and Dikov in the mid-20th century. Similarities to Scythian/Saka cultures of the Russian and Inner Asian steppe first led researchers to assign deer stones to the Early Iron Age (ca. 400-0 BCE) based on comparing tool styles on deer stones with artifacts in well-dated Russian kurgan burials. These typological comparisons led to the idea that deer stones and their art were based on Scythian/Saka prototypes of the 5th to 2nd centuries B.C. One of the first to question this view was Novgorodova (1989) who thought Classic deer stones dated to the late 2nd millennia, BC. Esther Jacobson (1993), also considered the possibility of a pre-Scythian age. Most considered her idea outrageous because the thought of Mongolian nomads initiating one of the great art styles of antiquity—Siberian Animal Style Art known largely from southern Russia—was inconceivable to Russian archaeologists, at least until our deer stone project radiocarbon dates began to accumulate.

Lacking c14, Volkov relied on typological dates for his views on deer stone chronology. He thought Sayan-Altai stones might be later than the classic Mongolian stones because they illustrated animals like horses, moose, pigs, and others not seen on classic stones, and because they were shown "floating" on the surface of the stone along with tools not attached to the belt. In his view, these stones demonstrated a "post-classic" breakdown of the classic deer stone structure, something that was even more pronounced in the case of the even more simplified Eurasian stones. His and others' views were based only on the idea of stylistic degeneration; none of the Sayan-Altai or Eurasian deer stones had ever been radiometrically dated, and the general absence of tool images made typological dating impossible. Volkov (1981, 1995) and Novgorodova (1989) also believed that stylistic features like deer with out-stretched legs seen standing "on tippy-toes" rather than crouched or folded, was a late, post-classic, development. This idea was reinforced when the golden statue of a classic style Mongolian deer was recovered from the Pazyryk Arzhan II royal grave in southern Russian, dendrochronologically dated to ca. 500 BCE. This animal, probably created as a headdress ornament, shows a standing deer whose features were classic Mongolian deer style except the absence of a bird's head and beak and the standing pose.

The golden deer ornament from the Arzhan II chiefly burial. (photo: Wikipedia Commons)

However, there is another approach to be considered that is not strictly chronological. As our field research progressed, the spatial distribution of Volkov's three types suggests there may be social and cultural as well as geographical and chronological components in the dating and function of these deer stone types. Sayan-Altai and Eurasian deer stones may date to the same chronological period as classic Type 1 deer stones, perhaps indicating geographic cultural variation with attenuated ritual belief and practice outside the DSK culture core area. But there is also evidence at sites like Khyadag East, described below, for later dates for Sayan-Altai and Eurasian deer stones, perhaps as late as cal. 2400 BP. If so, it could be that they represent weakened expression of the Deer Stone-Khirigsuur complex following its contact with Pazyryk in the west and replacement in the core area by the new regime that comes with the Slab/Square Burial culture following 2600 BP. Sorting out these issues will be discussed further below and will undoubtedly be a task for future research, but it will not be easy. We attempted to date Sayan-Altai and Eurasian deer stones many times but could not find suitable dating material because of the absence of horse graves and the uncertain context of charcoal and bone associations.

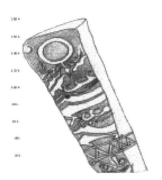

Sketch of Ulaan Tolgoi Deer Stone 5 by Andrea Neighbors.

Dating Deer Stones at Ulaan Tolgoi

Ulaan Tolgoi's Deer Stone 2, while huge and artistically impressive, was of less interest to us than the site's smaller monuments (DS4 and 5) because one of our primary research goals was to obtain radiocarbon samples, which required undisturbed deer stone settings. We selected Ulaan Tolgoi's DS4 and 5 because their carvings were clear and their settings seemed undisturbed. We hoped to find charcoal or bones associated with their setting foundations.

Deer stone art has been recorded in drawings made by T. Sanjmiatov, and more recently, Gary Tepfer photographed the Ulaan Tolgoi stones when he and Esther Jacobson visited the site in the late 1990s. Sanjmiatov, who worked there as part of a Soviet-led team, remarked that his group re-set at least one of the monuments that had fallen. When we arrived, we found DS1 set in concrete, and we suspected the huge DS2 had been re-erected at the same time. Following our brief visit in 2001, we returned in 2002 to map the smaller deer stone settings and survey the site surroundings. We found the valley floor packed with mounds and khirigsuurs that extended up the rocky southeast slopes of Ulaan Tolgoi. The hill and its surroundings were full of monuments and boulder features, including khirigsuur burial mounds, miniature khirigsuurs (called 'slope burials' by some researchers, but they are really just small khirigsuurs), slab/square burial features, numerous small one-meter-wide boulder mounds, and scores of circular or oval boulder hearth rings. Near the top of Ulaan Tolgoi hill, horse heads were tucked in among the rocks with their snouts facing east. Clearly the Erkhel region was an important area, within which Ulaan Tolgoi had special significance. We found this situation repeated in other areas of northern Mongolia: small hills rising out of a level plain often had DSK ritual sites around their eastern and southeastern flanks.

Ulaan Tolgoi deer stones west of Erkhel Lake; (photo: H.F. Beaubien)

Ulaan Tolgoi Deer Stones 1,2: south sides, both re-set during the Soviet period, and small khirigsuur 'slope burials' on southeast side of Ulaan Tolgoi.

With help from Bruno Frohlich in 2002, we completed a map of DS5 and its associated features and excavated a 1x2 m trench south of the stone and an oval hearth ring feature 50 m to the east. Having excavated deer stones earlier with Volkov, Sanjmiatav discouraged our plan, seeing it as a waste of time because he never found artifacts at deer stones or in the associated stone circles. Fortunately, we had some new tools not available to Russians and Mongolians in the 1970s, and besides, we were not particularly interested in artifacts. Instead, we sought organic materials, bones or charcoal, either

associated directly with deer stone foundation pits or in ritual fires, deposits, or other activities associated with deer stones. While determining a positive association of finds from a deer stone pit can be problematic due to rodent disturbance or later ritual activity, we might at least obtain a terminus *ante quem* date and eventually come closer to a true age for the deer stone art.

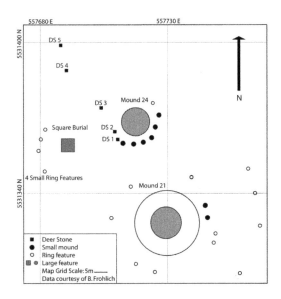

Bruno Frohlich using a satellite GPS receiver to map Ulaan Tolgoi DS4 in 2006. (photo: P. DePriest)

Ulaan Tolgoi deer stones and its closest two khirigsuurs and a looted square burial. (graphic: B. Frohlich)

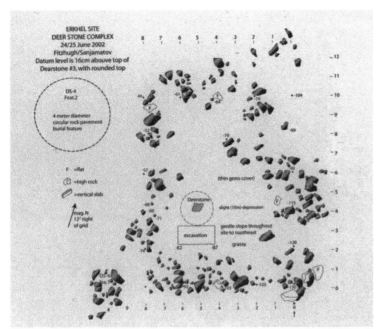

Ulaan Tolgoi features associated with DS5 and DS5 south side. (graphic: Frohlich)

Our first test trench was laid out 75 cm south of DS5 to avoid undermining its foundation. We soon determined that the stone was in its original position, but the excavation, which terminated 40cm below ground surface, failed to reveal the edge of its foundation pit, apparently because the pit was barely larger than the stone itself. Beneath a 1-2 cm thick turf zone we found four stratigraphic levels. From top to bottom they were: Level I, a 4 cm thick layer of loosely-packed gravelly sand that had accumulated as wind-blown deposits and contained no cultural material; Level II, a 5 cm thick buried old ground surface containing organic stains but no cultural material; Level III, a 20 cm thick layer of gravel-free light brown silty sand; and Level IV, a dark-stained zone reminiscent of an old ground surface which contained fragments of charcoal. While not illuminating our deer stone study, this stratigraphy turned out to be characteristic of undisturbed steppe soils in much of northern Mongolia. We collected two charcoal samples suitable for AMS dating from this zone, and one yielded cal. 2150-1960 BP (Appendix 1). Imme-

diately adjacent to the deer stone and clearly defined in the north wall of the trench was a rodent burrow that terminated on top of a flat slab 35 cm below the ground surface, 50 cm north of the charcoal find. While our first c14 date seemed to validate a post-Scythian age for DS5, the tables turned dramatically when we discovered a more accurate way to date deer stones than digging around rodent-infested deer stone foundations.

Ulaan Tolgoi DS5 excavation trench with Baterdene Sanjmiatav, Ishka, Adiyabold Namkhai, and Steven Young.

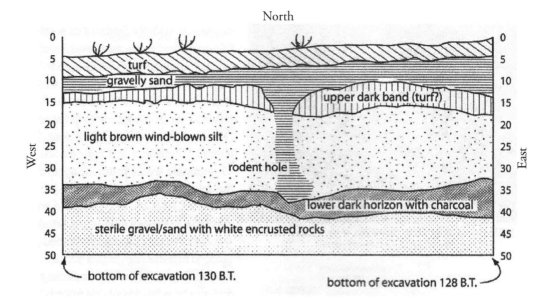

Stone Circles:
Altars vs. Hearths?

In 2002, we noticed that DS5 was surrounded by circular cobble rings that we presumed were hearths related to the deer stone installation. These cobble features were identical to ones also found surrounding khirigsuur structures. Excavating Feature 3, 47.5 m and 100° (mag.) from DS5, we found two soil levels: L1 being unconsolidated wind-blown sand, and L2 being a tan sandy soil 2-3 cm thick containing tiny fragments of charcoal and calcined bone that we later identified as sheep and goat remains. A charcoal sample was obtained but was not submitted for dating because at that time we were not certain about the hearth's association with DS5. So, by the end of the season we were still in the dark about the age of DS5.

In subsequent years, we came to understand that these rings are associated with deer stones and khirigsuurs and excavated many to obtain charcoal for radiocarbon dating when the sites did not have satellite mounds with horse remains. Horse teeth were our preferred dating

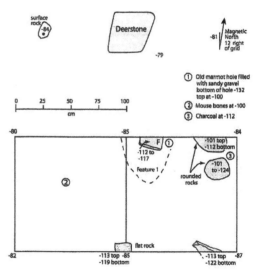

Ulaan Tolgoi DS5: excavation plan and test pit map; and north wall profile.

samples because their high density made them less susceptible to contamination from ground water. Since stone rings were almost always present at these sites, and almost always contained charcoal, the rings offered an alternate method for dating monuments without horse heads. Of the scores of rings we excavated, only a few did not contain at least small amounts of charcoal and calcined bone.

We later learned the function of these stone circles from descriptions of Scythian sacrifices as reported by Herodotus:

The manner of their sacrifices is everywhere and in every case the same; the victim [an animal] stands with its two fore-feet bound together by a cord, and the person who is about to offer, taking his station behind the victim, gives the rope a pull, and thereby throws the animal down; as it falls he invokes the god to whom he is offering; after which he puts a noose round the animal's neck, and, inserting a small stick, twists it round, and so strangles him. No fire is lighted, there is no con-secration, and no pouring out of drink-offerings; but directly after the beast is strangled the sacrificer flays him, and then sets to work to boil the flesh.

As Scythia, however, is utterly barren of fire-wood, a plan has had to be contrived for boiling the flesh, which is the following. After flaying the beasts, they take out all the bones, and (if they possess such gear) put the flesh into boilers made in the country, which are very like the cauldrons of the Lesbians, except that they are of a much larger size; then placing the bones of the animals beneath the cauldron, they set them alight, and so boil the meat. If they do not happen to possess a cauldron, they make the animal's paunch hold the flesh, and pouring in at the same time a little water, lay the bones under and light them. The bones burn beautifully; and the paunch easily contains all the flesh when it is stript from the bones, so that by this plan your ox is made to boil himself, and other victims also to do the like. When the meat is all cooked, the sacrificer offers a portion of the flesh and of the entrails, by casting it on the ground be-fore him. They sacrifice all sorts of cattle, but most commonly horses. (Macaulay 1904:314)

Ulaan Tolgoi DS5 with refilled trench and datum triangle, view NW toward Ulaan Tolgoi hill.

The function of the stone rings seemed clear enough. They were located around the fringes of deer stones and khirigsuurs, beyond satellite mounds (see below for more discussion) if they were present, and when found around square- or round-fenced khirigsuurs, were spaced at regular measured ranks and intervals rather than occurring in a haphazard arrangement. Their position seems to have been placed according to a predetermined or at least a conscious plan. Their location at sites with multiple, closely spaced deer stones is less clear than at khirig-suurs and or at deer stone sites that have only a single deer stone. Since most sites had multiple deer stones positioned in a north-south line with only a few meters between each stone, it is often difficult to assign individual horse mounds and stone circles to a particular deer stone. This problem does not occur with khirig-suurs, where most circles are found outside the fence on the west or northwest side of the khi-rigsuur. The function of the circles had to be for presenting animal offerings as part of organized khirigsuur or deer stone ceremonies.

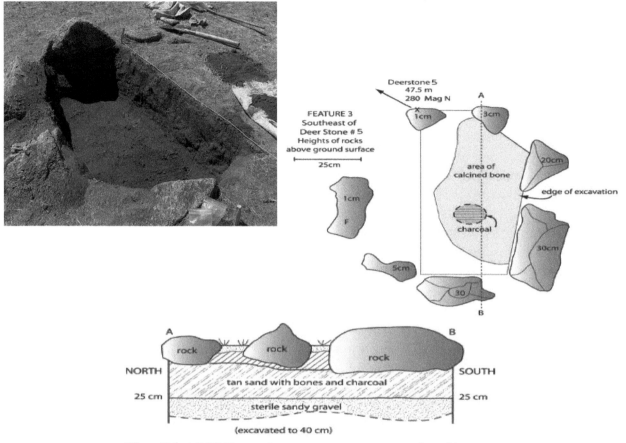

Ulaan Tolgoi DS5 Feature 3: a stone ring containing calcined bone and charcoal, view SW; Top plan of Feature 3 circle.

The presence of charcoal and calcined bone shows that the offerings were burned inside the stone rings. We imagined that animals were slaughtered at the ceremonial site, probably on the stone pavements that Volkov occasionally reported at deer stones sites. We later excavated several of these pavements, including one at Khydag East, and found fragments of unburned caprines and occasionally larger animals on their surfaces.

It turns out that the stone rings may be more complicated than we initially imagined. Broderick et al. (2014) made a detailed study by excavating four rings at the Urt Bulagiin KYR40 mound

in Khanuy Valley. Their study, titled "The Mystery of the Missing Caprines," confirmed a caprine (sheep/goat) dominated assemblage in all four, with a bovid bone present in one. They report only a small trace of charcoal, note the absence of fire-burnt earth, and cite the high heat required to calcine fresh bone, which led them to conclude that the bones were burned elsewhere and deposited later in the circles. They propose calling the circles 'altars', a term also used by Jacobson for the stone rings and horse head mounds, and recommend against describing the features as 'hearths', the term we have used in our research.

There is merit in using 'function-free' terminology like 'stone circle' rather than 'hearth ring' or 'stone hearth,' when the function is not or cannot be determined. But I believe there is sufficient evidence to interpret these features as active hearths. First, the rings almost always contain charcoal as well as calcined bone. Usually it occurs as small scattered chunks and flakes, never as a bed of coals as found in domestic hearths that had repeated, long-term use. Clearly these rings were not intensive, multiple-use features; instead, they must have been used only once as part of a single ritual. This is probably why charcoal layers and burned soil are not found. It is quite possible for a fire to be hot enough to calcine bone without producing burned earth, especially if animal fat was used as an accelerant.

We also need to consider the ritual behavior lying behind a bone offering. Depositing previously burned bone remains in a stone circle made to resemble a hearth seems like a poor excuse for a ritual. Animal offerings to deities would have required a more active process, commensurate with the careful spatial planning of the rings and the need to actually 'send off' the animal offered to the spirits of the upper world. Bayarsaikhan, referring to F. T. Van Straten's (1995:167; Naiden 2013) description of Greek sacrificial ritual, provides a convincing analogy from ancient Greek fire ritual—the sending of a signal or message to the sky spirits in the form of a plume of smoke from burning animal bones. Burning fresh animal bones is a smoky business. As in the Greek case, it is likely that the smoke itself was the sacrificial message to the gods; smoke would have been the embodiment of the sacrificed animal's spirit and the product of an act of devotion. It is not likely that the purpose of the circles was simply placing previously burned remains in a stone ring. I believe the function of the stone rings was for burning animal remains to produce smoke as a message to the gods, and that the ring features may legitimately be called 'hearths'—at least until experiments show otherwise. It is unlikely that

DSK people, with their highly ordered society and belief systems, would assemble around a monument made to honor a deceased leader and deposit bits of pre-burned bones fired in some off-site animal crematory into simulated hearths. This does not seem the proper way to honor gods and ancestors.

Having experimented with boulder circles, we planned to excavate and date a number of these and other features to determine their function, ritual, and species associations; their chronological relationships within individual deer stone settings and khirigsuurs; whether the structures resulted from ceremonial events at a single point in time or evolved over time with the addition to new ritual activity. Since the khirigsuur mounds at Ulaan Tolgoi were too large for us to excavate, mapping, sampling, and investigating their outlying features was a practical way to date them and explore their relationship to these structures as well as deer stones.

At this early stage in our investigation, in 2003, we could not offer sweeping generalizations about Ulaan Tolgoi. Nor could we argue with assurance that the charcoal date of 2150-1960 BP was an accurate age for DS5, as the sample might have resulted from rodent activity. However, it was a promising start; we had found that deer stone foundation stratigraphy could be compromised by rodents and that cobble rings associated with deer stones produced charcoal and burned animal bone. It seemed that future work at Ulaan Tolgoi could provide important data, not only on deer stones but also on Late Bronze Age ritual landscapes (Askarov et al. 1992; Bokovenko 1994; Bokovenko et al. 1995, 1996; Sementsov et al. 1998; Mon-Sol Project 1999/2000; Jacobson et al. 2001, 2002; National Museum of Korea 2002). It also offered the potential for studying differences in stone constructions, construction histories of khirigsuur features, studies of ring hearths and their relationship to deer stones and khirigsuurs, feature chronology, and a host of other questions.

5. Learning From the Dukha: Reindeer, Ritual and Religion

Dukha shaman Suyun displaying her outfit in her tent in Menge Bulag. (photo: Stephanie [Nef] Marik)

Khuvsgul Province includes the northernmost area of Mongolia and borders southern Siberia. The topography is mountainous, with some peaks reaching over 3,000 meters. The other main geomorphic features are two large north to south running valleys. The eastern valley contains Lake Khuvsgul, whose surface elevation is about 1,800 meters. To the west lies the Darkhad Valley, which is currently mainly dry, although it contains several large lakes. The valley floor, once the bed of a glacial lake, lies at about 1,600 meters. Pleistocene glaciation of the region appears to have been mostly localized, but alpine glaciation occurred in the mountains that separate the Darkhad from Lake Khuvsgul. At some time, the exit drainage from the north of the Darkhad was blocked by a glacier and a large ice-dammed lake formed. Old shoreline features can be seen on the sides of the surrounding hills up to elevations of 1,900 meters. In the mountains along the western border of the Darkhad there is evidence of numerous cirque glaciers and apparently some valley glaciers, but the overall landscape does not appear to have been overridden by ice sheets. (Steven B. Young, July 2001)

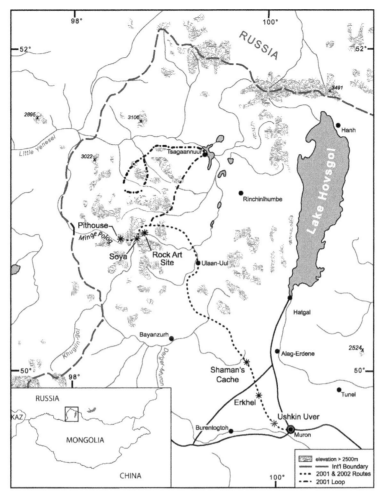

Darkhad Valley sites and routes of the 2003 expedition.

Menge Bulag 2001-2004

Our introduction to deer stones at Uushigiin Uvör and Ulaan Tolgoi raised questions about function and iconography. In addition to the dating problem, what role did deer stones have in DSK culture? What was the meaning of the deer image? And how widespread was the deer stone phenomenon? Our discussions with Mongolian colleagues, who were Buddhist and had a long history as a pastoral society, produced few clues, and despite decades of Soviet research, Deer Stone culture remained a mystery. Believing we might have more success exploring these questions with the Tsaatan, we joined Ed Nef who

had initiated a humanitarian project to deliver horses to the Tsaatan reindeer herders at their summer camps in the taiga forest of northern Mongolia. Among our goals was to determine if there were comparable rituals or parallels between DSK culture and ethnographic Dukha culture and belief. Were the Dukha lineal descendants of DSK people and culture? Were their ritual ovoo monuments derived from DSK khirigsuurs? Could their shamans help inform our interpretation of deer stone art and khirigsuur function? And were deer stones or khirigsuurs present in Dukha taiga territories?

Enroute to Minge Bulag

On the 26th of June we "jeeped" across the highlands south of the Darkhad valley, through the town of Ulaan Uul and across the southwest corner of the Darkhad plain, finally reaching Söyö, where the Khugiin Gol (Melody River, a headwater of the Little Yenesei) exits the mountains. Here we camped for the evening, meeting Tsaatan horsemen who were to escort us into the Sayan mountains. Ed Nef had arranged to purchase twenty horses from herders in Tsaaganuur, the northernmost town in Mongolia, as gifts to the West Taiga Dukha (known as Tsaatan, meaning 'reindeer herders' in Mongolian) who needed horses to help manage their reindeer herds and obtain supplies from town. On the morning of the 27th we departed on horseback into the hills, following the valley of the Khugiin Gol, noting several burial mounds on the north side of the river upstream from Söyö. After spending a night on the trail across from the last of the Mongol sheep-herding camps on the Khugiin Gol, we climbed over a 2500m high mountain pass and entered the Minge Bulag valley, a 2000m high lichen-rich basin where the Dukha spend summers camped in three clusters along the river. Subject to cloudy, wet 'mountain weather,' Minge Bulag receives a large amount of summer rainfall, making it an ideal climate for lichen growth, and therefore reindeer pasture. Its vegetation is a grassy tundra, with patches of dwarf birch and isolated young larch trees, both of which appear to be expanding their range north across the hillsides in response to the pronounced warming being experienced now in Mongolia. (27 June 2003)

The Dukha (Tsaatan) live as reindeer herders in the West Taiga country in the Eastern Sayan Mountains west of the Darkhad Valley. In addition to reindeer that supplied them with milk, meat, and fur, they needed horses so they could maintain contacts between their summer and winter camps and the village of Tsaganuur, where they obtained food, medical services, and schooling. I was eager to see how the Tsaatan reindeer adaptation differed from the Yamal Nenets herders I had been with in northwest Siberia in the 1990s. I also wanted to scout for archaeological sites in the taiga forest zone and see if Deer Stone-Khirigsuur culture or signs of Mesolithic or Neolithic peoples were present. Could the forest zone have been a conduit for cultural transmissions to the northeast and eventually to Bering Strait and Alaska? This region of Mongolia was also where Russian ethnologist Sevyan I. Vainshtein (1980, 1981) believed reindeer breeding began 2000 years ago as a result of contacts between Siberian forest hunters and steppe cultures to the south, whose peoples had been in the animal herding business since the mid-Holocene.

Loading the horses at Minge Bulag; and Sanjiim and other Dukha camped en route to Menge Bulag in 2005.

Birch bark technology. Bayamonkh showing the curved blade of his birch bark cutting tool, 2009; Enka sewing strips of birch bark into ortz panels, 2009; Birch-bark ortz at the Kharmai Valley meeting place, 2007. (photos: PDP).

Our team of American and Mongolian researchers and students visited the Tsaatan for a week each year between 2001 and 2004, at first to deliver Ed Nef's horses and later to contribute food and craft production tools like wood and bone carving sets, tent canvas, and other goods. Our last visit was in June, 2004. Our first excursion left Söyö Tolgoi (tooth hill) at noon and crossed the bridge over the Khugiin Gol River

The weather was chilly, windy, and cloudy. It took us four hours to reach the Evdei River. We continued our journey over Evdei Mountain Pass and then down into Menge Bulag Valley, walking on foot in rough or marshy areas. Menge Bulag is located in a high mountain zone of the Red Taiga Mountains and is one of the main Tsaatan summer reindeer herding areas. When we asked our Tsaatan guides what 'Menge Bulag' means, we

Adiya Namkhai (at left) distributing our donation of tent canvas and other goods to West Tsaatan herders.

Steven Young and Paula DePriest discuss fine points of riding technique during a travel break.

before heading north towards the Evdei River, whose name derives from the Uigur word "ivd" and "ivtsaa" and is translated as "reindeer" or "river with reindeer" in Mongolian. We climbed in our jeeps to the edge of the forest and there met the Tsaatan and set off on horse-back for Menge Bulag, their camp in the tundra above the forest edge.

got two different explanations: 'Monhk Bulag' means 'forever river', and 'Myangan Bulag' means 'a thousand rivers.' We arrived at the Dukha summer camp at around 8:30 in the evening. There were ten families present, and we pitched our tents next to the tents of Bayandalai, Zolzaya, and Batsaya.

Our Dukha hosts en route to Meng Bulag, with Batsaya, Bayandalai, and Adiya, Dukha families, Bayandalai's family, and Tartag. (photos: WF, PDP, BF)

Dukha summer reindeer camp at Menge Bulag in the Sayan Mountain tundra west of Tsaaganuur, and Mongolian ponies.

Dukha/Tsaatan—Mongolian Tuvans

The Dukha ethnic group is related to reindeer herders of the Tuva Autonomous Region of Russian South Siberia and traditionally remained in close contact with them through trading, intermarrying, and sharing of hunting territories (Plumley and Battulag 2000; Wheeler 2000). However, most recently they have been separated and had their herding ranges reduced by the closing of the Russian-Mongolian border. In part, the Dukha are descended from Tuvan reindeer herders that fled to Mongolia to avoid collectivization after 1944. The Dukha maintain their native language, 'Khuvsgul Uigur,' a dialect of Tuvan in the Turkic language family. 'Khuvsgul Uigur' is heavily influenced by Khalkha Mongolian and is not mutually intelligible with other Tuvan dialects. At present an estimated 200 people speak 'Khuvsgul Uigur' and 235,000 speak Tuvan in Russia. The Mongolian Dukha are also fluent and literate in Mongolian using either the traditional vertical Mongolian script or Russian Cyrillic alphabet.

Reindeer herding among the Dukha and Tuvan people probably dates back two thousand years (Vainshtein 1980; Solnoi et al. 2003) and is the most southern and probably the oldest reindeer -herding culture in Eurasia. The Darkhad region of northern Mongolia has been proposed as the region where reindeer were first domesticated 2-3,000 years ago and the source of their latter expansion throughout the Eurasian taiga and Arctic zones. (DePriest 2003:34)

The next morning, following draughts of milk-tea, I began interviewing Dukha about old camping places and artifacts. During my 2002 visit I was encouraged when Bayandalai showed me a small cylindrical microblade core, a Neolithic period implement, but he could not remember where he found it. I suspected it might have been from a depression in the center of the camp—perhaps an ancient house pit—and asked if we could test it. There followed a delicate negotiation with the assembled elders over concern that digging would offend the underground spirits of ancestors and reindeer. Hearing this, Sanjmiatov produced a well-worn antler tine from his pack and explained that since reindeer are always pawing the earth, using a reindeer antler might be acceptable—and so it was! The negotiation reminded me of a similar discussion I had with Yamal Nenets who also were reluctant to let us put trowel to earth—for the same reason—offending ancestors. As our dig proceeded, a circle of curious Dukha gathered around, amused as much by our slow, methodical procedures as by our scant finds. In the end, we came up with a few small microblades and some not-so-old bones from recent Dukha meals. We later learned that the core had been found on a nearby campsite while the microblades must have come from an undiscovered Neolithic site somewhere in the present camp. Clearly there was archaeological work to be done here, but the sites dated to a time long before deer stones. (20 June, 2002)

My 2004 survey ranged farther a-field, up and down Menge Bulag brook, this time on horseback! This was a first for me, and strangely image-building. Later I got a chance to ride a reindeer—the steeds Dukha kids were romping around on, playing their version of 'cowboys and indians'. But I made little progress because my feet were dragging on the ground. This rider and his reindeer were more comfortable standing still for photos.

Dukha herders lining up at the start of a reindeer race, and playing reindeer polo. (photos:PDP)

Batsaya, Sanjmyatav, and Steven Young inspect our excavation in a possible house pit at Menge Bulag camp in June 2002; Paula DePriest presenting Dukha herders with pictures she took the year before.

Our four visits to the Tsaatan were memorable and instructive. We made many friends and saw the reindeer economy close-up: how people tended and milked their animals; how they defended them against wolves prowling around the camp perimeter at night; how reindeer were still key transport animals carrying people, gear, and firewood; and how hunting, fishing, and gathering continues to provide crucial subsistence resources. We also saw how the fall of the Soviet regime in 1990 trashed the infrastructure that had supported the Tsaatan camps with helicopter transport for medical services, travel to school, and other services. The mountain-focused life of these reindeer people is very different from the Yamal Nenets whose huge territory is only a few meters above sea level and who are constantly on the move, winter and summer, migrating with huge herds hundreds of miles north and south every year. Dukha have a life more like Mongolian herders, more sedentary, with short vertical camp shifts rather than constant settlement relocation and long-distance seasonal moves. Several years later, American archaeologist Todd Surovell and his students returned to Minge Bulag and made a detailed ethnoarchaeological study of Dukha camp activity using elevated remote cameras to document camp life, material culture, and community patterning (Haas et al. 2019).

Shaman Suyun and Sanjiim in her Menge Bulag chum, 2006.

Dukha Traditional Knowledge

Dukha knowledge of reindeer diet includes their preference for feeding on certain lichens. For example, Sanjiim noted that reindeer will eat bujirach (Cladonia stellaris) and gatig hag (Cetraria) in all of the seasonal feeding grounds. In contrast, the lush mosses associated with lichens in the feeding grounds apparently are not eaten by the reindeer at any time of the year. Two lichens were noted as important for seasonal increases in the weight of reindeer and indication of their increased health, with lush colonies of bujirach and gatig hag leading to fattened reindeer. For this reason, the herders warn against disrupting these lichens or mosses from their loose rooting in the soil because they cannot become rooted again and will die. Although the feeding ground used in 2002 shows the effects of grazing by comparison to the Jamts area that has not been grazed for over 15 years, it is still adequate for the current level of around 700 reindeer. Increases in herd size will require moving the herd more often or into currently unused and more remote areas.

The Dukha and their traditional knowledge of lichens are on the verge of extinction. One of the major goals of the International Convention on Biological Diversity is that traditional knowledge about plants and animals held by indigenous peoples and local communities must be respected, preserved. Among the problems facing the Dukha are lack of veterinary care, loss of herder salaries provided during the Soviet regime, geopolitical partitioning of their traditional grazing grounds, and pressures for more sedentary life for schooling and medical care. Furthermore, large-scale global warming and landscape changes potentially will degrade reindeer feeding grounds. These limits threaten not only the ability of the herders to continue their hunting and gathering lifestyle, but also threaten the loss of their symbiotic knowledge of reindeer and lichens. Without domesticated reindeer and reindeer herding culture, Dukha traditional knowledge of lichens will be lost forever. (DePriest 2003)

vodka libations, khadags, prayers, new charms and artifact donations, and other types of offer-

Dukha scenes. Children in 'summer school' in a 'chum' (tent) in Menge Bulag with a teacher supplied by Ed Nef and a visit from Pamela Slutz, U.S. Ambassador to Mongolia, 2005; and Sukhbaatar reading Mongolia newspaper to herders, 2004.

Ovoo Worship Sites

In the Dukha taiga we garnered important ethnographic evidence for interpreting our archaeological finds. Although we found the taiga/tundra zone has no khirigsuurs, deer stones, or empire period monuments, we encountered numerous small ovoo rock-piles—worship sites adorned with blue, white, or green prayer ribbons called khadags, animal offerings consisting of bones, antlers, and sometimes whole heads, and a diverse array of artifacts, one of which was a wooden model of an airplane. Ovoos are a regional expression of landscape ritual traditions widespread among central Asian groups. Dukha and Darkhad Mongolian ovoos accumulate archaeological materials over time and resemble smaller versions of the larger mounded ovoos seen in steppe regions to the south. Dukha ovoos display donations such as articles of clothing, shoes, empty vodka bottles, animal bones, wood implements, and spirit carvings. They are renewed by yearly visits that include

tory behavior. There is no particular structure to the mounds, which grow by accretion of small rocks and sticks. Some of these worship sites are trees rather than rocks and stick constructions, all of which may be adorned with khadags and articles of clothing. In the Mongol steppes to the south, ovoos are often found at places where tracks and roads cross passes between valleys. Here travelers pause and walk three times around the structure, praying and adding rocks, crutches, coins, paper money, and other items to the mound, which can grow to immense size along popular routes. Much of the steppe ovoo tradition is related to Buddhist belief, but it certainly had earlier origins dating back at least a few thousand years. One of the largest ovoo sites in northern Mongolia is at Oliin Davaa ("Bald Pass") where the road enters the Darkhad Valley; this site consists of thirteen rock-based teepee-structures filled with all manner of material donations.

Ovoo examples. Larch tree ovoo maintained by the Dukha in the northern Darkhad decorated with khadag ribbons, poles, and rocks, 2005; One of the thirteen ovoos at Oliin Davaa at southern entry to the Darkhad Valley in a late spring storm.; Ancient rock ovoos at Ovoolog, which according to Dukha legend was built by Uighers 500 years ago (photos: PDP).

Oliin Davaa

The Darkhad Valley, as the former Buddhist ecclesiastical estate Darkhad Ikh Shav under the Jebtsundamba Khutuktu, is home to a number of Buddhist-influenced ovoos. They are character- ized by multicolored prayer scarves traditionally of Chinese silk (but now often of synthetic fab- ric), printed prayer flags with standard messages, wooden, seed, or stone prayer beads, and plaques with Tibetan script. The most important ceremoni- al sites, Öliin Davaa ('Bald Pass') at the southern entrance of the Darkhad Valley (N50°34.647' E 099°08.581'), Ongon Hill in Renchinlkhumbe Sum (N51°22.548'" E 099°34.988'), and the sacred Renchinlkhumbe Mountain (N51°32.575' E 099°12.270'), each have thirteen ovoos or altars– twelve small ovoos or altars in a row with one large ovoo at the south end. The ovoos are constructed of standing sticks in a teepee form. The number of ovoos and offerings is part of the "Cult of Thirteen Altai Mountains of West Mongolia", a ritual num- ber adopted by Buddhism as representing sacred Buddhist mountains. (DePriest 2007:105)

Our forays into the high taiga failed to locate any evidence of the DSK and demonstrated that this complex was limited to the grassy steppe where it was firmly linked to a pastoral economy similar to that of today's Mongolian Darkhad

herders. Despite the absence of deer stones and khirigsuurs, we learned much of importance from the Dukha. Our ethnographic work revealed what has probably been a long-standing interface between peoples of the taiga and steppe whose economies and cultures diverged dramatically after the steppe peoples domesticated the "five snouts": horses, camels, yaks, sheep, and goats as early as 5000 years ago, while Dukha ancestors maintained a nomadic hunting, fishing, and gathering life until they began domesticating reindeer. For taiga peoples, changes came much later, when reindeer began to be domesticated about 2000 years ago. Today both peoples contin- ue to practice herding supplemented by fishing and hunting while the Dukha depend also on foraging for plants, tubers, seeds, and nuts. his deer stone thesis.

Our taiga experience gave us an opportuni- ty to compare Dukha acquisition of horses for communication, trade, herding, and transport with the DSK culture which also was beginning to utilize horses for similar purposes, including war. While vastly different in context, the addi- tion of horses to Dukha life brought subsistence improvements to their reindeer herding economy and settlement patterns that were similar but on a smaller scale than that occurred when Deer Stone culture people began to control horses with bridles for mounted riding, allowing for a major expansion of pastoral economy, trade contacts, and political and military developments (Taylor 2017). Moreso than Khalka and Darkhad Mongolians, the Dukha provided a small-scale model of DSK culture when one took account of important differences like herding reindeer rather than sheep and goats, having smaller and more nomadic populations, and absence of a megalithic monument tradition. Dukha interactions with their cultural and linguistic neighbors across the Russian border in Tuva also served as examples of how DSK populations must have interacted with the taiga peoples across the steppe/taiga border in their times.

The Sailag Davaa Ovoo

In June-July 2005 and July 2007, our group visited the hunting ovoo at Sailag Davaa (N51°06.702'/E 098°08.961'), a trip of over two days by horse from the closest reindeer camp or settlement. According to my Dukha guides, the hunting ovoo became important during Mongolian independence in 1911 when, under increasing Russian influence, the local groups paid tribute in sables hunted or trapped in the pass. To meet this tribute, large groups of hunters camped at artells in the pass in the winter months, as described by Vainstein (1980:174). This pass is the eastern entrance to the Bussin Gol Depression, since the late 1950s an uninhabited border region that is the primary hunting and antler-gathering ground for both the Dukha and the Darkhads.

The ovoo, standing on a small hill in the center of the pass, is constructed of 2.0-1.5 meter long sticks anchored in a pile of rocks. The sticks are tied with as many as 300 strips of fabric in multiple colors...Attached to the sticks are over 60 carved ongons [spirit objects], almost all of wood. Half of these represent hunting equipment – knives (14), rifles (10), spikes (2), bullets for particular rifle models (2), a club, and a crossbow arrow. The remainder include wild animals – rabbits (2),

and bear, bird, deer, lynx, marmot, and squirrel; domestic animals – horses (5) and camel; commemorative plaques (13, including 10 that were produced during our July 2007 visit); and various items – skis (2), an airplane, a flour-mixer, and a vodka bottle. Other objects include bullets (10), vodka bottles (3), ibex antlers (1), cigarette lighter (1), and numerous matches and match boxes. Interestingly, this ovoo has no horse or animal skulls, although they are common on ovoos throughout the Darkhad Valley. The ovoo has two altars of flat rocks that are in current use for burning incense (documented in June 2005) and offerings of cheese and candy (June 2005 and July 2007). Milk offerings are made to the surrounding mountains and rivers and to animate the ongons and antlers on the ovoo. As with tools attached to Dukha and Darkhad shaman garments, the small weapons and animals serve as amulets as the hunter negotiates with the animal spirit master for good hunting. Animal figures are used to ask for exchange for actual animals, and to serve as repositories (ongons) for holding the spirits released from his earlier catches. The released spirits are then ready for rebirth under the control of their spirit-master. (DePriest 2007:107)

One of the thirteen ovoos at Oliin Davaa at southern entry to the Darkhad Valley.

Deer Stones, Dukha, and Shamans

Another important revelation from our acquaintance with the West Taiga Dukha was meeting their 100-year-old female shaman, Suyun, a specialist in reindeer ritual and medicine. During our several visits to her tent in Minge Bulag, Suyun demonstrated her shaman's clothing, drum, and ornaments. She could not conduct a séance for us because it was "the wrong time of the month [moon]". Suyun was renowned throughout the Darkhad for her knowledge of plant remedies. The year after our last visit we learned that she had died and her shamanic robe and ritual items had been cached in a special place in the country, separate from her remains to avoid spirit conflict.

to a hilltop at Baga Ertseg, sensing in it a place of tranquility and power. That evening, while exploring around the granite peak, I came across the weathered remains of a shaman's drum in a cleft in the rocks and recognized it as part of a shaman's 'sky' burial. The location was dramatic, with rock pinnacles emerging from the crest of the hill, a cave-like, wooded forest glen between the granite outcrops, and a view for miles around over the surrounding hills and valleys. Nearby I found the drum handle and beater, small iron tinkle bells and rattles, a cut-out human figure, and a small bronze drinking cup. The wooden handle and beater were incised with skeletal designs resembling the shield-like emblems on deer stones, and also like patterns on the chests of shamanic garments like Suyun's. We photographed the objects but did not disturb the cache. In 2004

A Dukha and Darkhad shaman hunting ovoo with carved images of weapons and animals at Sailag Davaa. Rainbows are considered both ongons and good omens; Darkhad shaman hunting ovoo above the Kharmai Valley decorated with blue and white prayer khadags on its lower branches. June 2007]
(photos: PDP)

Soon after leaving the Dukha in 2001, we chanced upon such a cache while camping near Arbulag, north of Murun. Passing nearby in the evening, we found ourselves drawn irresistibly

we re-visited the site and found many items had been removed during the past three years, so we collected the remaining objects for preservation in the Mongolia National Museum.

The 100-year old Dukha shaman, Suyun, a healer (photo: Stephanie [Nef] Marik); The Baga Ertseg shaman cache at Angarkhai Hill, view west from the cache; and the cleft containing the shaman cache.

Mongolia and Circumpolar Shamanism

Across the North American Arctic, skeletal markings are found on animal carvings, masks, shamanic clothing, and other ritual items of early Eskimo cultures. Skeletal frames are seen on shamanic items in 1500-year old Ipiutak and Old Bering Sea cultures in Bering Strait and northwest Alaska, where they are interpreted as Iron Age Siberian shamanic introductions. In Yamal, Arctic Russia, I found a cache of Nenets shamanic objects with similar skeletal designs (Fitzhugh and Golovnev 1998). The Baga Ertseg cache with its skeleton motifs demonstrates the widespread persistence of circumpolar shamanic tradition and iconography extending over 3,000 years, from deer stone times to the modern day.

The connection between deer, deer stones, and shamanic ritual has been studied extensively in Mongolia, where shamanism continues to be practiced today. O. Purev, one of the leading Mongolian scholars of shamanism, believed that "for a long time, shamans of Mongolian tribes considered the female deer as heavenly steeds" and identified them with their shamanic clothing and implements (Purev 1999). Given their prominence, it is logical to see the deer in deer stone art as having a similar function as in modern Mongolian shamanism. In the 2500-year old Pazyryk culture of western Mongolia and Russian southern Siberia, a warrior was buried with a horse wearing deer antler headdress (Rudenko 1970), and Esther Jacobson (1993) has written an entire book describing the "deer goddess" cult as reflected in Inner Asia archaeology. Central to these beliefs is the idea of the deer as a magical stallion that carries people's souls to heaven, also known as the "dark space". These thoughts guided our explorations as we began to decipher deer stone art and its function in Late Bronze Age Mongolia (Fitzhugh 2005:23; for more analysis see Bayarsaikhan 2022).

A cache of shamanic paraphernalia was found in a cache at Baga Ertseg near the top of Angarkhai Hill where it had been placed, probably decades ago, inside a wooden box found nearby: a drum hoop with rattles, a drum handle with chevron/skeletal engraving, rattles for a shaman's robe or belt, mouth harps, and a small bronze offering cup.

We returned to the steppe from Menge Bulag on the morning of June 16, separating into two groups so the botany crew could collect samples. Before we left, Paula DePriest created a competition among the Tsaatans, offering 5,000 tugrugs to the owner of the largest reindeer and horse. The largest reindeer was owned by Mandakh, whereas the largest horse was owned by Baasankhuu (nicknamed Tartag). At eleven o'clock in the morning, we mounted up and headed to Soyë Tolgoi, and by 3:30 pm arrived at our vehicles. On the way back, we stopped at Tsatstain Khuushuu, where we spent the next three days excavating its deer stone, one of the northernmost known in the Darkhad valley.

A Shishged Sky Burial

Walking in the forest near the top of the hill behind our camp on the Shishged River, I found a weathered horse skull in a tree at the edge of the open steppe. In the forest edge about 100 m southwest of the skull, clothing, boots, and prayer sashes were draped over a fallen tree, and hanging from a standing tree a meter to the south was a bag with turquoise-colored and clear plastic beads. "Is this a sky burial", I wondered? Then to the southwest, I found vodka bottles, an open, empty suitcase, and about 50 small white and blue khyadag prayer sashes tied to nearby trees. 100 m to the north, a female skull still wearing a braided cap rested on

Sky burial, perhaps of a woman shaman, south of the Shishged River with horse, clothes, suitcase, knitted cap, and many other objects, 2006.

the surface of the ground, with yellow and blue prayer sashes tied to nearby trees south and north. The skull faced east. A tube of lipstick was next to the hat; a porcelain bowl and a plastic bottle of cooking oil was alongside the skull, and a bundle of juniper twigs was tied with white sash to a tree 5 m south of the skull. Thirty meters southeast of the skull lay more clothing and a sweater, and 20 m to the southwest, a shawl. The burial area is in a larch grove 100 m in from the pasture. Marion and I made a map of this site on the 17th. (15/17 June 2006)

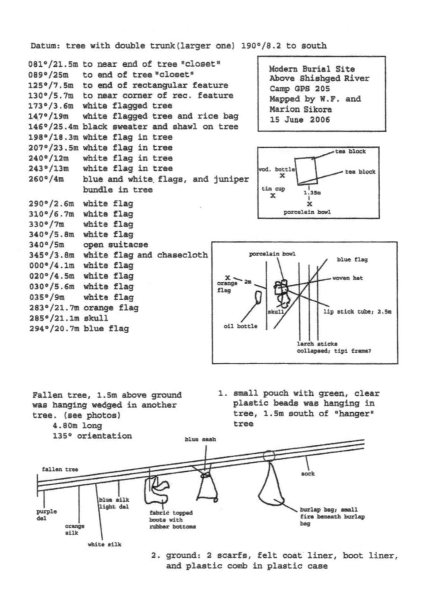

A Sky Burial at the Shishged River Ferry.

Mongolian Altai   *Khuvsgul Aimag*

6. Deer Stone Ancestors

Söyö: a Neolithic and Medieval Site

While staging our 2001 excursion into the mountains with the Dukha, we found a Neolithic site at Söyö Tolgoi ('Fang Hill') on the south bank of the Khugiin Gol river where it exits the mountain forest and emerges onto the Darkhad plain. Apparently, hunters using microblades and prismatic cores like those found at Minge Bulag were not confined to the mountain taiga zone. Two hearths were eroding at the terrace edge, revealing fire-cracked rock, charcoal, and carbonized bone. Among the bones were a large herbivore (deer or elk), small mammals, and sheep or goat. Artifacts included small conical flint cores, microblades, a ground stone bead, and friable, thin cord-marked ceramics, as well as a red-painted thick-walled ceramic bowl fragments. Excavation revealed

this to be a two-component site which was, in 2001, the first Neolithic site known from the Darkhad region. The lower horizon associated with the Neolithic tools produced a radiocarbon date of cal. 6510-5940 BP, conforming well with the flint tools, while Hearths 1 and 2 from the upper level dated to the Late Iron/Early Medieval period, cal. 1170±50 BP and cal. 1020±50 BP (see Radiocarbon Dates, Appendix 1). The presence in these hearths of both forest game and domestic sheep or goats provided a starting point for investigating the mixed hunting/pastoral economy that persists to this day, later studied by Julia Clark (2014). Initially we hoped that the Söyö Neolithic level, parts of which were still frozen when we excavated, would contain wild reindeer bones that could be used for assessing domestication, but when the ground thawed, we found no organics except charcoal. Vainshtein (1980, 1981) had hypothesized that northern Mongolia was the most likely location for the origin of Eurasian reindeer domestication because taiga peoples were in regular contact with steppe pastoralists. We hoped to test this idea by analyzing reindeer bones dating across the domestication threshold from 4000 to 1000 years ago, but we never found sites with large reindeer bone collections.

While working at Söyö, we visited a rock

The Söyö site has a Neolithic level containing flints, stone beads beneath a Medieval level with ceramics and domestic faunal remains, and Kevin Robinson and his lake sediment core samples for paleoenvironment reconstruction, a B.A. thesis for University of Pittsburgh.

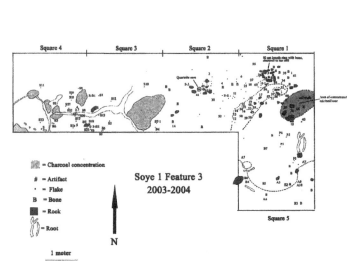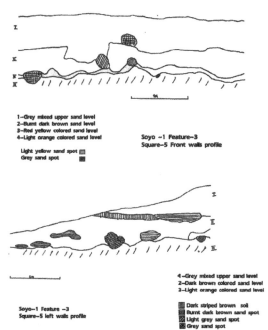

Söyö-1/F3 excavation plan map of Neolithic Layers 2,3; south wall profile of Square 5, Söyö-1/F3; and east wall profile of Square 5, Söyö-1/F3

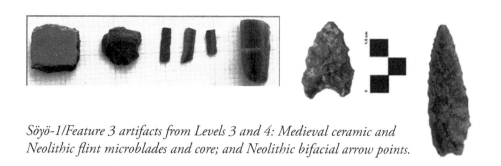

Söyö-1/Feature 3 artifacts from Levels 3 and 4: Medieval ceramic and Neolithic flint microblades and core; and Neolithic bifacial arrow points.

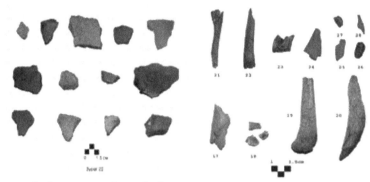

Söyö finds: ceramics from the lower Neolithic level; bone from the Medieval hearths.

art site at Tolijgii Boom north of the Khugiin Gol ford (Sanjmyatav 2005). The art showed a red-painted rectangular enclosure filled with dots and a human figure but had been vandalized recently by a looter attempting to pry it off the cliff face. This was my first exposure to Mongolian rock art, which I pursued later with Richard Kortum in the northern Darkhad and for several years in Altai Mountains of western Mongolia. When Richard and I returned to the Northern Darkhad in 2008, we discovered new rock art sites, including images of the iconic Mongolian deer, near a group of Shishged River khirigsuurs.

Tolijgii Buum rock art site north of Khug River at Söyö, and an art panel damaged by looters or vandals who had pried some of the art off the rock face.

The Khogorgo Gol-3 Burial

In 2007 we returned to the Darkhad Valley to continue investigating Late Bronze Age deer stones and khirigsuurs after conducting a preliminary survey of the lands around Bayan Ulgii in the Altai Mountains of western Mongolia. Reaching the Shishged River north of Tsaaganuur, we found a circular pavement feature near the mouth of the Khogorgo River, east of the ferry landing, with flint chips and microblades on the surface. As at Hort Azuur, Evdei, and other places, we had puzzled over the association between deer stones and chipped stone tools. Could that technology have persisted into the deer stone era at a time when bronze was available for tools, weapons, and pots? Or were the lithics the product of earlier occupations at these sites? Khogorgo offered a chance to explore and date stone tools associated with a riverside domestic

ping and starting an excavation at the stone pavement. The area was full of squirrel holes, and almost every hole was surrounded by flakes of chert that had been brought to the surface by the rodents. Our surface collection had produced few artifacts other than a microblade core and a tiny bifacial leaf-shaped point similar to ones at Söyö. The microblades were so small it was hard to imagine them being inset in bone points. This may be a chronological factor, possibly dating later than Söyö, whose radiocarbon dates were ca. 6200 BP.

The excavation turned out more complicated than we imagined. It produced many Neolithic flint tools and a variety of ceramics, including some thick Bronze Age ceramics and also thinner Neolithic sherds. These artifacts were scattered throughout the fill above and below the rock pavement, which was composed of large cobbles with a few large slabs in the center. After surface

Khogorgo Gol-3 finds: Clearing the circular burial pavement; surface-collected microblades and cores; check-stamped ceramic sherd. (photos: Elaine Ling, WF)

site and a stone pavement—possibly a grave. Such sites might also hold clues as to the origin of DSK khirigsuurs. The site had two features, Locus 1 (N51°24.733'/E99°18.464') and Locus 2 (N51°24.722'/E99°18.450').

Soon after setting up camp, we found the ground littered with flakes of black chert and a microblade core and spent the afternoon mapping and photographing, we removed the rocks from the center and found Neolithic artifacts and large amount of flakes in the brown silty soil below. Eventually, we worked down to rocks descending into a central pit about 3m in diameter excavated into tan, silty, sterile soil.

When we got below the last rocks, a leg bone showed up, then a skull, and then a well-pre-

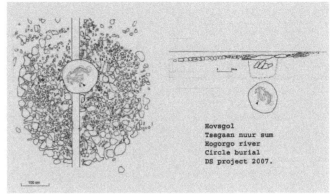

The Khogorgo-3 Mound, showing rocks at the top of the central burial pit, north at top, and plan and profile views.

served skeleton buried in a tightly flexed position, lying on its left side, head to the east, facing south. A few chert artifacts and flakes were associated directly with the burial, but there was no formal grave deposit, at least one that was preserved. The skull looked Mongolian and had only three teeth; otherwise, the skeleton was not remarkable other than being quite short in stature. Bayaraa thinks the burial style is early Bronze Age – about 4000 years old, and this makes sense of the tiny microblades and thin, poorly-fired pottery, with check-stamped or dentate decoration. At least here we had a clean Early Bronze age site without confusing Neolithic or LBA elements. The few thick ceramic sherds found near the surface are a post-burial component. A human tooth from the burial produced the very satisfactory date of cal. BP 3830-3620, several hundred years before the DSK period. From this time, it did not seem like a big jump for people to start piling up stone mounds on a stone foundation like the one at Kohogorgo. But what would be very different was the astronomical-like architecture of khirigsuurs with their stone fences, horse mounds, and circle hearths. These features must have been from a distant intervention.

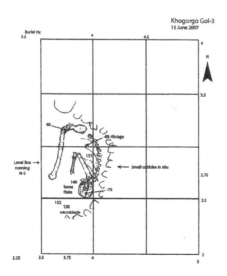

The Khogorgo Gol-3 burial map, and the burial in situ.

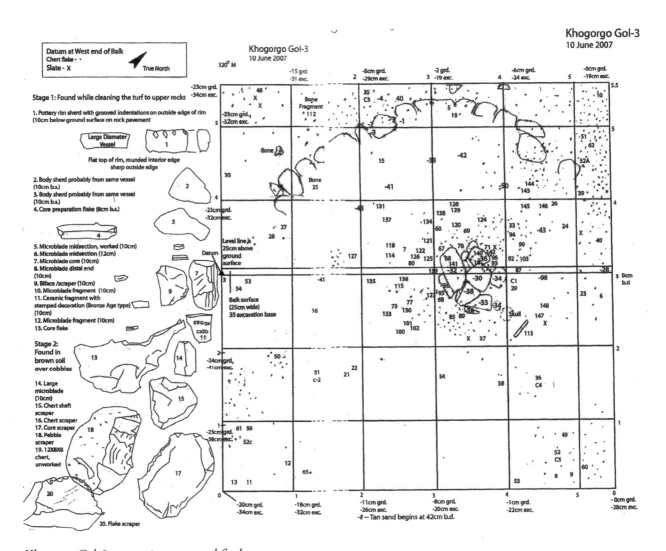

Khogorgo Gol-3 excavation map and finds.

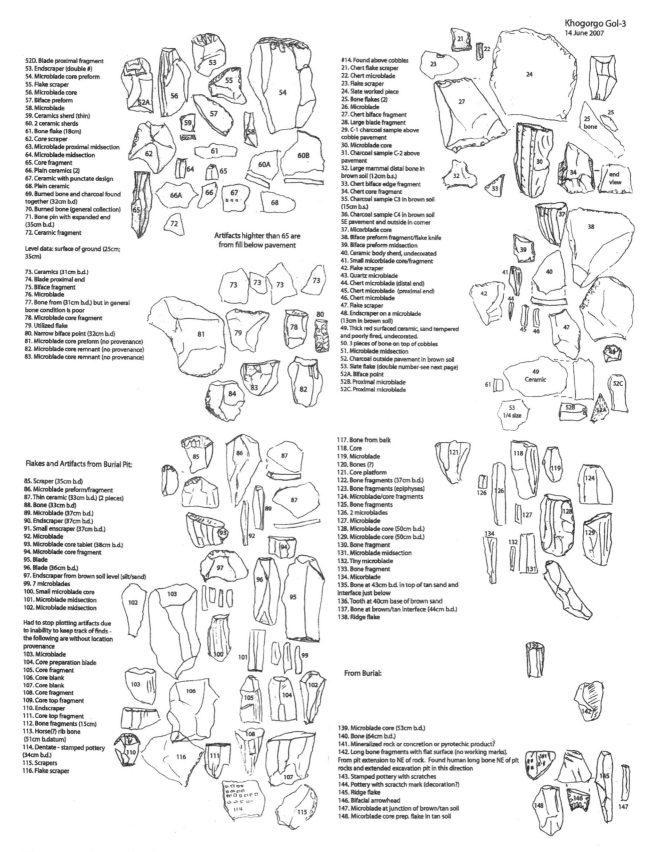

52D. Blade proximal fragment
53. Endscraper (double #)
54. Microblade core preform
55. Flake scraper
56. Microblade core
57. Biface preform
58. Microblade
59. Ceramics sherd (thin)
60. 2 ceramic sherds
61. Bone flake (18cm)
62. Core scraper
63. Microblade proximal midsection
64. Microblade midsection
65. Core fragment
66. Plain ceramics (2)
67. Ceramic with punctate design
68. Plain ceramic
69. Burned bone and charcoal found
together (32cm b.d)
70. Burned bone (general collection)
71. Bone pin with expanded end
(35cm b.d.)
72. Ceramic fragment

Level data: surface of ground (25cm;
35cm)

73. Ceramics (31cm b.d.)
74. Blade proximal end
75. Biface fragment
76. Microblade
77. Bone from (31cm b.d.) but in general
bone condition is poor
78. Microblade core fragment
79. Utilized flake
80. Narrow biface point (32cm b.d)
81. Microblade core preform (no provenance)
82. Microblade core remnant (no provenance)
83. Microblade core remnant (no provenance)

**Artifacts highter than 65 are
from fill below pavement**

#14. Found above cobbles
21. Chert flake scraper
22. Chert microblade
23. Flake scraper
24. Slate worked piece
25. Bone flakes (2)
26. Microblade
27. Chert biface fragment
28. Large blade fragment
29. C-1 charcoal sample above
cobble pavement
30. Microblade core
31. Charcoal sample C-2 above
pavement
32. Large mammal distal bone in
brown soil (12cm b.s.)
33. Chert biface edge fragment
34. Chert core fragment
35. Charcoal sample C3 in brown soil
(15cm b.s.)
36. Charcoal sample C4 in brown soil
SE pavement and outside in corner
37. Microblade core
38. Biface preform fragment/flake knife
39. Biface preform midsection
40. Ceramic body sherd, undecorated
41. Small microblade core/fragment
42. Flake scraper
43. Quartz microblade
44. Chert microblade (distal end)
45. Chert microblade (proximal end)
46. Chert microblade
47. Flake scraper
48. Endscraper on a microblade
(13cm in brown soil)
49. Thick red surfaced ceramic, sand tempered
and poorly fired, undecorated.
50. 3 pieces of bone on top of cobbles
51. Microblade midsection
52. Charcoal outside pavement in brown soil
53. Slate flake (double number-see next page)
52A. Biface point
52B. Proximal microblade
52C. Proximal microblade

end view

Ceramic

53
1/4 size

Flakes and Artifacts from Burial Pit:

85. Scraper (35cm b.d)
86. Microblade preform/fragment
87. Thin ceramic (33cm b.d.) (2 pieces)
88. Bone (33cm b.d)
89. Microblade (37cm b.d.)
90. Endscraper (37cm b.d.)
91. Small enscraper (37cm b.d.)
92. Microblade
93. Microblade core tablet (38cm b.d.)
94. Microblade core fragment
95. Blade
96. Blade (36cm b.d.)
97. Endscraper from brown soil level (silt/sand)
99. 7 microblades
100. Small microblade core
101. Microblade midsection
102. Microblade midsection

Had to stop plotting artifacts due
to inability to keep track of finds -
the following are without location
provenance
103. Microblade
104. Core preparation blade
105. Core fragment
106. Core blank
107. Core blank
108. Core fragment
109. Core top fragment
110. Endscraper
111. Core top fragment
112. Bone fragments (15cm)
113. Horse(?) rib bone
(51cm b.datum)
114. Dentate - stamped pottery
(34cm b.d.)
115. Scrapers
116. Flake scraper

117. Bone from balk
118. Core
119. Microblade
120. Bones (?)
121. Core platform
122. Bone fragments (37cm b.d.)
123. Bone fragments (epiphyses)
124. Microblade/core fragments
125. Bone fragments
126. 2 microblades
127. Microblade
128. Microblade core (50cm b.d.)
129. Microblade core (50cm b.d.)
130. Bone fragment
131. Microblade midsection
132. Tiny microblade
133. Bone fragment
134. Micorblade
135. Bone at 43cm b.d. in top of tan sand and
interface just below
136. Tooth at 40cm base of brown sand
137. Bone at brown/tan interface (44cm b.d.)
138. Ridge flake

From Burial:

139. Microblade core (53cm b.d.)
140. Bone (64cm b.d.)
141. Mineralized rock or concretion or pyrotechic product?
142. Long bone fragments with flat surface (no working marks).
From pit extension to NE of rock. Found human long bone NE of pit
rocks and extended excavation pit in this direction
143. Stamped pottery with scratches
144. Pottery with scratch mark (decoration?)
145. Ridge flake
146. Bifacial arrowhead
147. Microblade at junction of brown/tan soil
148. Micorblade core prep. flake in tan soil

Khogorgo Gol-3 artifact finds (a-e).

Coiled Sythian Panther.
(Wikipedia Commons)

7. Defining the Deer Stone Khirigsuur Culture

A Deer Stone at Tsatstain Khushuu

Returning from the Dukha excursion in 2004, J. Bayarsaikhan, T. Sanjmyatav, and L. Manlaibaatar, and I began a three-day excavation around a single deer stone at Tsatstain Khushuu N51°10'1428', E099°22'554' in Renchinlkhumbe sum, Khuvsgul Aimag. This deer stone had dimensions of 108 cm x 33 cm x 38 cm and was located south of Tsaaganuur in the northwestern part of the Darkhad, north of Evdei. The only carved design was a circular earring groove near the top of its east side. A dense cluster of surface rocks lay east of the deer stone, and we excavated this entire area, hoping it contained offering deposits that could date one of the northernmost deer stones in this region. While cleaning the surface we found a broken piece of deer antler.

The stones were heavily smashed and broken, making it difficult to identify individual offering features and to distinguish soil types. When we removed the stones, we found three horse heads buried a few meters from the deer stone. The first was near the east side of the stone under a thin layer of soil. It was not complete and consisted of only small fragments of the occiput and mandible. The second, southeast of the stone, had its head facing east, neck vertebrae along the south side of the skull, and four hooves beneath the mandible. The third was east of the stone, its head also facing east, and the neck vertebrae in anatomical order along the north side of the skull. We hoped to find cultural materials under a large flat rock buried north of the deer stone, but nothing was present.

Tsatstain Khushuu deer stone, and excavation with Adiya Namkhai reassuring a concerned local resident.

This was one of the first deer stone sites we had investigated, and we expected to find artifacts, but here and in our early work at Ulaan Tolgoi, we came to the same conclusion as Volkov and Sanjmyatav—nada! Both deer stones and khirigsuur burials were only rarely—and perhaps accidentally—accompanied by artifacts; the ceremonial ritual and architectural structures themselves were the "empty temples" of Late Bronze Age burial ritual. Unlike the Pazyryk and Slab Burial cultures that followed the DSK period, sending the deceased off with possessions was not part of DSK philosophy. Instead, status and honor were marked by the size of the khirigsuur, the artistry and size of the deer stone, and the number of horse sacrifices or hearth features accompanying their burial and memorial structures. A radiocarbon sample on the Tsatstain Feature 1 horse teeth produced dates of cal. B.P. 3300-2900 BP. This was the earliest date so far in our deer stone chronology. Could it be that the deer stone concept entered Mongolia from the Siberian forests to the north, we wondered? This idea had been offered by Karl Jettmar (1994), who proposed a Russian forest origin, suggesting deer stones and their art began as wood carvings before being transferred to stone after the advent of metal stone-working tools. This idea might explain the early dates and absence of deer images and other typically "Mongolian" designs on the Tsatstain deer stone.

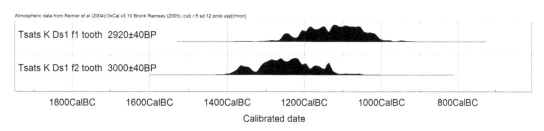

Radiocarbon dates from Tsatstain Khushuu.

While excavating the Tsatstain deer stone and its horse heads, a Darkhad Mongolian woman visited us from her nearby camp and berated us for tampering with ancestors. Adiya Namkhai explained that the site was 3000 years old and many ancestors lay between us and those from such an ancient time. "No matter, you will soon have to pay for intruding into their world." She could not be placated and was sure our excavation would bring disaster to her, her family, and to us. Her view that calamities result from lack of respect to ancestors is shared by many traditional Mongolians and was especially strong in the Darkhad. Perhaps this view helped protect archeological sites from being vandalized in the past. Today that fear has mostly vanished, and sites are being mined by local people for their grave goods, which in certain periods can be quite numerous and valuable. At artifact-free DSK sites, looting produces nothing but destruction of priceless scientific data, yet it continues.

Field camp at Ulaan Tolgoi, view south, 2005, and DS1, 2 with B. Sanjmyatav, Ts. Sanjmyatav, S. Young, W. Fitzhugh, Adiyabold Namkhai, and others.

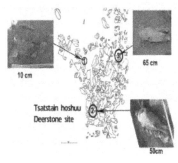

Khushuu deer stone site, viewed to north, cleared to the top of the rock deposit; Map of the rock layer showing locations and orientation of horse head offerings. View to north.

Ulaan Tolgoi II: Dating Deer Stones and Khiriguurs

Having attempted and failed to date DS5 at Ulaan Tolgoi in 2002 by excavating its base, we returned in 2003 to map its surroundings, which included 12 clusters of surface rocks surrounding the stone. But instead of further work here, we chose DS4 which was surrounded by a clearer arrangement of rock features, each about 2-3 meters in diameter and each only a few meters away from DS4. These clusters were easier to distinguish as separate features than at DS5.

Deer Stones 4 and 5 and their associated horse mound features before excavation; and excavation in progress at DS4 in 2004, view NE.

Archaeologists too frequently concentrate their efforts on excavating individual features— be it a dwelling interior, a grave, or a midden or hearth. Such spatially-restricted work often fails to identify the functional and social context of a particular feature and contributes little information on site organization and settlement patterns. We planned to contextualize deer stones by expanding the excavation area several meters beyond the deer stone. To our knowledge, this had not been done before, even though some of Volkov's maps showed extensive distributions of rock pavements, small mounds, and circle hearths at deer stone sites. The fact that sites with

multiple deer stones, such as Uushigiin Uvör, had monuments only a few meters apart made it difficult to determine the relationship between a particular deer stone and nearby rock features. Ulaan Tolgoi had the advantage of 'small site archaeology'; its features were more distinct because they were not crowded together and had not been so extensively re-modelled or cannibalized. Ulaan Tolgoi's deer stones were far enough apart to identify which features were associated with which deer stones.

Deer Stone 4 offered our best chance for contextual work. Like DS5, it was surrounded by several rock clusters, some of which appeared

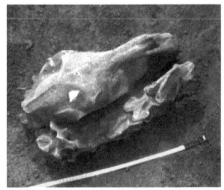

Ulaan Tolgoi Deer Stone 4, north side; south side; and an east-facing horse head and cervical vertebrae from one of the horse mound features around DS4. (photos: HB, PDP, WF)

as small mounds while others were less distinct rock scatters. As we began excavating, the clusters turned out to be the remains of mounds whose surface rocks were partially buried. Our goal was to try to reveal the broader spatial context for deer stone ritual. In 2003, we excavated three cobble features (F-1,2,3) located south and west of DS4. Each appeared on the surface as a low, circular cobble mound ca. 1.5-2.0 meters in diameter covering a one-meter diameter cobble ring 15-20 cm below the surface. In the middle of each one of these rings we found identical

the deer stone. After removing the turf, we found a rock ring containing charcoal and small pieces of broken bone but no artifacts or horse remains. However, north of DS4 we found two horse heads. F5 in the western part of unit 4N/0E contained an east-facing skull and mandible lying upside-down with six articulated cervical vertebrae and a single hoof along the north side of the skull, which was oriented 101°(mag.). A small fragment of Bronze Age ceramic was recovered just above the sterile soil. F6 in the northeast

  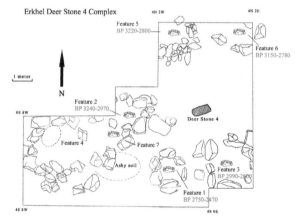

Horse head burial at Ulaan Tolgoi, DS4, Feature 5, an upside-down, east-facing (crushed) skull and solid mandible; excavation map of horse head features surrounding Ulaan Tolgoi DS4.

'packages': tightly nested bundles of horse bones that included a skull, mandible, seven cervical vertebrae (sometimes with atlas and axis), and four (or sometimes less) hoofs. The heads were placed with their muzzles facing east or southeast. Most were well-preserved, but some had been disturbed by rodents or later human activity or suffered natural decomposition. In each case, the cervical vertebrae were touching the skull bones, indicating that the flesh was missing at burial and the bones were positioned following a strict protocol. Hooves were in their 'anatomical' position at the four corners of the bundle.

We returned to complete excavating around DS4 in 2004 and opened areas west and north of

corner of unit 4N/2E also contained an east-facing horse head accompanied by six cervical vertebrae and two hooves along the south side of the skull. This head was aligned 120°(mag) and like F5 was up-side-down, and the vertebrae and hooves were on the south side of the skull. Finally, while excavating between F1 and F4, we discovered a poorly preserved horse head beneath rocks forming the west wall of F1. This feature, designated F7, probably pre-dates F1 because its setting was disturbed when F1 was constructed. Radiocarbon dating (see below) confirmed this stratigraphic inference. It would appear that the Feature 1 horse head was buried at a later time.

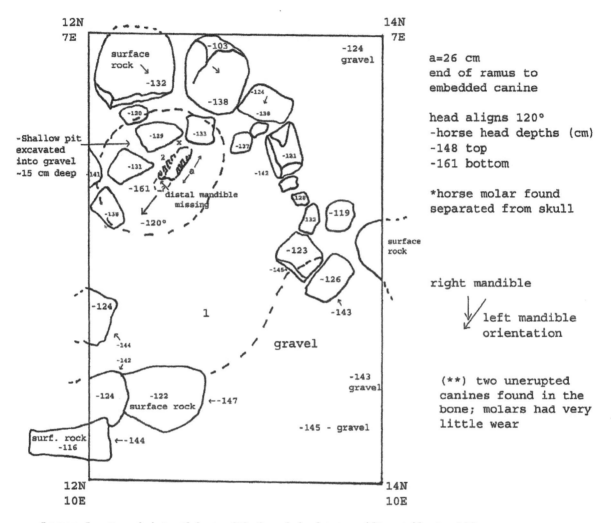

12N 7E ... 14N 7E

surface rock
-132
-103
-124 gravel
-138
-124
-138
-120
-129
-133
-137
-121
-Shallow pit excavated into gravel ~15 cm deep
-131
x
2
a
-142
141
-161
?
distal mandible missing
-138
-120°
-120
-119
132
surface rock
-123
-145
-126
-124
1
-143
-144
gravel
-142
-143 gravel
-124
-122 surface rock
←-147
-145 - gravel
surf. rock -116
←-144

12N 10E ... 14N 10E

a=26 cm
end of ramus to
embedded canine

head aligns 120°
-horse head depths (cm)
-148 top
-161 bottom

*horse molar found
separated from skull

right mandible

left mandible
orientation

(**) two unerupted
canines found in the
bone; molars had very
little wear

Locus 1: Leg joint of horse(?) found in brown silty soil at -148
below datum - does is belong to horse burial in Locus 2?

Locus 2: Crushed and badly preserved young male horse (**) skull found
between -148 and -161 cm. B.D. in brown silty soil. The
skull was not intact and had been crushed during/after burial,
displacing its original position, but the general orientation
of 120° was observed. The distal end of the mandible was eroded
away and 2 ramuses had different orientations. One molar 10cm to
west of skull-no hooves or vertebrae present.

Ulaan Tolgoi, Deer Stone 4, Feature 3.

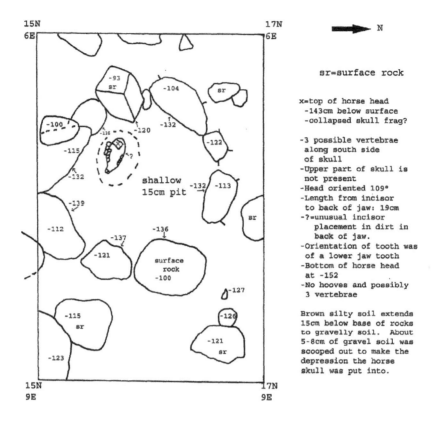

```
sr=surface rock

x=top of horse head
 -143cm below surface
 -collapsed skull frag?

-3 possible vertebrae
 along south side
 of skull
-Upper part of skull is
 not present
-Head oriented 109°
-Length from incisor
 to back of jaw: 19cm
-?=unusual incisor
   placement in dirt in
   back of jaw.
-Orientation of tooth was
 of a lower jaw tooth
-Bottom of horse head
 at -152
-No hooves and possibly
 3 vertebrae

Brown silty soil extends
15cm below base of rocks
to gravelly soil.  About
5-8cm of gravel soil was
scooped out to make the
depression the horse
skull was put into.
```

```
The base of the feature rocks is probably the original
level of the surface ground, into which the buried pit
was excavated.  If so, about 25cm of soil has developed
here in the past 3,000 years.
```

Ulaan Tolgoi Deer Stone 4, Feature 4; north to right.

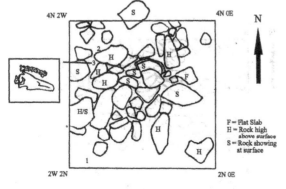

1. Bronze age ceramic fragment in lower brown soil above sterile gravel

2. Horse head bone fragment

3. Horse head burial

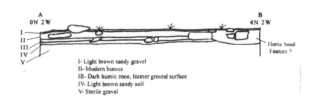

Ulaan Tolgoi DS4, Feature 5: Square 4N 0E upper level rocks and finds with insert showing east-facing horse head burial in lower level; Feature 5 west wall soil profile 0N 2W to 4N 2W.

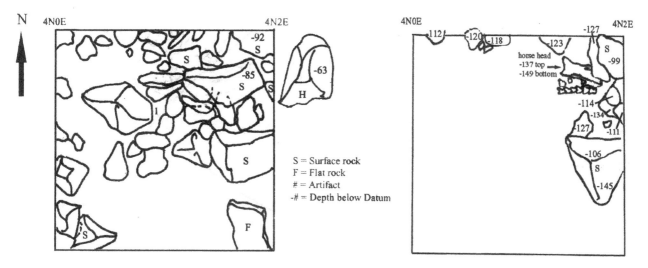

S = Surface rock
F = Flat rock
# = Artifact
-# = Depth below Datum

1. Bone fragment (Metacarpal?) at -102, at ledge of a large rock in lower brown soil.

Ulaan Tolgoi Deer Stone 4, Feature 6: upper level rocks and finds in Square 4N 2E; lower level rocks and horse head burial in Square 4N 2E. (Numbers indicate depth below datum.)

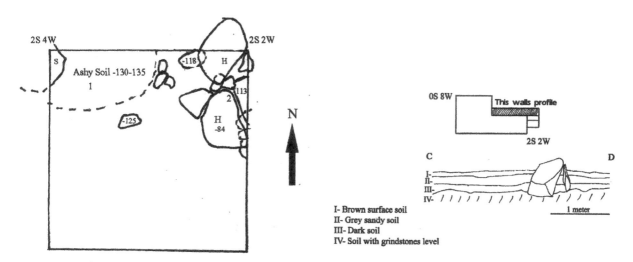

I- Brown surface soil
II- Grey sandy soil
III- Dark soil
IV- Soil with grindstones level

1. Charcoal sample starting at -130 to -135 in upper tan soil without gravel.

2. Horse vertebra - only one at -142cm. On top of sterile gravel.

Ulaan Tolgoi Deer Stone 4, Feature 7: upper level map of Feature 7; wall profile from 2S/4W to 2S/1W.

By the end of the 2004 season, it was obvious that the horse head features encircling DS4 had all been placed with their muzzles pointing to the east, and most had cervical vertebrae along the north side of the skulls and hooves beneath the four corners of the skulls. No charcoal or artifacts except the single Bronze Age sherd and stone abraders were found in any of the horse head features. The spacing between features was relatively regular, suggesting a planned arrangement. However, as noted above, one horse head on the west side of the stone had been disturbed by intrusion of a later feature.

Dating Horse Heads and Deer Stones: Post- or Pre-Scythian/ Saka?

Our first radiocarbon date of ca. cal. 2000 BP on charcoal from the DS5 trench had agreed with the views of Russian scholars, whose dating was based on typological comparisons of deer stone belt implements—primarily daggers and axe forms—with finds from Russian kurgan excavations. This idea was called into question by Esther

Excavation northwest of the Ulaan Tolgoi deer stones revealed a stone circle and Bronze Age ceramics.

While we were excavating the last of the DS4 features, Bayaraa and the Mongolian students opened a large area ten meters northwest of the deer stones where surface rocks suggested something other than horse head mounds and stone circles. The dig revealed one of the circle hearths and produced poorly-fired ceramics with linear surface decoration dating to the Late Bronze Age. Apparently, activities surrounding deer stones included use of ceramics for feasting or food preparation. Future work at these sites should employ more broad-scale area excavations as one can expect a wider range of activities than just deer stones, horse heads, and circle hearths.

Jacobson, an art historian, who thought deer stone art, particularly the iconic deer form, was stylistically pre-Scythian (Jacobson 1995). Space does not permit full exploration of the historiography and major features of Scytho-Sakaian art, but we need to be aware of some of its main characteristics to understand its relationship to deer stones. We will return to this topic in our concluding discussions.

Images illustrating common Scythian-Saka animal style motifs: pedation; coiled animals (see Chapter header); stag; and Chinese beast. (Wikipedia.Commons)

Scythian art is associated with the kurgan burials and funerary art of the Scyths, a sheep- and goat-herding nomadic warrior culture located around the Pontic lands east and north of the Black Sea in the 5-4th centuries BCE where they were described historically by Herodotus (Loehr 1955; Bunker et al. 1970, 1997; Farkas 1975; Sher 1988; Cunliffe 2019). They are known especially for their gold foil-covered ornaments made for personal use and horse gear, although their art played a major role in many categories of their material culture. The art of the Scyths and their eastern neighbors, Saka, emphasized animals in vigorous activity, running, jumping, or engaged in predator-prey interactions, presented on small plaques, jewelry, clothes and belt ornaments. Sometimes animal bodies are shown coiled or with their necks or bodies twisted back 180° making it possible for display in confined spaces like circular medallions and horse gear. Early art historians described these nomadic cultures as displaying a "Scythian triad": an emphasis on horses, weaponry, and animal art. Interactions between animal, humans, and nature might well be considered as a fourth element. Its origins were initially thought to lie in Pontic Scythia, but when similar art was discovered in graves across the steppe lands of Western Asia and southern

Russia, it became clear that animal style art was not a culturally specific diagnostic limited to Scyths or Saka. Rather, it represented a widespread 'horizon style' carried by several nomadic cultures and their neighbors throughout the western and central steppe. Its eastern boundary produced the most spectacular finds from the frozen royal tombs of Arzhan I (Rudenko 1970; Gryazhnov 1984), and later Arzhan II (Chuganov et al. 2003), in the Altai and Sayan mountains of southern Siberia, north of the western Mongolian border. Beneath huge stone mounds, Russian archaeologists found warriors whose preserved bodies were tattooed with animal style art and buried with horses and saddlery ornaments, richly embroidered textiles and clothing, and elaborate ritual objects including horse 'crowns' or masks with deer antlers. Many of these materials displayed designs and elements of animal style art. Dated by dendrochronology and radiocarbon to 8-7th centuries BCE, these tombs were 3-400 years earlier than the Pontic finds. And among the rubble and rocks capping one of the Arzhan II mounds was a deer stone fragment bearing the image of the 'Mongolian' deer. Apparently Arzhan II had been constructed on an earlier deer stone site.

Deer Stones and Horse Ritual

Imagine our surprise when charcoal from Structure 7 collected in 2003 at the base of the cultural deposit south of DS4 came back from the radiocarbon laboratory at ca. 3100 cal. BP! Another sample from Structure 17, a rock feature near DS4, produced a later date, 2200 cal. BP, agreeing with the charcoal date from DS5. This confusion began to sort out when samples of horse bone from DS4 Features 1, 2, and 3 returned dates of 2600, 3100, and cal. 2900 BP (below, and Appendix 1). The discrepancies between charcoal and horse bone apparently resulted from intrusive charcoal unrelated to the deer stone installation, perhaps from rodents like squirrels, mice, and marmots which frequently burrow in the loose soil fill around the base of deer stones and cobble features. Later we learned to select horse teeth as the most reliable dating material because their dense ivory and dentin helped seal the inner tissue from humic acid and other types of soil and ground water contamination. As a result, our subsequent dates for DS4 Features 5 and 6 produced consistent dates in the 2900-3100 cal. BP range.

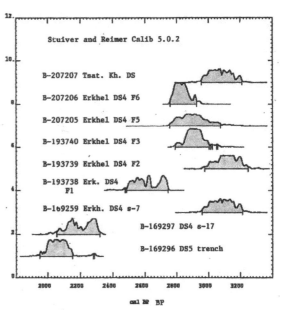

Calibrated radiocarbon dates from Ulaan Tolgoi deer stones and related features. See Appendix 1 for the full list of Deer Stone Project radiocarbon dates.

Pecking and grinding stones were found while excavating horse features around Ulaan Tolgoi DS 4.

Besides a horse head, Feature 1 contained several fist-sized cobbles made of tough greenstone rock whose surfaces showed areas of extensive abrasion. These rocks were unlike others in the surrounding soil; their surfaces had been rounded by stream action but displayed areas that had signs of repeated impacts. These rocks had been used as pecking stones. Some of their more pointed pecked surfaces fit the broad U-shaped grooves carved on DS4, while other areas displayed evidence of grinding rather than pecking, apparently from smoothing areas of recessed carvings like the bodies of the deer or mirrors. Small pecking depressions could be seen all over the surface of DS4, and its grooved decoration seems to have been produced by impact pecking followed by grinding with the tips of pointed rocks. We detected no sign of metal tools but did not have the means or official permission for sampling. Today a hand-held XRF detector could be used to quickly identify minute pieces from the tips of metal chisels or picks. Most deer stones display wide-groove carving that could have been produced by hammerstone pecking and grinding. However, some like those at Jargalant, Khushuutiin Gol, Shuvuutiin Am, and others have carvings whose inner edges have right angles that must have been formed by metal rather than stone implements. Presumably, these deer stones date toward the end of the DSK period when iron chisels may have become available. Analysis of finely carved deer stones that have been buried for centuries at the sites noted above might possibly retain traces of metal or paint on their less weathered surfaces.

Finding pecking and grinding stones demonstrated that at least some of the final phase of deer stone production occurred after the stones were erected, or possibly on-site immediately before. Their presence in and near horse head features provided further evidence not only that the horse features were directly associated with the deer stones but that they were probably concurrent events. Our excavations at Targon Nuur

and Zunii Gol also recovered fragments of rock removed by percussion while shaping deer stones. While it is possible that some horse head burials at DS4 may date to different periods, as indicated by stratigraphic evidence from Features 1 and 7 and a several hundred year spread of radiocarbon dates, the presence of pecking stones within horse features is certain evidence that those horse head burials date to the time when the monument was erected.

A similar inference can be made from the spatial distribution of horse heads. Although we did not have time to extend our excavation area more widely than 4-5m from DS4, the seven horse head burials ringing the monument can without question be associated with DS4, and the presence of other outlying rock features not excavated suggests they, too, contain horse heads related to DS4 ceremonialism. The nearest deer stone, DS5, is 9 meters to the north and has its own cluster of encircling horse head features. While there is some evidence for later horse burial features, such as the disturbance of F7 by F1 construction, a strong argument can be made for most of the horse head features dating to a single period, ca. 2900-3100 cal. BCE. In pages below we discuss further evidence for the contemporaneity of sacrificial events from the large khirigsuur and horse

Deer stones at the Jargalant site displaying art that must have been accomplished at least partly with bronze or iron tools; (c) shows the top of (b) with a pendant earring with rays, supporting their dual interpretation symbolizing sun and moon as well as earrings.

head mounds at Urt Bulagiin.

If this pattern is verified by future research at other deer stone sites and installations, it would appear that deer stone ceremonialism includes a general ritual pattern in which a stone is created to honor a distinguished warrior, leader, or perhaps shaman (see below). The installation involves final finishing work on the stone using stone hammers and grindstones followed by ceremonial offerings—not of artifacts or human remains—but of horses that were brought to the site, sacrificed, and had their heads, neck vertebrae, and hooves buried a few meters from the deer stone. At least some horses seem to have been offered when the stone was erected, but additional sacrifices may have been made at a later date, accounting for later c14 dates and disturbance of earlier features. The sacrifice consisted of a prescribed 'package' containing the skull, mandible, cervical vertebrae, and hoofs, whose close juxtaposition in the ground indicates the neck had no flesh. East-facing orientation was required, and at DS4 at Ulaan Tolgoi there was a tendency for the neck vertebrae to be placed along the north side of the skull and mandible while at many other sites investigated later a south-side placement was more common. Variations of these patterns exist, but in cases where skulls or mandibles are found upside-down, we suspect disturbance when rocks were placed above the skulls or some other post-burial activity occurred. While the pattern suggests live horse sacrifice at deer stone installations, there are instances in which the skull, mandible, vertebrae, and hooves were incomplete, entirely missing, or included weathered remains, suggesting use of previously deceased horses.

The question of seasonal timing of deer stone ritual has been explored using the azimuth (compass) direction of horse head interments, most of which align between 100°-120° mag. Ethnographic data gathered by Francis Allard (Allard and Erdenbaatar 2005) indicate that even today modern herders honor the spirits of their favorite horses by placing their head or skulls at the tops of hills near their camps, and positing them where they receive the rays of the rising sun. A similar principle is thought to explain the eastern orientation of khirigsuurs (see below), whose fence lines, entry paths, and fence gates align east/southeast. Ritual practices and beliefs relating to the rising sun governing the orientation of Chinese ritual architecture provide a comparative basis possibly explaining the 'honor east' practice in Bronze Age Mongolia. If the rising sun determined the orientation of khirigsuurs and horse head graves, their orientation might suggest the horses were buried from May to June, and deer stone installations may also have taken place at this time. We discuss this further in the khirigsuur section below.

Modern horse head ritual in a hilltop larch tree in the Darkhad valley.

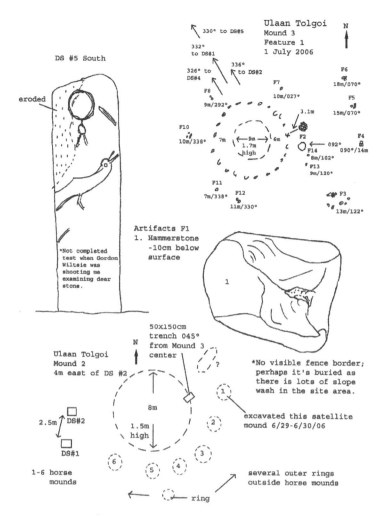

Sketch of Ulaan Tolgoi DS5 and K2 Feature 1 with our fence trench, and K3 Feature 1 investigations in 2006.

The Ulaan Tolgoi Khirigsuurs

Our return to Ulaan Tolgoi in 2005 included study of its khirigsuurs and their relationship to deer stones. Deer stones and khirigsuurs are not always found together, and until recently some Russian and Mongolian archaeologists believed they belonged to different cultures and time periods. This supposition was sustained because both types of sites had lacked chronological control and contained no artifacts to clarify their cultural affiliation. At large sites, both can be found together, although usually with some spatial separation; at small sites, each can be found separately without the other. Ulaan Tolgoi was unusual in having deer stones and some mounds only a few meters away, and this raised the question: do deer stones represent individuals buried in nearby khirigsuurs? As discussed in the previous section regarding the Mongolian Altai, where deer stones sometimes are part of khirigsuur constructions, this would appear to be so, but this was not evident at Ulaan Tolgoi where two khirigsuurs, K2 and K3, were next to five deer stones while others like K1 were at a considerable distance.

To resolve questions about culture and chronology we began excavations at Ulaan Tolgoi Khirigsuurs 2 and 3, both being round-fenced stone mounds east and southeast of the deer stone group. As this was our first exploration of khirigsuurs, we did not know what to expect and decided to excavate a 50cm wide trench across the fence of K2, and a satellite mound (Feature 1) a few meters east of the fence ring, which produced a caprid scapula and a microblade core. This structure had two satellite mounds east of the fence and 8 to 10 hearth rings encircling the mound. K2 was unusual for not having a visible fence (perhaps it had become buried), but it had several satellite mounds around its eastern perimeter and many stone hearth circles beyond the small mounds. Its Feature 1 produced a horse hoof.

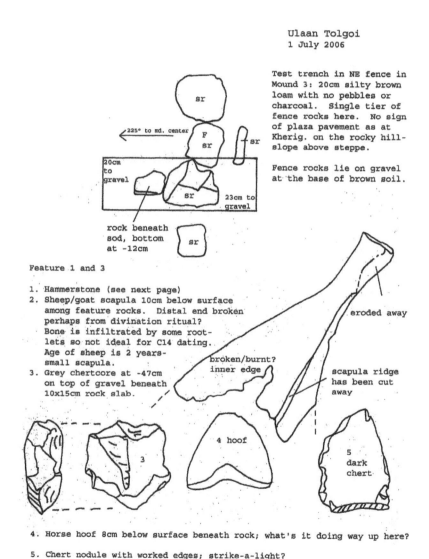

Excavations and finds from Ulaan Tolgoi Khirigsuur 3.

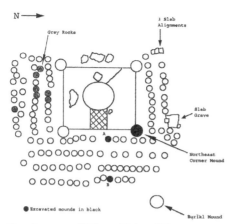

Sketch map of Ulaan Tolgoi Khirigsuur 1 and northeast fence corner mound top rocks.

Ulaan Tolgoi Khirigsuur 3. Frustrated by the lack of finds at khirigsuurs close to the deer stone, we turned to Khirigsuur 1, a large square-fenced structure south of the deer stone cluster and spent several days mapping and excavating three of its many satellite features. The central mound was too large to tackle, but with the assistance of Bruno Froelich we mapped the site and its mounds and stone circles.

Ulaan Tolgoi Khirigsuur 1, Northeast Fence Corner Mound. We began by excavating three small mounds on the east side of Khirigsuur 1, also known as Mound A in some reports, a large square-fenced mound south of the Ulaan Tolgoi deer stones. Since we could not excavate the mound itself, excavating a few of its 117 satellite mounds might date the khirigsuur as accurately as the contents of the mound. We had no previous experience excavating khirigsuur satellite mounds and hoped the northeast corner mound would not be an empty pile of rocks.

After mapping the surface of the corner mound, we removed the upper rocks and began finding charcoal and pieces of split long bones, ribs, and bone fragments from a medium-sized animal. The base of the mound rested on undisturbed ground surface and consisted of a meter-wide ring of flat rocks around a cobble floor with more caprid-sized bones on it, including a mandible fragment. The bones suggested a single

animal, and the mandible was sheep or goat. There were no artifacts or horse head remains as in deer stone mounds. The finds indicated ritual consumption or burning of meat and bones as part of khirigsuur fence construction or dedication. We supposed similar finds would be present in the other three corner mounds, which we did not excavate.

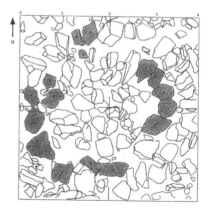

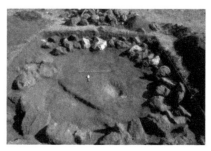

Map of upper rocks, and photo of bottom of Ulaan Tolgoi K-1 northeast fence corner mound showing a hearth floor where caprid bones were found.

Ulaan Tolgoi Khirigsuur 1 Horse Mound A.
Our second excavation explored Satellite Mound
A, one of several first rank mounds positioned
in the first row of horse mounds alongside the
K1 east fence, straddling the 'gateway' gap in the
fence. Mound A, immediately north of the entry,
was 4m in diameter, larger and more heavily

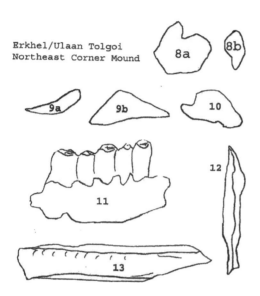

Bone fragments from the Khirigsuur 1 north-east corner fence mound.

constructed than the other satellite mounds, but
about the same size as the fence corner mound.
Large rocks covered its center. The other mounds
in the first rank east of the fence were somewhat
smaller and had fewer large rocks. Mound sizes
and their rocks grew smaller as one proceeds
outward away from the fence in ranks 2, 3, and 4.
Bayaraa's Mound B feature in the fourth rank was
barely more than a circular pavement.

After removing surface rocks in Mound A,
a pattern similar to the northeast corner mound
emerged – a circular outer ring of large stones,
with an intermediate ring of inward sloping slabs
and a central core of smaller round rocks. A canid
(dog/fox?) mandible was among the upper rocks
along with fragments of small split long bones,
and near the base of the mound, a bovid calcane-

um and phalange. Charcoal lumps were throughout the upper mound. In addition, there was a
20-30cm thick layer of black charcoal under the
western side of the mound that had a few small
bone fragments and the joint fragment of a cow
or some other large ungulate at its base. Parts of
the left and right mandibles of a horse were lying
in a shallow depression at ground surface in the
center of the ring of rocks. The larger right fragment was missing its distal end, and the smaller
left fragment was only the molar portion. Both
were greyed and cracked from exposure before
burial; only one molar remained in its socket and
another was found nearby. The deposit seems to
have been from a horse that died long before the
khirigsuur was constructed. No cardinal orientation could be ascertained because the mandibles
arms were disarticulated.

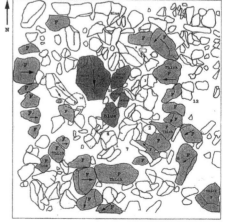

Ulaan Tolgoi K1 East Gate Satellite Mound A be-ginning excavation, and mapped with surface rocks removed showing basal rocks and inclined slabs.

Ulaan Tolgoi K1 East Gate Mound A showing depression in which weathered horse mandible fragments were found.

Ulaan Tolgoi Khirigsuur 1, Fourth (outside) row Satellite Mound B and its poorly preserved horse head which conservators consolidated for preservation. (photo:HRB)

Khirigsuur1 Satellite Mound B Bayaraa excavated one of the smallest mounds in the fourth rank of satellite mounds outside the east fence of Khirigsuur-1. Our method was based on the assumption that the outer rank mounds would have been the latest additions to the khirigsuur's construction and dating both the first and fourth rank mounds might indicate the elapsed time between the mound's initial dedication and when the last mounds were added. Some have argued that building khirigsuurs—particularly the largest ones—must have taken years and that its ceremonial deposits might span a considerable period (Wright 2015, 2017). If, on the other hand, khirigsuurs were constructed and horses were sacrificed as part of a single interment ceremony, the dates between the inner and outer horse burials would be the same, or within the range of c14 error.

Bayaraa completed Mound B in one day and found it barely more than a small scatter of rocks on the surface, with the crushed skull of an east-facing horse lying in the center beneath one of the larger rocks. Smithsonian conservators used the opportunity to demonstrate to our Mongolian colleagues how to extract and preserve a damaged specimen using Japanese conservation paper and water-soluble glue to create a package that could be block-lifted from the ground and transported to the laboratory. In the process, we extracted the left canine for radiocarbon dating. The lab results on the horse tooth and charcoal came back for Mound A at cal. 3080-2870 BP (a tooth from the weathered horse jaw) and 3260-3000 cal. BP (charcoal) and for Mound B, 3320-2940 cal. BP (a horse tooth). The Mound B tooth date was slightly earlier than the Mound A charcoal and Mound B tooth, but both were within the range of c14 probability for concurrent activities. This date closely matched the date from the Tsatstain deer stone and lies at the early end of our deer stone chronology.

Conservators Rescue Mound B Horse Head

Basiliki Vick Karas and Harriet Rae Beaubien provided conservation assistance to the archaeological team when a horse head deposit was discovered on 9 July in a small mound associated with the big khirigsuur at the Ulaan Tolgoi. The deposit contained a careful arrangement of skull, cervical vertebrae, and hooves. Because the skull was somewhat crushed, it was not considered exhibit-worthy. However, it did provide an excellent opportunity for demonstrating techniques for stabilizing fragile finds or removing complex deposits so that they could be excavated and analyzed more carefully in a laboratory setting. Fragile areas of the bone were stabilized by attaching small pieces of a very fine but strong tissue with an easy-to-remove adhesive. This facing held bone fragments together and protected the vulnerable portions as in situ cleaning progressed. Once the surrounding soil was cleared from around the sides, the conservators demonstrated the process of jacketing the deposit to hold it securely together for lifting. With their assistance, several of the archaeologists shaped a protective layer of plastic wrap and then aluminum foil closely around the deposit. Several layers

of plaster-coated gauze bandage were applied, which dried to form a rigid shell. A board was slid underneath and the whole deposit was safely lifted, labeled, and secured to a wooden plank for transport to the museum. (Beaubien and Karass 2005:62)

A recent forensic analysis of the horse remains from 21 DSK horse head burials (Taylor et al. 2020) identified evidence of killing, butchery, and sacrificial practices. Cut-marks on the cervical vertebrae showed that most horses were killed and the neck flesh was stripped at the time of burial, making it possible for the cervical vertebrae to be placed tightly against the skull and mandible bones. The absence of head impacts suggested that most animals were stunned by severing the spinal cord between the axis and atlas vertebrae followed by cut-throat bleeding into a container. None of the DSK horse graves contained burned remains, but the presence of weathered horse bones in some burials indicated that instead of always killing a living horse, they occasionally used animals that died long before.

Khirigsuur Form and Function

Our Ulaan Tolgoi Mound 1 exploration confirmed what Volkov and Mongolian archaeologists determined years earlier and added new insight. Despite superficial similarities to the Russian kurgan burials, Mongolian khirigsuurs are architecturally highly distinctive. "Kurgan" is a generic term for burial mounds on the Russian steppe. Its more specific use describes burials from the Bronze Age Karasuk culture of the Middle Yenesei ca. 1400-1000 BCE. LeGrand (2006) identifies mounds with circular or rectangular borders or curbs that resemble Mongolian khirigsuurs but lack the 'plaza' space between the central mound and the fence/border/curb; they also have no horse or hearth features outside the fence and no marked eastern orientation. The succeeding Middle Yenesei Tagar culture ca. 1000-200 BCE (Bokovenko 2006) buried their dead in slab-walled cists beneath stone mounds edged by a rectangular border of vertical slabs. Although overlapping Mongolian DSK chronology, Tagar graves more closely resemble those of the Slab Burial culture that follows the Mongolian DSK period. The fact that the term 'khiorigsuur' is a Khirgiz word may point toward its origin in Khirgizstan.

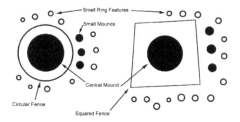

Schematic plan and photos of round-fenced and square-fenced khirigsuurs and their horse head satellite mounds and hearth circles. (credits: BF, RK, WF)

Mongolian khirigsuurs have a highly complex structure. Its essential elements include a central mound of boulders covering a shallow grave surrounded by a low rectangular or circular stone border or fence that usually has a gap or opening in its east side. The area between the mound and the fence, often appearing as an empty plaza or sacred space, may have a rough stone pavement, but there is usually a well-defined pavement connecting the east side of the mound with a corresponding gap in the fence. A few khirigsuurs in northern Mongolia have stone alignments or radials connecting the burial mound with the fence. Around the east side of the fence are a variable number of small 1-2m diameter "satellite" mounds spaced a few meters apart. In cases where there are many satellite mounds, they build outward from the fence in regular rows or ranks and may wrap around the south and north sides of the fence. Beyond the satellite mounds is an array of small, 1-2m diameter stone ring features. The ring features tend to be ten or more meters beyond the fence, outside the satellite mounds, and are concentrated on the west side of khirigsuurs, although they sometimes encircle the entire structure. Rock rings may also vary in number, with similar attention to regular position and spacing. Orientation is a crucial feature of khirigsuur construction; like deer stones, they always "face" east as determined by the east-side mound pavement, the gap in the east-side fence, and the east-side centering of satellite mounds. Some khirigsuurs have a single 'range' rock positioned many meters east of the mound. Deer stones are not part of khirigsuur constructions in north-central Mongolia, but they are found in some mounds in the Mongolian Altai.

Almost all khirigsuurs follow this architectural plan, although the number of satellite mounds and stone rings can vary from zero to hundreds or more. An average might be 3-8 satellite mounds and 10-15 stone rings. At khirigsuurs and deer stone sites, the satellite mounds and rings have identical structures and functions—to celebrate a revered, deceased leader with the sacrifice of horses, whose heads, necks, and hooves are buried in the satellite mounds, and ritual burning of animal flesh and bones in ring-shaped stone hearths.

There is no reason why khirigsuurs could not have served all these purposes. The matter of a mortuary function was laid to rest when Bruno Frohlich, working with Tugsoo and others at the

Bruno Frohlich excavating a shallow khirigsuur burial that displayed poorly preserved human remains as seen in most LBA khirigsuurs, such as this individual from Biluut 1C in the Mongolian Altai. In many instances, all bones are lost.

The complicated architecture of khirigsuurs begs the question: what were they for? This issue has inspired archaeological debate for decades. The long tradition of mound burials in East and Central Asia suggested to early scholars that khirigsuurs were grave mounds, like kurgans, although they had more elaborate architecture. But when Russian researchers began excavating, they rarely found human remains. In Esther Jacobson's writings she referred to khirigsuurs as 'altars'—places where important rituals were performed that were of a non-mortuary character. After 1990, when Mongolian archaeologists began working independently and with western scientists, this idea continued and was briefly supported by William Honeychurch (2015) and others. If khirigsuurs are mortuary, they asked, why don't they contain human burials? Others like Joshua Wright (2007, 2014, 2015, 2017) saw khirigsuurs as serving a community-building and social process function, following a line of thought being discussed with regard to European megaliths and British henge monuments.

Mongolian Institute of Archaeology, began a systematic survey of khirigsuurs in Khuvsgul and excavated scores of khirigsuurs between 2005-2009. Careful attention was taken to record their architecture and contents (Frohlich and Barzarsad 2005; Frohlich et al. 2008, 2009, 2010; Littleton et al. 2012). The largest Class 1 mounds were too big to excavate, but most of the Class 2 and 3 mounds contained human burials at their centers. In the larger mounds, human remains were often in stone-lined boxes with large covering stones, while smaller mounds had burials just under the surface or less than a meter deep. Many of the skeletons were in a poor state of preservation, and in some mounds only tooth enamel was recovered from screened earth. As Littleton et al. (2012) demonstrated, preservation is the most important factor explaining the absence of human remains, while rodents, and in some cases human disturbance, accounts for displacement or loss of bones. Preservation was better in sites on the river bottoms than on or near hillslopes where soils are sandier, more acidic, and better drained.

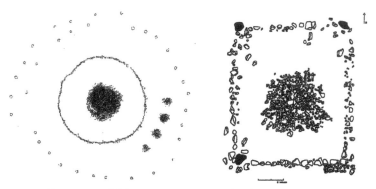

Large Class I round khirigsuur M-52, and Class II rectangular khirigsuur M-01. (credit: B. Frohlich).

M-52 had a central burial mound surrounded by a circular fence. Four external mounds are located outside the fence to the southeast, and 34 stone rings are positioned in two irregular circles beyond the horse mounds. The mound was fully excavated and yielded the body of an adult male. The fence has a diameter of 37 meters. No horse skeletal remains were found in the external mounds. A rectangular khirigsuur M-01 excavated by Bruno Frohlich has a central burial mound with a single burial chamber. The chamber, covered by nine capstones, was empty. A body was later found below the chamber floor, apparently positioned to deter detection from desecration. A square fence surrounds the burial mound. Maximum length of the eastern north – south fence side is circa 11 meters. Each corner is marked with a large boulder. A raised platform made from smaller rocks separates the center burial mound from the fence.

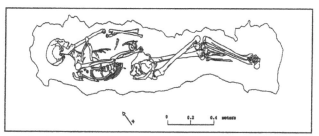 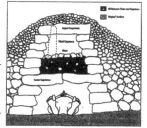

Skeletal remains of a 20-year old male from M-01; schematic of the round khirigsuur M-52 at the time of burial. (credit: B. Frohlich)

Mound M-01 contained the skeletal remains of an adult male, circa 20 years old, found in square khirigsuur. The body was originally placed in a supine position with the head toward the west. In order to secure the body from potential intruders, the mound builders added small boulders around the chamber, two layers of capstones, and a faked chamber positioned on top of the real chamber. The lower layer of capstones is secured by being locked between the larger stones making up the chamber walls and the large boulders surrounding the chamber. Intruders succeeded in entering the upper chamber but failed to break through the upper chamber's floor and the locked capstones covering the lower chamber. Although they failed entering from the top, they later succeeded in breaking into the lower chamber through the western sidewall. The body was severely desecrated. Later, some bone elements were removed by animals. Some of these elements were found between the rocks making up the center burial mound.

A hearth circle at Zeerdegchingiin Khoshuu Khirigsuur 1, north of Tsaaganuur contained charcoal and has a stone missing or displaced in its south or southeast side. Most hearths also contain burned bone fragments. The same ritual is seen in the Mongolian Altai as seen in the second photos. Hearth rings probably served to allow 'ritual release' of the spirits of the animals burned as a smoke offering.

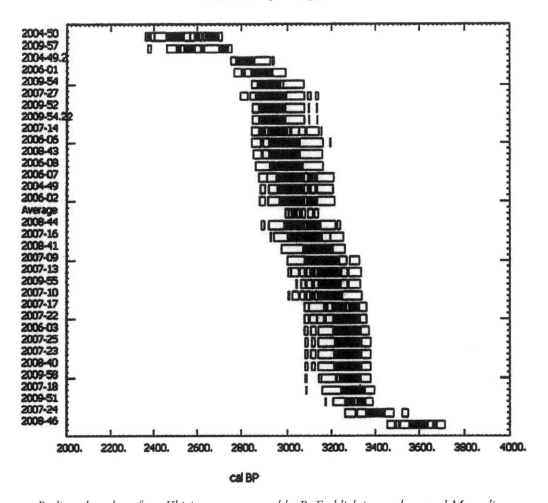

Radiocarbon dates from Khirigsuurs excavated by B. Frohlich in north-central Mongolia.

Frohlich and his partners mapped more than 1600 khirigsuurs in northern Mongolia and excavated and dated more than fifty. This figure plots calibrated AMS dates obtained and demonstrated that khirigsuurs begin to be built between 3400 years ago and ceased to be used ca. 2700-2500 years ago. Horizontal bars include the Sigma 1 range in black and the Sigma 2 range in white. M-2004-50 and M-2009-57 yield significantly younger age estimates. This may have been caused by very poor sample quality. M-2008-46 is significantly older than all other dates and has been classified as a 'pre-khirigsuur' structure based on both mound architecture and AMS date. Radiometric dates were produced by Beta Analytical, Miami, Florida (n=3), and the NSF AMS laboratory at the University of Arizona, Tucson, Arizona (n=31). (edited from Frohlich et al. 2010)

There is now no doubt that the primary function of khirisguurs was for human burial, but it is also clear that their construction and architecture served other functions as well, like the cathedrals of Europe that contain the bodies of saints, leaders, and heroes while also being places of worship that served as centers of social and cultural life. In addition to honoring the deceased, khirigsuur construction ranged from small mounds with no horse sacrifices or ring hearths to vast complexes that required hierarchical organization in order to maintain their architectural integrity. Social hierarchy must have been an important principle governing khirigsuur size and complexity and the conduct and scale of rituals conducted at these sites.

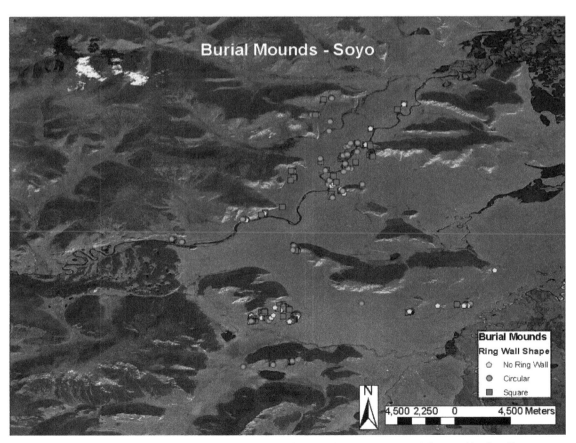

Khirigsuur mound sites—many with multiple mounds—in the Soyö region of the Darkhad valley. (map: B. Frohlich)

Herodotus Describes a Pontic Scyth Burial

Herodotus' description of 5th century (440 BCE) royal Scythian burials provides comparative context for understanding DSK khirigsuurs, which are a likely prototype for 8th century Pazyryk and 4-6th century Scythian-Saka mortuary practices:

The body of the dead king is laid in the grave prepared for it, stretched upon a mattress; spears are fixed in the ground on either side of the corpse, and beams stretched across above it to form a roof, which is covered with a thatching of osier twigs. In the open space around the body of the king they bury one of his concubines, first killing her by strangling, and also his cup-bearer, his cook, his groom, his lacquey, his messenger, some of his horses, firstlings of all his other possessions, and some golden cups; for they use neither silver nor brass. After this they set to work, and raise a vast mound above the grave, all of them vying with each other and seeking to make it as tall as possible.

When a year is gone by, further ceremonies take place. Fifty of the best of the late king's attendants are taken, all native Scythians—for, as bought slaves are unknown in the country, the Scythian kings choose any of their subjects that they like, to wait on them. Fifty of these are taken and strangled, with fifty of the most beautiful horses. When they are dead, their bowels are taken out, and the cavity cleaned, filled full of chaff, and straightway sewn up again. This done, a number of posts are driven into the ground, in sets of two pairs each, and on every pair half the felly of a wheel is placed archwise; then strong stakes are run lengthways through the bodies of the horses from tail to neck, and they are mounted up upon the fellies, so that the felly in front supports the shoulders of the horse, while that behind sustains the belly and quarters, the legs dangling in mid-air; each horse is furnished with a bit and bridle, which latter is stretched out

in front of the horse, and fastened to a peg. The fifty strangled youths are then mounted severally on the fifty horses. To effect this, a second stake is passed through their bodies along the course of the spine to the neck; the lower end of which projects from the body, and is fixed into a socket, made in the stake that runs lengthwise down the horse. The fifty riders are thus ranged in a circle round the tomb, and so left. (Herodotus, 440 BCE, Book IV).

Many similarities can be noted between the burial customs of the Scyths and the Pazyryk culture, that dates four hundred years earlier, and the DSK of ca. 1000 BCE. The Pazyryk custom of dressing sacrificed horses and chiefs in elaborate regalia including gold-ornamented clothing and jewelry, embroidered saddle pads, and disguising sacrificed horses behind antlered deer masks is not part of DSK ritual. Nevertheless, reference to deer symbolism suggests continuities with deer stone tradition. One can easily imagine the evolution from DSK belief in a nature-based deer master cosmology to rituals more suited to the new economic and political structure of a horse-dominated Pazyryk warrior culture. While khirigsuurs and deer stones do not display the ostentatious finery of Pazyryk and later Scythian-Saka ritual, we see in DSK the beginnings of a shift from a world order governed by nature-dominated spirits to one focused on more earthly concerns.

Khirigsuurs as Chariots for the Dead

When Soviet and Mongolian archaeologists began investigating khirigsuurs in Mongolia, they saw them as an extension of the kurgan burial tradition in southern Russia even though their architecture was more complex. Interest in exploring Mongolian khirigsuurs waned when the mounds and deer stones produced no artifacts or human remains. Nevertheless, stimulated by the Pazyryk finds, surveys continued in the Russia Altai, and there khirigsuurs were found to have radial lines connecting the central mound with the khirigsuur fence. In addition some khirgsuurs had deer stones set within the khirigsuur orbit or in the central mound itself (Savinov 1994). Russian archaeologists hypothesized the radials represented spokes on chariot wheels. The radials were always even-numbered in sets of 4, 6, and 8, leaving a strong impression of a spoked chariot wheel. Our Deer Stone Project surveys in 2009-2012 in the Khoton Lake-Bayan Ulgii region also documented spoked khirigsuurs as well as khirigsuurs with embedded deer stones, which extended their distribution from central into western Mongolia. We also began to find rock art images of chariots in the vicinity of spoked khirigsuurs. While it appeared that the khirigsuur-chariot connection was centered in southern Russia and western Mongolia, chariot references were also appearing as research progressed in central Mongolia. The east-side horse mounds, east-facing horse skulls, and the eastern orientation of khirigsuurs and deer stones all suggested individuals were being sent off on an eastward spiritual journey in the company of horses, sometimes hundreds of horses.

A break-through came when Jerome Magail's Monoco-Mongolian project proposed that the horses sacrificed and buried in the horse mounds of khirigsuur B-40 in Tsatsiin Ereg functioned as

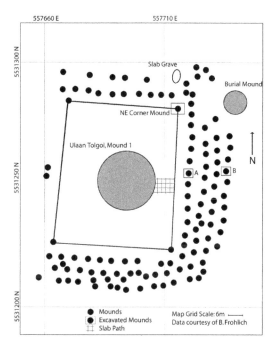

Ulaan Tolgoi Khirigsuur 1 showing distribution of horse mounds. (graphic: B. Frohlich)

a team of spiritual horses that carried the mound's proprietor eastward toward the rising sun (Lepetz et al. 2019). The purpose of DSK horse sacrifice could now be seen as much more specific than 'donations' to the deceased's afterlife by relatives or supporters; they were present at khirigsuurs and deer stones to perform a particular task, ensuring that the deceased maintained a connection between the living and the ancestors. It is in this sense that the Monaco project and others like Wright who believe that khirigsuurs were 'living' structures maintained and renewed over years and perhaps decades, are certainly correct, at least for larger khirigsuur installations with hundreds or thousands of horses.

Based on other architectural features, the concept of khirigsuurs as chariots for the dead can be taken several steps further than spoked wheels. I initially thought the pavement from the central mound to the east fence entry was for the procession of the burial party delivering the deceased to the burial place in the mound. We may now consider this pavement as the central shaft connecting the mound—the charioteer's driving platform—to the horses. The mound itself may then be considered as the round image of the platform seen in rock art depictions. What has not been documented in the Russian or Western Mongolia sites is deer stones positioned at the top of a burial mound in the place of a charioteer. Seeing the khirigsuur as a symbolic chariot helps explain why horse mounds are never found on the west side of the khirigsuur, where they would be unable to 'pull' in the right direction. Even when horse mounds wrap around the north and south sides of the khirigsuur, horse skulls always face east. We can now also understand the purpose of including horse hoofs as an important component in horse head deposits. Their presence seems peculiar as part of the sacrificial deposit until we recognize the need for traction.

This expanded view of the khirigsuur will change the way archaeologists look at khirigsuurs, including how they document and explore the internal structure of the central burial mound. No longer should we be excavating only to find and document the burial feature—be it a stone crypt or a simple near surface interment; care should be given to investigate what other structures might represent a chariot's physical or ritual features. The position of the body and number of individuals present may reflect the existence of a chariot team or assistants, something that becomes explicit in Xiongnu ceremony when an arc of secondary human burials is found along the east side at largest grave mounds like Gol Mod.

As with Scythian and Pazyryk kurgans, khirigsuurs provide a key to understanding DSK cosmology and religious belief. They were the symbolic 'chariots' that carried the departed into the next world, toward the rising sun. It has taken archaeologists several decades to recognize the symbolism involved in this interpretation, which was not so evident in early work on khirigsuurs in northern Mongolia because these structures lacked the radial stone alignments seen more commonly in Russian Siberia and the Mongolian Altai. Their size, whether small or huge, depend-

A chariot seen in a rare side view, from Biluut-2, Bayan Ulgii Aimag, and other chariot images. (photos: RK)

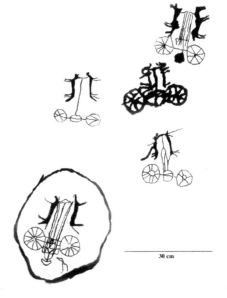

30 cm

ed on the status of the deceased, but all shared the same eastward orientation, and if important enough, the deceased was sent off with ranks of sacrificed horses "pulling" the khirigsuur 'chariot' from the east side of the mound, while around the khirigsuur, families conducted smoke offerings of burned animal remains at small circle hearths. Khirigsuurs functioned in all of these roles—as burial places that connected humans to their revered ancestors in the other world, as 'altars' for expressing religious devotion, and as ceremonial centers for sharing social and cultural values and strengthened social cohesion at social scales from bottom to top. From the many hundreds of khirigsuurs Frohlich mapped in Khuvsgul alone, it would seem that almost every member in DSK society other than slaves might have received a khirigsuur send-off.

DSK Cultures, East and West: Steppe vs. Altai

The Deer Stone Project's 2007 season extended our knowledge of deer stone rites into the northern Darkhad by finding smaller and differently-marked deer stones associated with charcoal or tooth samples that should date these sites. Most deer stone sites investigated produced bone, tooth, or charcoal samples, but only one horse head was found—from Deer Stone 2 at Khushuutiin Devseg. Our scanning team recorded lots of deer stones, and we found many new small as well as some large stones, small ones for the first time south of Darkhad at the Khyadag East site.

Our excursion into the Mongolian Altai (Fitzhugh et al. 2013) added an important comparative dimension by demonstrating different deer stone and khirigsuur traditions between central/northern and western (Altai) Mongolia. DSK sites in central and western Mongolia date to the same period, cal 3100-2700 BCE, but have different features, suggesting a cultural boundary existed

between the two regions. Altai deer stones display different motifs and organization (Types 2, 3), use slate and metamorphosed rock instead of granite and basalt, and often set deer stones inside khirigsuur fences or into the central mound rather than being apart from khirigsuurs. This custom, in particular, adds evidence to the idea that deer stones (1) represent specific deceased individuals, and (2) represent the individuals buried in those khirigsuurs. Thus, we may surmise that in central Mongolia, khirigsuur burials can be linked to nearby deer stones, and possibly to individual deer stones. Another difference is the near universal absence of horse head burials in western khirigsuur and deer stones sites. The explanation may lie in ecology and geography, such as a deficiency of available horses, since the mountainous Altai does not support the huge herds found on the Central Mongolian steppe. As a result, we had to date Altaian deer stones and khirigsuurs using charcoal from stone hearth circles.

While adhering to this general plan in central Mongolia, khirigsuurs in Tavan Bogt of the Mongolian Altai Mountains and neighboring regions of Russian South Siberia and Xinjiang in northwestern China display their own distinctive styles. All have central mounds and square or round boulder fences, and most have circle hearths. But only in exceptional cases are satellite horse mounds present. In several years of surveys in the Tavan Bogt region around Khoton Lake, we found only one khirigsuur, On Khot, at Magoit, had horse mounds. Many of these western khirigsuurs display from 4 to 10 radial boulder lines extending from the central mound to the fence.

Unlike khirigsuurs in central Mongolia, khirigsuurs in western Mongolian and in nearby Russian Altai and Sayan mountains often have deer stones embedded in the east side of the central mounds or right outside their eastern fences. Here we have certain evidence that these deer stones represent the individual buried in the mound, as well as strong indication that deer

Excavation of a horse head mound at On Khot, Magoit, Bayan Ulgii Aimag, the only khirgsuur we found in the Mongolian Altai having sacrificed horses, 2008, and a small khirigsuur at Khuiten Gol Delta, Khoton Lake, with four radial spokes at whose center we found a human burial in 2012.

stones in central Mongolia represent individuals buried in nearby khirigsuurs. One possible reason for mortuary 'social distancing' might be to protect the grave from being linked to individuals known because of their deer stone images. It is now widely recognized that the opening of Bronze Age mounds was not only to procure valuable grave goods, but also to break the ancestral link between the individual and a group's ancestral territorial claims (Littleton et al. 2012). This purpose is especially cogent in the case of khirigsuurs because potential rivals, enemies, and vandals must have known these burials never contained artifacts.

Khirigsuur Size and Symbolism

The meaning of the basic division among khirigsuurs—the shape of the surrounding fence, square or slightly trapezoidal, or round—has never been adequately explained. Bruno Frohlich excavated scores khirigsuurs in Khuvsgul Aimag to see if square or round khirigsuurs signified gender. Results showed no statistical difference;

males and females were buried in approximately the same numbers in round and quadrilateral khirigsuurs (Frohlich et al. 2005). A different kind of explanation is suggested by analogy to the round and quadrilateral symbolism seen in early Chinese ritual architecture, where round symbolized the heavenly domain and square represents the earthly domain. In later history, Chinese influence dominates Mongolian ceremonial architecture, and this may have been the case in DSK times, but it may not be the case in pre-empire times. Could khirigsuur architecture have originated from the round- and square-bordered Karasuk kurgans of southern Russia? Or was the Karasuk influenced by DSK forms since both date ca. 1500-800 BCE? More likely not, as we have a clue in the etymology of the word 'khirigsuur', which is not Mongolian but Khirgiz, a people whose ethnic origin lies in a region of southern Russia that was the Karasuk homeland.

Our data agree with Frohlich's mound description which classified mounds according to size: Class 1 (largest), Class 2 (medium-size), and Class 3 (smallest). Class 1 khirigsuurs occur in prime pasture lands in river valleys and where small hills like Ulaan Tolgoi rise in the middle of broad valleys. Class 2 khirigsuurs cluster around the eastern or southeastern bases of these hills. On the eastern slopes above such sites, we found Class 3 khirigsuurs (called "slope burials" by some archaeologists) diminishing in size with increasing elevation, occurring even on 20-30° slopes. Some of the Ulaan Tolgoi hillside khirigsuurs are only a few meters across yet still retain a circular or square fence and a central mound or rock cluster over a shallow human burial. Only a few of these "commoner" khirigsuurs have been excavated (Frohlich et al. 2005). Nevertheless, they are evidence of the hierarchical nature of khirigsuur architecture and allow cautious inference on social status. The presence of simple graves also implies that nearly all members of DSK society, other than salves, which we presume were present, were given some type of khirigsuur burial.

One of the other pervasive beliefs—that khirigsuurs were ceremonial structures and not mortuary mounds—also had to be abandoned after Frohlich's team began excavating Class 2 and 3 khirigsuur mounds around Murun and in the Darkhad valley. In these mounds, human burials were usually in shallow pits in the center of the mound. However, the remains were often poorly preserved because the bodies were either placed on the surface or in shallow pits that provided little protection against decay. Sometimes only tooth enamel was preserved. In some mounds, bodies were placed in stone lined crypts but rarely were deeply buried. In some cases, bodies were not in the center of the mound where one would expect them, but near the edge, possibly to keep looters from finding them. In others, bones were

Hillside Class 3 khirigsuur burials for "commoners": Bruno Frohlich excavating a 'slope' burial in the rocky hills above the plain, and a square fence khirigsuur burial with corner posts on a hillside near Galt. (photos: PDP, WF)

Frohlich's extensive region-based survey data allows one to begin to reconstruct DSK demographic structure and population size (Frohlich et al. 2008, 2009; Frohlich and Bazarsad 2005), because most khirigsuurs are visible on the surface and can even be seen clearly in satellite photographs. One of the interesting results of Frohlich's mound excavations is that children or young adults are sometimes found in Class 2 khirigsuurs, a fact that suggests DSK society was beginning to develop hereditary class distinctions, an early stage of hierarchical social status.

scattered, or not in proper anatomical position. Rodent activity was probably the most common cause of grave disruption, but in some cases, they may have been ransacked by intruders intent on erasing a prior or rival group's territorial claims by destroying the bones and graves of their ancestors (Littleton et al. 2012). Today, khirigsuurs have come under attack by looters motivated by financial gain, despite the fact that they do not contain artifacts.

Our excavations at Ulaan Tolgoi Mound 1 resolved the question of the cultural identity and contemporaneity of deer stones and khirigsuurs. These data constitute a strong argument for seeing khirigsuurs and deer stones as ritual components of a single culture and belief system. Mound 1 was a classic of the khirigsuur type, probably built as a grave for a powerful leader. This mound had more than 100 satellite mounds wrapped around three sides of the fence and had hearth circles beyond the horse mounds. Excavations here and at Deer Stones 4 and 5 revealed identical patterns of burying east-facing horse heads in both types of sites, and both were surrounded by circular hearths containing burned animal bone. These finds confirmed that both khirigsuurs and deer stones followed the same ritual practices, burying sacrificed horses in small mounds east of the central burial mound and around deer stones, and that both had ceremonies that included ritual burning of animal flesh and bones and/or consumption of these offerings at peripheral ring hearths.

The presence of both ceremonial forms at khirigsuurs and deer stones not only link these features as part of a single cultural system of mortuary practice; they also provide evidence of a unifying religious philosophy that called for standardized construction and behavior. Adherence to the 'rules' of khirigsuur architecture, horse sacrifice, and hearth rituals is seen also in deer stone installations. It is also seen in the 'rules' governing deer stone art that required east-facing orientation, circles for earrings, slashes for faces, placement of the pentagonal shield/chevron motif on the west side of the stone, and the standard iconic form of the Mongolian deer with its set of distinctive iconographic features. Rules seem to have governed nearly every aspect of these ritual systems. Yet within these strictures, there was room for experimentation in the exact placement of deer images, or whether a living or dead horse could

Salvaging remains from a looted burial mound in Erkhel.

be used in an offering mound, or whether the neck vertebrae was placed on the north or south side of the horse skull. Many of the most basic features of these ceremonial sites, like their physical location, square or round khirigsuur type, and placement of horse and hearth features, must have been created and enforced by a ranked system of DSK leadership, not by personal initiative alone.

Although we are not cognizant of all aspects of DSK ceremonialism, one cannot miss the symbolic nature of these two feature types whose architecture take a geometric and strangely cosmological structure, proceeding outward from a central mound or deer stone in concentric rings. Round khirigsuurs are geometrically accurate and their fences must have been measured; horse mounds follow in symmetrical ranks and mounds are evenly spaced. Square khirgsuurs are not always perfectly square and some appear to have been laid out by sight lines from nearby hills, resulting in a trapezoidal shape. Standard rules on the placement of horse mounds are apparent, with the first and most 'important' donations centered outside the east fence. The Monaco research team's proposal that the east-side horse burials served symbolically as chariot steeds to carry the soul of the deceased individual toward the rising sun (Lepetz et al. 2019) adds an integrative understanding to khirigsuur ritual. Deer stones do not always have east-side horse mounds and west-side hearths, but at some sites like Khooshootiin Am this khirigsuur pattern is seen: oval hearths lie to the west of the deer stone line and horse mounds to the east. Despite some variation, DSK ritual practice as it pertained to mortuary and honorific ceremonialism suggests a highly centralized body of thought and standard rules of behavior governed by a centralized political-religious plan.

Having settled the controversy over the deer stone-khirigsuur relationship, we confronted a terminological problem: what to call this now-unified culture?

Building the Deer Stone Story

One of the peculiar aspects of Late Bronze Age archaeology, and of the Deer Stone period in general, has been the absence of a culture name. In Russia, a series of Late Bronze Age cultures had been defined, mostly based on artifacts from cemeteries and grave mounds known as 'kurgans' that included human remains, ceramics, and bone and metal artifacts and ornaments. The Andronovo (2000-900 BCE) and Karasuk (1500-800 BCE) cultures date to the deer stone period, while a third, Afanasievo (3300-2500 BCE), precedes deer stones by a thousand years. A fourth, Pazyryk, dates to the Early Iron Age ca 700-500 BCE (Jacobson 1995; Honeychurch 2015). Before the Deer Stone Project began in 2001, most Mongolian and Russian scholars thought deer stones belonged to a later Mongolian version of Karasuk based on the Pazyryk-like deer images and the types of tools and weapons seen on deer stones. But even with all the fieldwork and publications on deer stones by V.V. Volkov in the 1970s, neither he nor others define the deer stone culture specifically. The basic reason for hesitation was the absence of diagnostic artifacts, identifiable dwellings, and human remains at deer stone sites. So, who were these people?

The archaeological standard of the time required cultural descriptions like house forms, an inventory of bone, metal, and ceramic artifact types, decorative objects, art styles, and information on mortuary practices such as grave structures, grave goods, and the position and orientation of the body. The surprising thing about the deer stones was the absence of most of these features; it was deer stones, and deer stones only that formed a coherent core. The same was true for khirigsuurs: no artifacts and no recognizable human remains or grave goods except for a few bronze knives and broken ceramics. Another cultural component that was glaringly missing was evidence of houses and settlement features, which were known for the preceding Late Neolithic period. Where were people in the Late Bronze Age living? People might have been suspicious about the strange coincidence of artifacts missing from both deer stone and khirigsuur sites, but this link remained unexplored. This absence of artifacts caused Volkov, Novgorodova, and others to explore this period strictly from an art historical and ritual landscape perspective, using deer stone art and surface features only.

We have seen above what was uncovered when we began to dig. My initial interest in deer stones was stimulated by Volkov's publication of deer stone art in which I saw similarities in content and form to early (Iron Age) Eskimo art. To understand the relationship, we needed to date the deer stones and understand the meaning of its imagery and symbols and the "ground context" of its settings. Volkov's maps showed that the areas around deer stone sites were filled with surface features; some were horse head mounds while others were hearth circles and stone pavements. But further explorations seemed fruitless without more tangible archaeological finds.

Like others before me, I did not have a good handle on how to place deer stones and khirigsuurs in a broader cultural context. Deer stones were completely unique as an Inner Asian phenomenon. The same was true of khirigsuurs; neither had real prototypes in Andronovo or Karasuk cultures, or the little-known Late Bronze Age cultures of eastern Kazakhstan, northern China, or Korea. On the other hand, Andronovo cultures from the southern Russian steppe utilized kurgan burials that included horse head ritual dating to the same period as the DSK complex. Having learned more about the LBA in Mongolia and the sharing of identical horse and hearth rituals at deer stones and khirigsuurs, knowing we were dealing with a single culture, people, and time period, what should it be called?

Given the absence of a full cultural description I decided to use the term "Deer Stone-Khirigsuur Complex" to signify that it described only the landscape and ceremonial mortuary ritual of a broader cultural entity still to be identified. What was missing was everything else about this unnamed culture: its material culture, dwellings, and subsistence pattern, although we knew it was a pastoral economy based on sheep, goat, bovids, and horses. Calling it the DSK Complex left room for future work that might define the larger culture this floating ritual complex was anchored in, and who they were as people: Asian, Caucasian, Korean, or Chinese-Manchurian.

We still do not have a grip on a suitable nomenclature solution. Although the past decade has seen acceptance of the term DSK Complex, we still have not resolved whether its parent culture is Andronovo or Karasuk, and who their descendants were (Slab/Square Burial people, Tagar? Pazyryk?). One solution would be to simply call it the Deer Stone Culture or its

Mongolian equivalent, Khoshoo Culture.

Dating and structural correspondence between the two site types establish that khirigsuurs and deer stones are integral components of a single ceremonial system central to the definition of the DSK complex. A large series of radiocarbon dates show these features dating 300 to 500 years earlier than Arzhan and other early Scythian horizon sites. The early deer stone dates from Khuvsgul province raise interesting questions about their origins and their impacts on later cultural developments, including the development of Scythian/Saka culture and art, for which the earliest dates at present come from the large mound complex west of the Mongolian border at Arzhan I in the Russian Gorni Altai region (Gryaznov 1980). Deer stone art, particularly representations of the Mongolian deer motif, has been frequently cited for its Scythian-related style. Mongolian deer stones, now dated securely for the first time, established that deer stone art is pre- and possibly proto-Scythian rather than Scythian-related or Scythian derived.

Scanning Deer Stones: Science, Conservation, Documentation, and Preservation

In 2008 we returned to Khydag, planning to excavate large areas at both Khyadag West and Khydag East. A family that was camped near the site offered us some shelter and hospitality when we arrived during a rain storm. While we waited, I read a draft of a proposal Bayaraa and Ts. Turbat were preparing to send to the US Embassy in Ulaanbaatar for an Ambassador's Grant to excavate, conserve, and reconstruct the large Jargalant deer stone site (KYR-119) associated with the Urt Bulagiin (KYR-40) khirigsuur in Khanuy Valley. (The grant was awarded, and they produced a fine publication, Turbat et al. 2011). Conserving and protecting deer stone sites need much attention today but are complicated by the need to balance research, conservation, heritage, environmental values, public interest, tourism, and economic development. Maybe a first step should be a special conference devoted to the subject with leaders from a variety of fields. Almost any proposal for DS site protection would be controversial to some, but just to let the monuments to languish in the countryside and deteriorate or be lost to theft is also unacceptable. I've had conversations about this with petroglyph experts, Esther Jacobson and Richard Kortum, and many of the same issues face rock art, except for the fact that they are not so portable as artifacts and deer stones. In the case of deer stones, perhaps the solutions will have to be on a case by case basis, depending on the condition of the stones, their environmental setting, potential significance, tourism interest, research, and other factors. Many of these issues were addressed in a special rock art conference convened by Mongolian President Elbegdorj with UNESCO support in 2016.

After Amraa cooked a lunch of hot soup in our neighbor's ger, we set up our camp about 500m away on the east side of the deer stone site. While most of the crew napped, Kyle and I walked around the country east of the site, discovering more ger camps and old winter places. The eroded granite outcrops breaking through the smooth contours of the steppe gave a mysterious quality to the landscape. A couple herders on a motorbike stopped to say hello, wearing warm deels and complaining about the cold weather and poor grass. The problem is not survival of their animals now, but if they're in a bad way when winter arrives, many won't make it through. Amraa prepared another great meal working at the iron stove in the whistling wind, and everyone went in for an early night hoping for better weather tomorrow.

In 2005 we began experimenting with methods to produce more accurate documentation of deer stones and their art. We had discovered that Volkov's published deer stone drawings were often incomplete, missing important elements and information, and were graphically inaccurate. His method relied on visual inspection, often under adverse lighting conditions,

Mongolia's time-worn granite outcrops seem spiritually alive. Amraa adopts a lamb abandoned by its mother.

and depended on the quality of the artist making the drawings. His renderings were, in effect, just sketches of the most visible deer stone motifs and spatial organization of their sites. So, we engaged the Smithsonian's Museum Conservation Institute to assist us in developing a more accurate method combining photography, photogrammetry, and eventually laser scanning.

With the fall of the authoritarian Soviet-dominated regime in 1990, the loss of a secure, state-guaranteed income had resulted in a rise in the looting of archaeological sites, graves, rock art, and monuments. Deer stones were an obvious target, since they could easily be removed and transported to China, and from there to destinations around the world. We had heard of one case in which a deer stone taken from Uushigiin Uvör was found in pieces in the Murun Museum after recovery by the police. Our conservators discovered the pieces matched Volkov's drawing of the complete stone (2002:fig 12, p.90), allowing its identity to be discovered as the missing DS15. Accurate inventory, mapping, and photographic documentation of deer stones and deer stone sites was needed to provide authorities with baseline data for apprehension and recovery. Creating an accurate photographic record would be a crucial component of site and deer stone preservation. For the next three years a team of Smithsonian conservators directed by Rae Beaubien led a pioneering effort to experiment with methods that would not only provide scholars with accurate images for research purposes but would also aid authorities in managing this critical asset of Mongolian heritage.

Our 2002 conservation effort resulted in a latex mold of the most famous deer stone in Mongolia: Uushigiin Uvör Deer Stone 14 (N49°39,925', E99°56,206') in Burentogtokh suum, Khuvsgul Aimag, which stands 256 cm high, the southernmost in a north-south rank of deer stones (see p. xx). DS14 shows the modelled face of a person, likely a male sha-

man, with an open mouth as though engaged in a ritual chant or exhortation. This stone is unique not only for the human face and ears; it also displays a cross-hatched belt with an axe, dagger, fire-starter, gortus (quiver), whetstone, shaman's mirror, pentagonal shield-chevron, and chariot rein hooks. Racks of deer are seen both above and below the belt. Paul Rhymer and Carolyn Thome made a cast of this imposing stelae in 2002 and Carolyn produced a fiberglass replica that was displayed at the Smithsonian in the *Modern Mongolia* exhibition produced by Paula Sabloff for the University of Pennsylvania. Following the exhibition, the model was accessioned by the SI National Museum of Natural History and a second replica made by Carolyn was sent to Ulaanbaatar to become a permanent feature at the Mongolia National Museum. In 2005 the conservation team returned to Mongolia and began systematically describing and recording deer stones at several of the sites we were then excavating. Ulaan Tolgoi, Uushigiin Uvör, and other sites became targets for an experiment using laser scanning as a method for detailed documentation.

Modeling Uushigiin Uvör Deer Stone 14

This deer stone is the most famous of Mongolia's deer stone monuments. Others have more beautiful and legible carving, but what make it unique is the presence of a finely modelled human face at the top of the east-facing side of the stone. Less than 10 or 12 deer stones have human faces, and all are poor representations except for Deer Stone 14, so it became a logical target for a replication project. We also wanted to demonstrate the capability of latex casting as a method for documenting and preserving deer stone monuments in the field, where deer stones and other monuments are being degraded by erosion, lightning, animal rubbing, and even out-right vandalism and theft. The procedure is not difficult to learn and could be accomplished by training museum specialists in Mongolia. However, care must be taken to ensure that the surface of the stone is sufficiently intact, solid, clean, and without crevices and pores that could be damaged while separating the latex mold from the stone. For this reason, an experienced conservator familiar with the procedure is necessary. While the discussion continues in Mongolia and elsewhere about the best method to preserve deer stones and other exposed monuments from damage from natural and human causes, latex casting provides a relatively safe, simple, and inexpensive method of replication. This method can accurately docu-

preserve and document Mongolia's monuments, whether by removing them after careful archaeological excavation and replacing them with exact replicas, or by making replicas to serve as 'voucher' copies of originals in the field, stored in museums or other secure locations. Uushigiin Uvör Deer Stone 14 was cast in the field by Smithsonian artist Carolyn Thome and taxidermist Paul Rhymer and constructed by Carolyn Thome at the Smithsonian Exhibit Central Office in Washington D.C.

In 2005 we returned to Mongolia with a team from the Smithsonian Museum Conservation Institute to find a more accurate way to document deer stones using new laser scanning technology. Laser scanning required deer stones to be scanned from different directions to create

Uushigiin Uvör Deer Stone 14 being prepared for casting by Smithsonian staff (l-r: Paul Rhymer, Carolyn Thome, Ts. Ochirkhuyag, and Ts. Ayush; DS14 has a Mongolian face with a pursed mouth as if shown chanting or singing.

ment carved decoration and inscriptionsand can also faithfully record the surface qualities and granularity of the stone. Once cast, an experienced model-maker can then accurately render even the color and surface texture. Latex casting thus may facilitate decisions about how best to

a 360-degree image and had to be done under nearly dark conditions since direct or even ambient light degraded the result. We experimented erecting a tent of dark cloth over the deer stone but found this cumbersome, especially with tall stones like DS2 at Ulaan Tolgoi

Scanning Ulaan Tolgoi DS2. Cleaning and preparing the stone; scanning under cover to eliminate competing light, 2005. (photos: HFB)

and DS14 at Uushigiin Uvör. Wind was also a complicating factor. Nevertheless, we succeeded in creating some excellent files that, with post-processing, enabled full-round images to be created with a high degree of accuracy. Lasar scanning also allows one to tailor the degree and direction of the light source to enhance shadow effects, change levels of illumination and contrast, and add colors, lines, and other elements to aid interpretation. In the end, we discovered that the field scanning process was best done at night, when the wind was down and equipment could be moved around the stone without encumbering structure and tenting. The results were spectacular, as seen in the final images of

Uushigiin Uvör DS14, which clearly show the difference between a photogrammetrically accurate scan and Volkov's drawing of this iconic object—an object he was attempting to render as accurately as possible.

Laser Scanning Experiments

For the 2005 field tests, a Polhemus FastS-CAN Cobra™ laser system, in conjunction with a lap-top computer and small gas-powered generator, was used for scanning. The equipment's portability and compactness were ideal for use in the field, but its light sensitivity and inability to be used in the vicinity of metal objects posed challenges in creat-

Laser scanning is the most accurate method for documenting three-dimensional monuments like deer stones and other types of sculpture because it can distinguish sub-millimeter changes in surface topography. Conservators check scan data after completing a daytime scan at the North Erkhel Lake site. Night scanning had the advantage of a windless time and no need for a dark tent.

Uushigiin Uvör DS14; SI/MCI laser scan; and Volkov's published illustration showing corrections in blue based on scanned image (after Beaubien et al. 2006; Volkov 2002: fig 79)

ing a suitable scanning environment for each deer stone. The solution the ACP group developed was to construct a temporary shelter using wooden poles, including 5-meter lengths borrowed from nearby animal corrals, draped with medium weight canvas and supplemented inside with light weight black fabric. This provided sufficient shade for scanning and accommodated people and equipment involved in the process. Over a three-week period, scanning tests were conducted on twelve deer stones at six sites: Uushigiin Uvör (#1), Tsatstain Khoshuu (#1), Evdei Valley (#1), Erkhel/Ulaan Tolgoi (#1-#5), Erkhel East (#1-#2), and Erkhel North (#1-#2). The process typically included mechanical removal of dimensional accretions (mostly bird droppings and bulky lichen) and intrusive grass or stones around the base, prior to scanning. Once the logistics of operating the instrument in the field had been worked out, the ACP group succeeded in producing complete raw data files for the ten deer stones from the Evdei and three Erkhel sites. (Beaubien and Karass 2006:59)

Between 2003-2006 the Smithsonian conservation team working in the field with Mongolian assistants scanned dozens of deer stones at major sites across northern Mongolia. Their reports, data logs, field photos, laser scans, descriptions, and condition reports are on file at the Smithsonian's Museum Conservation Institute. Funds did not permit production of final post-processing images of all deer stone laser scans, such as done experimentally for Uushigiin Uvör DS14. However, all data is stored and accessible for researchers in the future and Bayarsaikhan (2017/2022) illustrated many of the resulting scans. Because deer stones are high-value national treasures that exist unprotected across the steppe, they need careful documentation, conservation, and protection to ensure these treasures of Mongolian heritage can be preserved for future generations.

For a detailed discussion of the Uushigiin Uvör site and its deer stones, see the entry in the site description section below.

Looting: A Scourge on Heritage

At the close of our initial studies in the Darkhad Valley, we became aware of a growing threat to the preservation of archaeological sites and resources. During the Soviet era, historical sites were assiduously protected and revered for their cultural and artistic heritage, but with the new capitalistic economy and relaxation of authority structures, archaeological sites began to be seen as exploitable resources. Unscrupulous local residents working on commission from UB and Chinese antiquities dealers, inspired by the market values of some of the prestige goods of the post-DSK culture tombs, began systematic looting of sites. Bruno Frohlich encountered some of these diggers during his wide-ranging khirigsuur surveys and found them digging openly without any fear of reprisal from local authorities. We returned to Ulaan Tolgoi one year to find one of its khirigsuurs ransacked, with a skull and bones tossed back into the bottom of the looters' pit. We reported the activities locally and in Ulaanbaatar, but police showed little interest in investigating. Khirigsuurs, of course, have no grave goods, so this was an unnecessary tragedy, but soon Darkhad looters discovered medieval grave mounds where they found large caches of artifacts including carvings in ivory, bone, and stone, and even whole garments that were preserved in permafrost. Since 2018 J. Bayarsaikhan and teams of American and Mongolian students have been combing through the looter spoil piles in Medieval period cemeteries and recovered fragments of garments and small or broken artifacts looters left behind. The brazen nature of the enterprise is illustrated by a fancy publication of professionally conserved materials that appeared in 2018 containing near-complete, richly embroidered garments described in great detail by scholars paid by the owners of the looted collections. Bayarsaikhan's salvage team found a fragment that fit one of the published garments. While conservation scientists and archaeologists can learn much from shreds and fragments, the loss to cultural heritage and recognition of the proud past that is Mongolia's is irreparable.

A looted khirigsuur at Ulaan Tolgoi, skull lying at pit bottom; and Bayambajargal salvaging a looted medieval grave at Khuigiin Am, Darkhad Valley in 2017. (photo: WF, W. Taylor)

8. Chasing Deer Stones: Initial Surveys

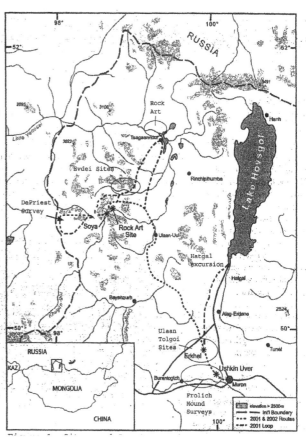

Deer Stone Project survey and research locations in northern and western Mongolia, 2001-2012.

Getting There

Tsogoo took us on a different route after Arbulag, climbing into the hills west of our usual way, and as it happened, into snowfields, following a new track he had chosen to avoid the mudholes in the old route. After stopping for pictures at the snowy pass, we descended through some high pastures, where Tseree got his van stuck in a half-frozen bog. We had to cut down a 25 cm thick larch tree strong enough to lever the van up, hooking the tree under the rear wheel axle hub, so we could get stones under the wheel for traction. After a couple hours in cold whipping wind, we succeeded and soon were lunching with a family Tsogoo knew named Tunendemberel.

After leaving Tooms Brigade, we got into snow

again and found pingos (volcano-shaped permafrost mounds) in the valley leading up to Tooms Davaa pass. The government has been running electrical lines from Murun to Ulaan Uul, but most of the poles are still lying on the ground. At Tooms Davaa, the ground was covered with snow and the trees and bushes all around had burned from a spring fire some say was set by miners. We have been hearing stories about the gold strike in the mountains 50 km up the Khugiin Gol River above Söyö, our old Darkhad field camp from a few years ago. Some large chunks of gold have been found, and "Ninja" miners are working illegally in the middle of Tsaatan reindeer-herding country. It's a rough and tumble operation, as is always the case in gold mining, and attracts all kinds of characters—good and bad. I wondered what effect this will have on the Tsaatan. Later we heard one of our Tsaatan friends was killed defending his claim.

Entering the Darkhad valley was exciting after a three-year absence—the overcast ceiling had begun to lift, and we could see the Khoridol Saridag Mountains and the hills to the west, and the Sayan Mountains looking like they had been sculpted with a knife, so sharp were their shapes with patches of forest flowing over the hills. The Khugiin Gol bridge was in better repair than last time when we took our lives in our hands crossing, ignoring the warning sign.

We arrived at Tsagaan Nuur at dusk and piled into the 'hotel' which had been built in 1960 as a

culture center for the Dukha. It later became a hospital and now is a hotel with the Soviet hammer and sickle insignia still over the door, together with the Mongol national emblem. There was only one room available for all 15 of us, including the baby rabbit we had found under a rock when we dug

Harriet (Rae) Beaubien enjoying lunch with team members (photo: C. Leece); Lunch with the Tunendumberel family north of Oliin Davaa; an unstable wooden bridge over the Khug River, people and vans make separate crossings; killer mud and the required remedy; and Amaraa rescues a baby rabbit. (photos: WF, CL)

The Tsaagannuur Hotel, once a Dukha culture center in Soviet days, was now a hotel, but with a lingering sign from the Soviet era. Our kitchen and dining tent looked like this after a new sheep arrived.

the van out of the mud. For the past two days, this little creature has been living in Amaraa's winter coat pocket. Several of us decided to tent outside to make room for the rabbit.

jeeps, tractors, and trucks were left behind and acquired by Mongolian urban and rural peoples.

An agricultural plot at Nukhtiin Am. Lack of sufficient water makes Mongolian farms a chancy business, especially in a time of climate warming, and motorcycles are replacing horses for those with money.

Transport Transitions

For nearly 4000 years, the herding peoples of the Mongolian steppe have maintained an economy based on the "five noses"—sheep, goats, yaks, horses, and camels. Today the subsistence economy of herders throughout the Mongolian countryside remains based largely on these animals. Although grain agriculture—mostly millet—was periodically practiced at small scale in the larger river valleys, it was not until the Soviet era when agriculture expanded with the assistance of tractors and pumps, the latter opening grazing possibilities in the northern Gobi and arid regions. However, these introductions also produced disasters when plowing broke up the sod for farming without sufficient water, resulting in massive wind erosion and weed introduction that ruined the land for both herders and farmers.

Following 1990 and the departure of Soviet infrastructure, large numbers of Russian vans,

We observed the transition to new transport systems everywhere we travelled. Poorer families continued to use age-old yak-drawn carts or rented camels to make their seasonal household moves from winter to summer quarters. Yaks, cattle, or reindeer continued to haul firewood to camp or logs to a local sawmill and occasionally pulled turnstile pumps, drawing water for livestock. Families with more resources began to rent trucks instead of yaks or camels, while exceptional herders began to buy jeeps or trucks on credit as banks began to function as lenders. During our travels we also saw the introduction of solar-powered electric lights in gers, and soon televisions could be watched for a few hours in the evening, catching signals from satellites. The old tradition of long evenings of traditional music and story-telling began to be eroded by soap operas and decadent satellite-signal western programming. We watched globalization start changing 'outback Mongolia' as people were pulled into the 21st century without their previous Soviet-guaranteed safety net.

Transport Change: Horsemen with yaks hauling logs; a camel transporting a herder camp across Khug River; fuel-tank cable ferry crossing the Shishged River; Soviet era truck replacing camels and ox-carts; nomad camp with ox-cart, truck, and solar collector; and yak delivery service.

Shishged River farm owned by a prosperous Darkhad Mongol seen here with Tsogoo.

Gunj (Khairkhan)

Heading north into the field in 2007, we took a route west of the normal run between Khairkhan and Ulziit because our drivers were on the prowl for airag (fermented mare's milk). This is good horse country and it was the right time of year for airag, a few days before Naadam, the annual national holiday. East of Khairhan, we came across a well-preserved deer stone whose base was guarded by a growth of nettles (N48°23.709', E402°11.860', Khairkhan suum, Arkhangai Aimag). The site is on a small bench on the east-facing side of the hill overlooking a horse-grazed plain and a herder's camp. Mongolian deer carvings encircled the stone, but it had been damaged by erosion, especially on its north side. The west side has a shield-like chevron emblem; the south has a circle groove at its top, and there are

three right-ascending deer on its east side. Boulder features are present around the east and south sides of the stone. Dimensions: 175(tall)cm, 44(w), 40(t). This stone had not been moved since its installation 3000 years ago.

Further east in the same valley, a solitary craggy hill rising above the plain had eroded slabs of granite tumbling down its sides 560-600ft above the valley floor. At the base of the hill, we found a string of khirigsuurs and a Tibetan rock inscription (N48°20.229', E102°19.602'). Slightly further to the southeast, an abandoned threshing mill stood in ruins beside a large tract of land farmed in the Soviet era that had turned into a wasteland due to lack of rainfall or sufficient irrigation. On all sides around this weedy, ruined field the natural pastureland was in fine condition—another example of the many disastrous foreign-funded agricultural development schemes.

A well-preserved solitary DS near Khairkhan; Crossing a weak Shishged bridge, passengers separate from the van.

Square/Slab Burials and Repurposed Deer Stones at Sakhalt Khairkhan (Burdnii Ekh)

In 2005 while traveling north to the Dark-had, we found an open Square Burial grave at Burdnii Ekh ('The Source,' N48°20.783', E102°22.578') on the east side of the road, a kilometer east of Sakhalt ('Mustache Hill'), in Saikhan suum, Bulgan Aimag, a few kilometers south of the ferry landing on the Selenge River. Sometimes called 'Slab Graves' when they are surrounded by standing slabs, this one was constructed using re-purposed deer stones as construction material. Four deer stones were standing at the corners of the grave while others had been used to make a square crib lining the subsurface walls,

period. Radiocarbon dates on these sites date to the period ca. 2600-2400 cal. BP, immediately following the DSK period (Taylor et al. 2019). At Urt Bulagiin, square burials are found along the southeast outer tier of the ca. 2300 satellite horse mounds, indicating that they were among the latest additions to the site's ritual features. Their use of deer stones as building materials seems incongruous given the placement of the graves at such an important DSK site, because it implies sensitivity to or acknowledgement of the cultural or spiritual power of the location. This iconoclastic juxtaposition seems all the more extraordinary given the diametrically different religious philosophies and belief systems of these two cultures—the DSK culture whose burials were beneath stone mounds and did not

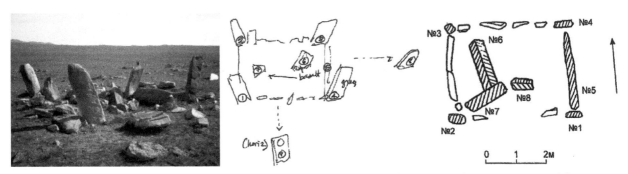

Burdnii Ekh Square/Slab Burial with re-purposed deer stones at corners, looking north, 21 June 2005 (photo: Ts. Sanjmyatav); Beaubien sketch on 7 June, 2006; and Volkov sketch (2002:162, fig. 47).

essentially using deer stones as 'logs' to line the burial crypt. In 2006 we saw a similar square burial constructed with deer stones at Jargalant (Turbat et al. 2011). The latter was excavated by Volkov and Sanjmyatov in 1990, and Sasha's excavation notes tell of finding the remains of horse, cow, sheep, goat, and fowl, and many artifacts. These graves also contained well-preserved human remains that were identified as having Asian physical features.

The use of deer stones at these sites provides evidence on the transition from the DSK culture to the succeeding Square/Slab Burial

generally include grave goods or animal deposits, while Square Burial leaders were buried in deer stone-lined crypts with deer stone corner posts, large amounts of earthly possessions and animals sacrificed for food, company, and service in the afterlife.

The contrast between DSK and Square Burial mortuary ritual and belief could hardly be more striking, especially as the time interval between the two is minimal—in fact they appear to have overlapped. Obviously, the SB people knew and respected or perhaps feared the power of DSK beliefs to some degree or they would not have chosen to locate their leaders' graves at Urt Bulagiin and other DSK burial sites. The unusual nature of the SB appearance is also manifested by the re-emergence of the mound burial tradition 400 years later when the

Turkic figure with khadag devotional prayer ribbons and offering objects; and the accompanying Turkic ritual site/temple foundation at Dalkha, south of the Selenge River.

Xiongnu culture appears. Xiongnu burials continue the DSK tradition of mound burial, but in this case, they built huge mounds over burial pits as deep as 30 meters, filled with a lavish array of grave goods, including horses and chariots; and instead of DSK-type satellite mounds of sacrificed horses, their leaders' mounds had east-side satellite burials of sacrificed retainers. Xiongnu graves suggest a melding of SB and DSK traditions by this incipient empire society dating ca. 200 BCE-200 CE. The inevitable question raised is whether SB culture appeared as an in situ evolution in which DSK peo-

ple adopted a radically new belief system and ceremonial architecture, or was it forced upon them by external invaders, with demographic replacement, or some combination of the two (Honeychurch 2015).

Also, south of the Selenge River is the 7-8th C. Turkic ritual site at Dalkha (N48°20.783'/ E102°22.578') which consists of the square temple foundation with a central passage or hall beside a beautifully carved Turkic memorial figure. This site was excavated by the Russians in the early 1970s and was left open, revealing the intricate architectural plan of the building. Over the years, as we passed this site, the figure was always draped with blue khadags.

Evdei-1, a Turkic Slab Memorial

Traveling south from our Tsaatan visit in June 2005, we discovered several sites in the Evdei region south of Tsaaganuur. Evdei-1 (N51°7,310', E99°13,300') in Renchinlkhumbe suum, Khuvsgul Aimag, presented two irregularly shaped and unmodified standing slabs of greenish greywacke placed in north-south alignment at the base of a hill bordering the north side of the valley. Superficially, these standing stones resembled deer stones because they followed the same pattern of north-south alignment, but closer inspection revealed an absence of deer stone iconography—i.e., no belt, tools, necklace, or circular earrings. The presentation of the stones was also different; they were flat, two-sided slabs with untrimmed edges and were not the usual 4-sided plinths of granite or basalt. Could these stones be an unusual variant of the standard deer stone, we wondered? (See General Notes for the Evdei-1 excavations in Appendix A, and 28 June diary notes in our 2005 Field Report.)

Evdei 1 Turkic Stone 1 excavation, and 2005 field team.

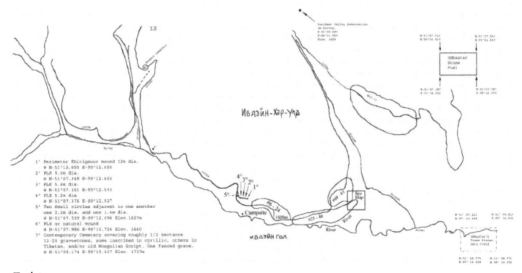

Evdei survey map.

Evdei 1 Standing Stone 1 excavation, view southwest.

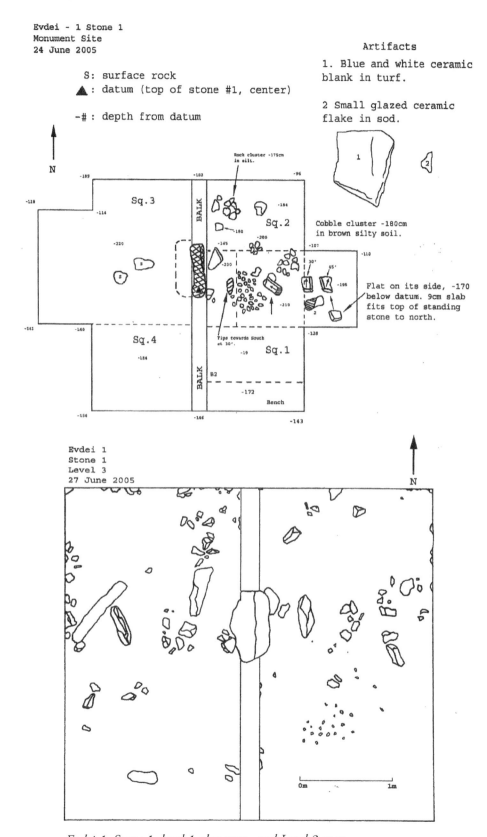

Evdei 1, Stone 1, level 1 plan map, and Level 3 map.

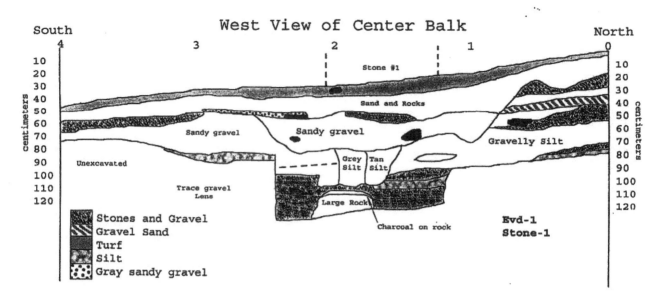

West View of Center Balk

South
4   3   2   1   0   North

Stone #1

Sand and Rocks

Sandy gravel   Sandy gravel   Gravelly Silt

Unexcavated   Grey Silt   Tan Silt

Trace gravel Lens

Large Rock

Charcoal on rock   Evd-1 Stone-1

Stones and Gravel
Gravel Sand
Turf
Silt
Gray sandy gravel

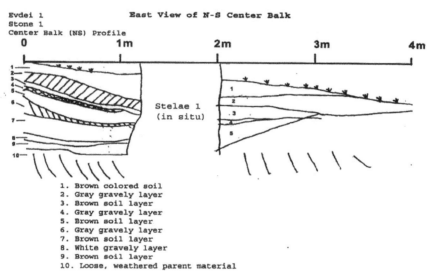

Evdei 1
Stone 1
Center Balk (NS) Profile

East View of N-S Center Balk

0   1m   2m   3m   4m

Stelae 1 (in situ)

1. Brown colored soil
2. Gray gravely layer
3. Brown soil layer
4. Gray gravely layer
5. Brown soil layer
6. Gray gravely layer
7. Brown soil layer
8. White gravely layer
9. Brown soil layer
10. Loose, weathered parent material

West view of the Evdei central N-S balk, and east profile of the N-S balk.

The Evdei stones had no associated horse mounds or hearth circles, but excavation of four square meters around Stone 1 revealed animal bone fragments. We also found a series of small standing rock slabs extending east and west of the stones that had been partially buried in slope-wash from the hill above. These small standing slabs enabled us to identify Stones 1 and 2 as Turkic memorial features dating to ca. 7-8th centuries CE. Later when we studied similar Turkic memorials where sedimentation was minimal, we found small flat slabs spaced a meter or two apart and extending many meters east of the standing stones, which often had a face and torso of a man carved on their east sides. The small slab alignments, called *balbals*, are believed to represent individuals killed by the man-stone figure. Some of these memorials have hundreds of *balbals*. The central standing stones at these sites are prepared in a variety of ways, depending on the importance or wealth of the leader represented. Some like the Evdei stones are undecorated, while others may show only an engraved face, arms, and torso outline or may be carved in the full-round showing a clothed human with the left hand on a sword and the right hand holding a libation cup. The Evdei stones were at the rude end of the spectrum, and we were not able to count all the *balbals* because some were probably buried by slope-wash. By comparison, the Burdni Ekh figure south of the Darhad near the Selenge River was a full-round torso, but without *balbals*. The Evdei stones more closely resemble ones we found north of Tsaaganuur on the north side of the Shishiged River in 2004. As in the case of deer stones, the Turkic memorial figures are not found with human remains or grave goods. Most of these figures are positioned at the east side of a square slab-lined box with a cobblestone pavement upon which we found animal bone fragment from memorial offerings.

Evdei is toward the northern limit of Turkic memorial installations, whose core area is in the Altai Mountain region of western Mongolia. Our excavation helped us distinguish deer stones from at least one other type of standing stone. We also began to recognize a degree of continuity in the history of standing stone memorials, since the Turkic type ca. 1500 years later carries forward deer stone features like east-facing orientation of stone figures of leaders or warriors showing the upper body, belt, and weapons. Other similarities include the presence of burned animal offerings and absence of human interments and grave offerings. At Turkic figure installations, instead of horse sacrifices and circle hearths, there are *balbals*. L.N. Ermolenko (2006) has argued that Turkic figures are stylized representations of Turkic leaders or ancestors and are not personalized to specific historical figures. G.V. Kubarev 2007) disputes this idea, citing the considerable variation in facial features, poses, clothing and apparel. We argue here that deer stones are also personalized historical figures, and it would seem that this

feature of Turkic statuary may have been carried forward from DSK protoypes. Turkic figures have a similar distribution as deer stones and range from Kazakhstan to Baikal and southern Russia. The similarities between deer stone and Turkic figures suggest the mechanism for transmission of this ritual model from the past was the physical presence of deer stones standing throughout much of what became the Turkic culture area.

Evdei 2 looters pit where we found ceramic Buddhist devotional figures recovered from back-dirt excavation in 2005.

Evdei-2: A Buddhist Enclosure Site

In addition to excavating the Turkic memorial site we conducted a regional survey that recorded 75 mounds and other surface features in the Evdei area. One of the most imposing was a gridded pattern on the surface of the ground that local people reported had been the site of a Buddhist temple dating to the late 19th and early 20th centuries. We spent a day mapping its rectilinear features and excavated the back-dirt from three looters' pits, finding animal bones and small ceramic devotion figurines.

A full digging day out at the Evdei-2 site where we found looter's pits inside large enclosures marked by 5-10 cm deep trenches which probably are the remains of slotted logs into which fence boards were fitted. Similar constructions are still used today in Tsaaganuur as property boundary fences. The pits inside some of the enclosures, which measured up to 50-60 x 45 m and were strictly measured rectangles, had all been dug to a depth of 2-3 feet. One contained Buddhist ceramic relics (miniature hands, feet, torsos, etc) and many other artifacts overlooked by the looters. It was not clear whether these pits were domestic pits or ritual dumps. We collected from two of the pits, and Melanie and I excavated another that seemed to be a well that had been re-used as a trash pit and contained a few artifacts and many food bones, from which we collected a full trash bag. We surmised that those enclosures were animal pens, but why the trash pits? And in some cases, there were indications of structures or dwelling foundations. Od, Dennis, and Betsy mapped 8-10 of these enclosures. Their dates seem to be early 20th century. Local people report there was a monastery established in the valley north of Evdei, but after one of the monks died in the first year, they decided that location was not favored and moved to our site at the opening of the valley. Later this monastery was burned, perhaps during the purges in the 1930s. There should be good records of this in UB. (2 July 2005)

Evdei-3 Deer Stones

Two fallen deer stones are in the northern Evdei-2 site area at (N51°7.402', E99°14.827'). In 2005 we excavated DS1 and found a second unmarked slab lying a few cm. lower in the same pit. Two circular hearth features associated with DS1 were excavated, and a hearth circle at DS2 produced a charcoal date of 3050-2850

cal. BP, similar to the dates at Ulaan Tolgoi DS4 (Appendix 1). DS1 Feature 1 also produced a dark chert end scraper made on a thick prismatic blade. This was the first chipped stone artifact we have found associated with deer stones, raising the question of whether Late Neolithic lithic technology persisted into the Late Bronze Age. In this case, we believe the deer stones were placed on the location of an earlier Neolithic site.

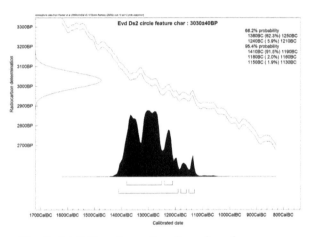

The Evdei-3 Deer Stone 2 radiocarbon date on charcoal.

Evdei-3, DS1, tipped up in preparation for scanning. (photo: H.F. Beaubien)

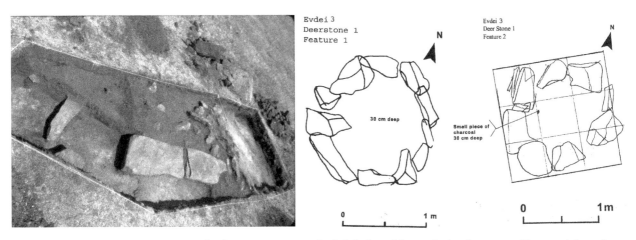

Evdei 3 Deer Stone 1 Pit, view south, showing an unmarked slab found beneath the deer stone; Feature 1 hearth ring; and Feature 2 hearth ring.

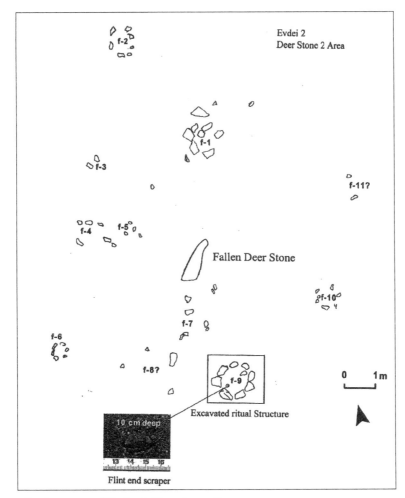

Surface map of Evdei-2 Deer Stone 2 area.

Erkhel Lake North

We briefly investigated a small deer stone site located on a low terrace on the north shore of Erkhel Lake at N49°58.373', E99°56.521'. The standing deer stone had faint but unmistakable deer stone markings, and the other, fallen, was a few meters to the north. We excavated the fallen stone and a circular boulder feature near DS1, but no bone, charcoal, or artifacts were recovered. Both stones were laser-scanned by our conservation team.

Khushuutiin Devseg

In 2005 a local herder told us about a deer stone site in the hills a kilometer east of the Erkhel Lake tourist ger camp at N49°55.031', E100°03.164'. Located in Alag-Erdene suum, Khuvsgul Aimag, the site had not been reported by Volkov or others. We found two deer stones in the middle of the herder's winter camp in the hills overlooking the east shore of Erkhel Lake. The stones have excellent carvings but are on roughly finished and eroded granite. We returned in 2006 and 2007 to search for horse head features and excavated an area containing three boulder features and a third, fallen, deer stone.

Erkhel North 1 DS1, in as-found position; and Erkhel North 1 DS2. (photos: H.F. Beaubien)

Sanjmyatav and Enkbold recording DS1 using a lined grid. (photo: DePriest)

In mid-June, 2007, we returned for proper excavations at Erkhel East, whose site name became Khushuutiin Devseg and set up camp on a plateau between the lowland and the hills over-

looking Lake Erkhel. There are several well-kept herder winter camps here, and after we got the excavation going, we met herders who told us of other standing stones nearby. The weather warmed in the afternoon, bringing out the midges, and my midge-bite polka-dots started emerging such that by the end of the day I was looking 'clownish'. Enkhbold began drawing DS1, and by evening we had cleared and mapped the rocks in a 5x4 m area that has a ring feature looking like it might be a horse head burial, and a mostly buried deer stone that so far has no marks showing. So far, we've seen none of the abundant pottery we found in last year's dig near the northern deer stone.

Excavations at Khushuutgiin Devseg produced our first information on a DSK deer stone site with a domestic settlement.

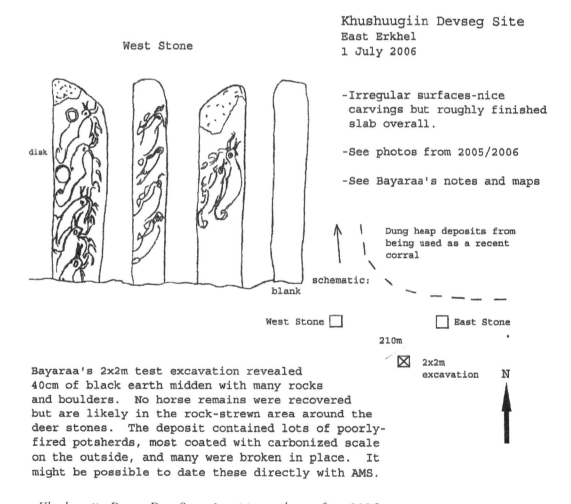

West Stone

disk

blank

Khushuugiin Devseg Site
East Erkhel
1 July 2006

-Irregular surfaces-nice carvings but roughly finished slab overall.

-See photos from 2005/2006

-See Bayaraa's notes and maps

Dung heap deposits from being used as a recent corral

schematic:

West Stone ☐   ☐ East Stone

210m

☒ 2x2m excavation   N

Bayaraa's 2x2m test excavation revealed 40cm of black earth midden with many rocks and boulders. No horse remains were recovered but are likely in the rock-strewn area around the deer stones. The deposit contained lots of poorly-fired potsherds, most coated with carbonized scale on the outside, and many were broken in place. It might be possible to date these directly with AMS.

Khushuugiin Devseg Deer Stone 1 position and notes from 2006.

Enkhbold spent all day drawing Deer Stone 1, the southern and most beautiful and well-preserved of the two standing stones, providing us with at least one excellent controlled representation of deer stone art. He went about it systematically by gridding out the entire stone in ten centimeter blocks using white thread, and then drew from this controlled surface. Deer Stone 1 has a top surface sloping up toward the east, four right-ascending deer and a partial earring groove on its badly eroded south side, five ascending east-facing deer and an earring groove and mirror on its north side, and four ascending right-facing deer and a bow on its east side.

The day was tremendously productive. Feature 1 turned out to be a horse head that produced a tooth date with several intercepts ranging from between cal. 2720-2350 BP as well as an unprovenanced horse tooth dating cal. 2320-1990 BP. Outside and stratigraphically above the base of the horse mound we recovered a large collection of ceramics in black midden earth. The Feature 2 mound had some large slab rocks at the bottom and a horse head oriented 145°, one hoof, and a set of neck vertebrae. A horse tooth from this feature dated cal. BP 2720-2350. Feature 3 was a tight ring of large rocks about the same size as the horse

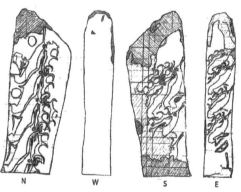

Khushuugiin Devseg DS1 and DS2, right. (graphic: Enkhbold; photo: JB)

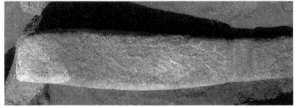

Khushuugiin Devseg DS3a, b which was found beneath the ground. (photos: WF JB)

mound and contained a single horse hoof and a tooth dating cal. BP 2860-2740. Just northeast of this ring was a small box-like hearth, and next to it the fallen DS3 whose upper corner was just protruding from the surface. Upon excavation, deer figures began to appear, and the stone was found to be heavily ornamented. The Feature 3 date is the only one we may securely tie to the deer stones; the others likely date the domestic winter occupation several hundred years later.

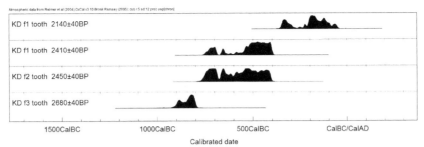

Radiocarbon dates from Khushuugiin Devseg.

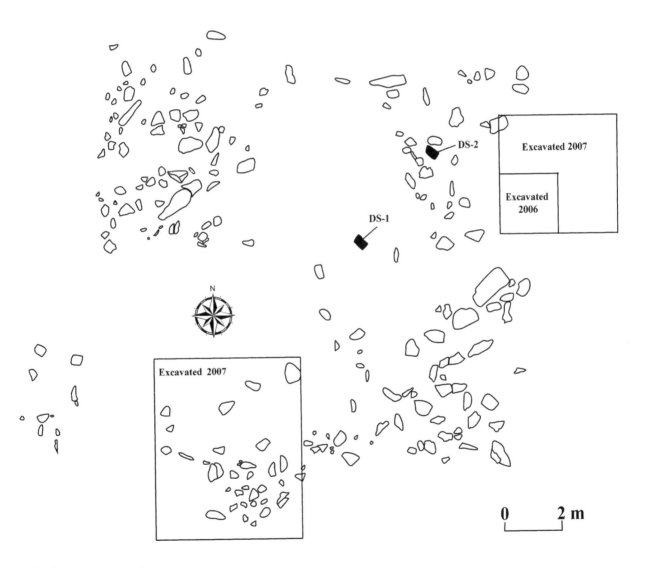

Khushuugiin Devseg deer stone site excavation map.

Khushuugiin Devseg with fallen DS3 (left), Feature 2 (rear), and Feature 3 (foreground); Feature 2 with horse head remains; Decorated rim of a large Late Bronze Age ceramic bowl. (photos: WF and JB)

2006: Excavating near the buried deer stone, Bayaraa found a rim sherd of a large ceramic jar, probably some sort of feast bowl, with interesting decoration. This is the finest piece of decorated ceramic we have found in five years! Mat Sagi, Bill Stewart, and I worked on expanding last year's excavation near the northernmost deer stone, where we found lots of utilitarian ceramics. This pottery *was not an exact match with the type Bayaraa found in Feature 2B, but it was a similar and had some decorative bands instead of incised designs. We were able to fit several pieces together, including some rim sherds, and could tell the vessel must have been quite large, perhaps a festival feast bowl. We now have one such bowl from each feature area, and the means for dating both.*

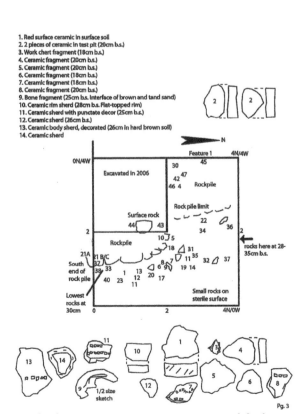

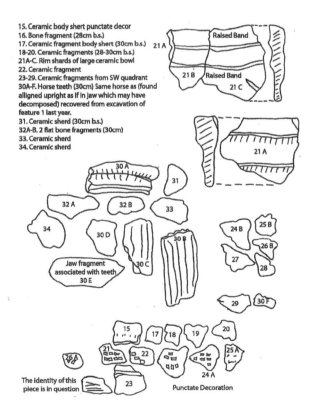

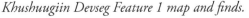

Khushuugiin Devseg Feature 1 map and finds.

While we were excavating, the herder who owns this camp returned from his summer pasture in the hills when he saw us digging in his farmyard. After getting a tour and look at the collections, we were relieved to find him thrilled by the finds and encouraged us to return. It must be strange to live with ancient deer stones in your farmyard and not to know what to make of them, or what harm or good they might bring. This site would be an excellent target for future research since it is one of the few Late Bronze/Early Iron Age winter settlement sites known in northern Mongolia.

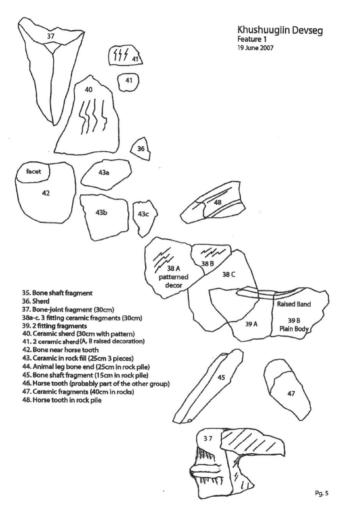

Khushuugiin Devseg
Feature 1
19 June 2007

35. Bone shaft fragment
36. Sherd
37. Bone-joint fragment (30cm)
38a-c. 3 fitting ceramic fragments (30cm)
39. 2 fitting fragments
40. Ceramic sherd (30cm with pattern)
41. 2 ceramic sherd (A, B raised decoration)
42. Bone near horse tooth
43. Ceramic in rock fill (25cm 3 pieces)
44. Animal leg bone end (25cm in rock pile)
45. Bone shaft fragment (15cm in rock pile)
46. Horse tooth (probably part of the other group)
47. Ceramic fragments (40cm in rocks)
48. Horse tooth in rock pile

Pg. 5

Khushuugiin Devseg Feature 1 finds (con't), and Features 2 and 3 map, following page, with c14 dates.

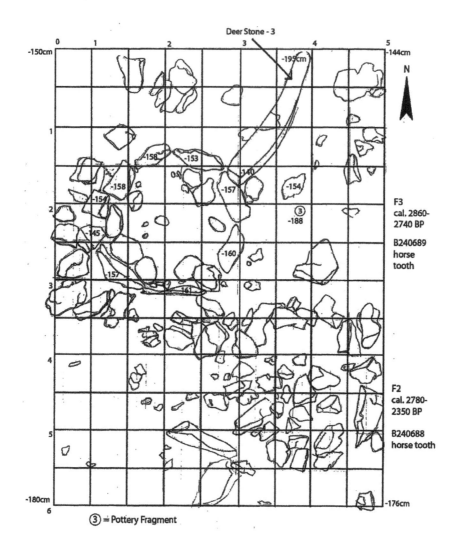

Deer Stone - 3

-150cm   -144cm
-195cm

N

-158 -153
-158   -140
-154   -157   -154

F3
cal. 2860-
2740 BP

③
-145   -188

B240689
horse
tooth

-160

-157
-161

F2
cal. 2780-
2350 BP

B240688
horse
tooth

-180cm   -176cm

③ = Pottery Fragment

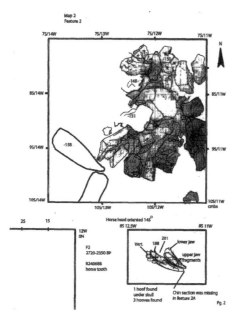

Map 2
Feature 2

7S/14W   7S/13W   7S/12W   7S/11W

N

-150

8S/14W   8S/11W

-148

-151

9S/14W   9S/11W

-158

10S/14W   10S/11W
10S/13W   10S/12W   cmbs

25   15
12W
0N

Horse head oriented 145°
85 12.5W   85 11W

F2
2720-2350 BP

Vert. 188 201 lower jaw
B240688
horse tooth   upper jaw
fragments

1 hoof found
under skull
3 hooves found   Chin section was missing
in feature 2A

Pg. 2

Khushuugiin Devseg Feature 2A second layer rocks overlying horse head remains, Bayarsaikhan with gnat protection gear.

Erkhel 1

Erkhel 2

Erkhel 3

Erkhel 4

Erkhel 5

Erkhel 6

Erkhel 7

Erkhel 8

Erkhel 9

Erkhel 10

Erkhel E Stone 1, Side 1

Erkhel E Stone 1, Side 1 i

UshkinUver Stone 6

UshkinUver Stone 6 i

UshkinUver Stone 6 ii

UshkinUver Stone 6 iii

UshkinUver Stone 9

UshkinUver Stone 9 i

UshkinUver Stone 9 ii

UshkinUver Stone 9 iii

Deer stone motifs drawn by field volunteer Elizabeth Eldredge in 2005.

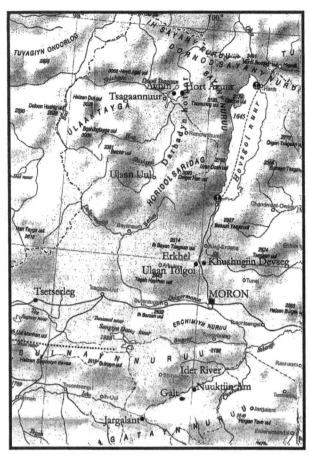

Map of northern Mongolia showing sites visited in 2002-2009.

ing butchered animal remains on the pavement stones. Later in the day we visited the French excavation site at Gol Mod I Xiongnu cemetery, finding a huge hole where the burial mound had been excavated down to reach the burial chamber. The pit was still open, awaiting final excavation, and on the west side of the mound, there was a ramp leading to what had been the center of the mound.

French excavations at Gol Mod-1, a huge khirigsuur-type tomb of the Xiongnu empire. (photo: PDP)

Khanuy Valley Excursions

En route to the Darkhad valley in June 2006, accompanied by Francis Allard, then of Washington University in Pittsburgh, Pennsylvania, we visited several sites along the road, including the large square burial at Burdnii Ekh (previously described) that used re-purposed deer stones from a nearby deer stone site as retaining walls and vertical corner posts. West of the deer stone/slab grave site is a large khirigsuur that has a rectangular pavement east of the mound and beyond that, horse mounds. Volkov recognized similar pavements at a few deer stone sites, and we have excavated such features at Hort Azuur and Khyadag East, find-

Naadam Day Races

The drive to Allard's camp was interesting because it occurred on Naadam Day, and we encountered two horse races as we passed through the countryside to the Khanuy Valley. The first race was at the first suum center south of Murun in To-son. We stopped here for about an hour while the horse-riders came in. I was invited to film from the finish line tower. Just at the crucial moment, the lead horse stopped running when it reached the crowd lined up in the final 100 meters, thinking that the race was over. This caused an outburst from the crowd and frantic efforts by the rider, for he was only a few lengths ahead of the second-place horse. He managed to win, nevertheless. As each horse and rider finished, the families converged to offer praise and support for the winners. Lat-

er, there would be a parade for the champions, probably at the beginning of the wrestling matches, as was done at the Naadam in Söyö we attended a couple years ago. We became caught up in a second race as we crossed the pass in Rashaant suum near the Turkic site we visited on the way north, and found ourselves in the middle of the race, catching up with the front-runner just at the finish-line. It was almost like we were also in the race, seeing the horses and riders struggling, gaining, or losing ground, watching the efforts of some riders pay off and other fall behind. (11 July 2005)

Bayaraa and one of his family's horses ornamented with medals from previous victories, ready for the 2009 Naadam race; and Scythian horse reconstructed from finds from the IV-Vth c. BCE Berel kurgan.

Approaching the finish line at a youngsters' horse race during Naadam festival near Lake Erkhel in 2006. Naadam, Mongolia's national holiday, features wrestling tournaments (b) in which special boots and open-fronted shirts are required. The winner must perform an eagle dance and gets pummeled with chunks of cheese. In addition to wrestling, the other two "manly sports" competed are horse racing and archery. (photos: C. Leece)

In the Khanuy Valley north of Gol Mod we found Urt Bulagiin (KYR40, N48°05.546', E101°03'), a huge khirigsuur with more than 2300 satellite horse mounds and 1000 stone hearth circles (Allard and Erdenbaatar 2005; Broderick et al. 2014). The horse mounds were carefully placed to provide evenly spaced lanes between the mounds and radial pathways extending out from the corners of the khirigsuur fence. Having established the architecture of the khirigsuur features at Ulaan Tolgoi, our purpose at Urt Bulagiin was to test whether the horse mounds were installed as part of a single ceremony at the time of khiriguur construction and burial ceremony, or represented an extended process of mortuary ritual perhaps lasting years or even decades.

This question had arisen because of the wide disparity in the sizes of khirigsuurs, ranging from small hillside constructions like those at Ulaan Tolgoi having no satellite mounds or ring hearths, to huge constructions like Urt Bulagiin with thousands of horse mounds and circular hearths. At issue was not only the labor required to build a huge mound, but the social and political organization needed to carry out a large-scale architectural plan, and the need to maintain organizational control over the out-years following the burial of a revered leader. As we have seen, khirigsuurs and deer stone installations follow a specific, codified plan. The architecture—and we have to assume the conduct of related ritual—conformed to a standard pattern in the types and placement of features and building elements; they were not free-form constructions. The patterning seen in layout of satellite mounds at large khirigsuurs suggests centralized planning and control. One can imagine the construction of a massive mound and fence like Urt Bulagiin being created to honor the burial of a major leader, as in the case of Egyptian pyramids. What type of organized control might be needed if the accretion of horse sacrifice mounds was to take place over the course of years, decades, or longer? How would such a plan be organized? What would compel the owners of horses to continue sacrificing their animals to a leader long departed, especially when young leaders would want to be honored instead?

It was these types of questions that we pondered as we looked over the vast array of horse mounds at Urt Bulagiin. One way to test the question of khirigsuurs as 'event-based' (or hierarchical) ceremonialism vs. a 'egalitarian-based' function was to determine the age differential between the horse mounds that were laid down in the first inner rank of satellite mounds against those established in the

outermost ranks. We tested this method in our excavation of Mound 1 satellite mounds at Ulaan Tolgoi and found identical dates from both inner and outer horse mounds, but that mound only had four ranks of horse mounds, not 13 as at Urt Bulagiin. At Urt Bulagiin we had a better chance of determining chronological separation if the mounds were installed over a longer period. Assuming that those in the first rank date the earliest horse sacrifices, how much time might have passed before the 2300th horse was killed and buried?

Urt Bulagiin

After lunch, while the Mongolian students were setting up their Naadam wrestling match grounds and determining who would wrestle whom in the first round, Francis took us for a tour of the huge khirigsuur he worked at down in the valley and explained his theories about it. This mound has almost 3000 stone features outside its fence – perhaps as many as 2300 horse head mounds and a huge number of small round hearth rings. The pattern is almost the same as we observed at Ulaan Tolgoi and in the Darkhad to the north: east-facing horse skulls with 30 degrees of azimuth variation, which Allard attributes to the advancing season when the sun rises farther to the south, and then shifts back north. He finds some small horse mounds linked to larger ones— perhaps representing a colt sacrificed together with its mother. He's inclined toward a non-hierarchical model with horse mounds being added over many years, and he thinks variation in the east and west wall lengths relate to the "keystone" effect of an observer fixing the square corners by sight lines to four people lined up and viewed from a vantage point on the hill west of the site. This would explain why he finds the east walls of khirigsuurs to be 13% longer than west walls.

Urt Bulagiin has several slab graves construc-

tions along the east side of the mound outside the horse head mounds. Allard and Erdenbaatar suggest this results from syncretism, new people or customs building upon a local khirigsuur religious base, as is also suggested by the re-use of deer stones in slab graves at sites like Jargalant deer stone site that Sasha [Sanjmyatav] worked on with V.V. Volkov in 1990. The amazing thing about these sites is the large number of horse head mounds organized in ranks of hundreds, even at the Jargalant deer stone site, something we have not seen to this extent in Khuvsgul sites. We saw some beautifully carved deer stones at Jargalant, a few made of basalt that had remarkable deer carvings. This site's destruction—in antiquity as well as by archaeologists—is a tragedy that should inspire new research and reconstruction. [see Turbat and Bayarsaikhan 2011] (12 July 2005)

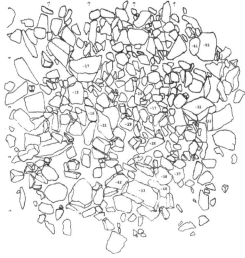

On 9-10 June we excavated two horse mounds and chose mound KYR40-1-21 in the middle of the east fence in the first rank at N48°05.547'/E101°03.465'. The second excavation was a horse head mound KYR40-1-22 in

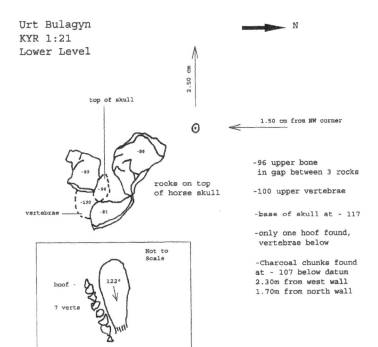

Urt Bulagyn
KYR 1:21
Lower Level

N

2.50 cm

top of skull

1.50 cm from NW corner

rocks on top of horse skull

vertebrae

-96 upper bone
in gap between 3 rocks

-100 upper vertebrae

-base of skull at - 117

-only one hoof found,
vertebrae below

-Charcoal chunks found
at - 107 below datum
2.30m from west wall
1.70m from north wall

Not to Scale

hoof -

122°

7 verts

Urt Bulagiin mound KYR40-1-21 on the inner row of horse mounds just outside the east fence before excavation. Finds included a poorly preserved skull, seven vertebrae, one hoof, and charcoal.

the outermost row at N48°05.546'/ E101°03.504', 13 ranks beyond the fence rank. We found horse heads in both mounds and a charcoal in mound 21. The radiocarbon dates on horse teeth turned out to be identical: cal. 2980-2770 BP (KYR40-1-21) and cal. 2970-2780 BP (KYR40-1-22) (Appendix 1). These dates support the idea of a single event ceremony in which invited attendees representing a very wide geographical region assembled to honor a powerful leader. In this case, Khanuy would have been near or at the center of DSK power, occupying one of the most economically favorable regions of the Mongolian steppe, which would also have been a major trade crossroads. It is debatable whether two samples could do more than suggest confirmation of our single-event hypothesis, and more analysis using a large series of dating samples using Bayesian interpretation methods would be required, but it is interesting that the Rank 1 horse dated 10 c14 years older than the Rank 13 horse. Perhaps this shows that a more mature, respectable horse gained first honors beside the east fence!

The discussion of khirigsuur chronology and hierarchical vs. egalitarian interpretations has been considered by Joshua Wright (2014, 2015, 2017a, b) in a series of papers devoted to social theory. He argues for an egalitarian model by modeling labor requirements for moving stone, the economic cost of sacrificing horses, and the efficiency of communal organization. Similar arguments have been advanced for megalith-building in northern Europe. Lepetz et al. (2019) and Zazzo et al. (2019) come to similar conclusions based on their intensive study of khirigsuur chronology at the large Tsatsyn Ereg B10 khirigsuur in Arkhangai. Using Bayesian modeling and a large suite of c14 dates, Zazzo and Lepetz argue for a lengthy span of horse burials at this large khirigsuur. Their analysis of 100 radiocarbon dates from the B10 khirigsuur, which has ca. 1100 horse mounds and a similar number of hearth circles,

suggests its horse donations occurred over a period of 50 years rather than in a single event. Assuming yearly events, only 24 horses would need to be sacrificed each year over a period of 50 years. Such losses could be managed by a relatively small local kin group without widespread regional contributions.

On the other hand, this analysis can be questioned on the basis of variations in the age range of living horses, the possible inclusion of deceased animals, sample contamination, standard deviation, counting or machine error, and other factors. Even if one accepts the conclusion, questions remain concerning how such a multi-generational honorific practice could be sustained and managed socially and politically over several decades. I would still maintain that at the peak period of DSK activity, with its widespread regional integration, trade, military activity, and diplomacy, the death of powerful leaders may occasionally have called forth a huge regional response. This could be tested by analyzing horse teeth strontium and oxygen isotope ratios to determine whether the horses are of local or distant origin, as determined in a study by Makarowicz et al. (2018).

In related research, Lazzerini and colleagues (2018) reported on a preliminary study of ritually sacrificed horse heads from a khirigsuur in Burgast, western Mongolia, using oxygen isotope ratios to determine the season of death. Their findings indicate these horses were killed in November, whereas the ritual calendar probably resulted in the horse heads being deposited in their mound features in the spring. Their results need testing from a larger sample, but if the pattern holds up, it suggests horses were not slaughtered in a single large event at the consecration of the khirigsuur burial as our original model proposed, but during fall and early winter when herders today usually kill horses for food and other purposes. This would make sense as it would allow the neck vertebrae to be defleshed so they could be packaged tightly, as found in excavation, alongside the skull and mandible.

While at Urt Bulagiin, we inspected the paved area along the north side of KRY40 that Francis Allard calls the "killing area", where horses and other animals were slaughtered for ceremonies. Later in the summer we found a similar pavement at a large khirigsuur west of the two deer stones at Nukht Am on the Ider River that consisted of a rectangular paved area outside the fence along the north side of the mound. We excavated one of these pavements at Khydag East between Murun and Lake Erkhel and found the remains of butchered cattle and caprids. We excavated a similar feature at Hort Azuur, and another was found when large-scale excavations were conducted at Uushigiin Uvör (Takahama et al. 2006).

so we packed our camp into the vans. After the storm, Francis, Brian Miller, and Christine Lee gave us a tour of the Gol Mod 2 cemetery. This is a truly spectacular site in a high valley filled with sand hundreds of meters deep that was blown up against the hills by northern winds during Pleistocene storms. Blown to where it could be blown no further, it packed a small pocket valley full, creating the preferred cemetery situation for the Xiongnu.

Brian thinks this is the northern branch of an early empire that formed under Chinese influence, separate from the southern group that became the population of modern inner-Mongolia. The site is fantastic! Not only is there one huge ramped mound at the entrance of the valley, but there are several more of slightly smaller size all oriented north with square stone-walled foundations, a site

 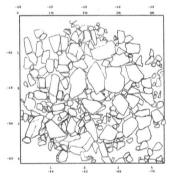 

Urt Bulagiin Khirigsuur KRY-40-1-22 in the 13th outermost rank of horse mounds before excavation. In the background are some of the 2300 satellite mound features around the south, east, and north side of this huge burial installation. North is 'up' on the surface rock map viewed toward east. The horse head faces east (top).

Gol Mod-2: A Royal Xiongnu Cemetery

It was a very silent camp at 7:00 am with the Pittsburgh group snoring soundly after the night's party, but the sky to the west was dark and rumblings of thunder gave an ominous cast to the morning. We snuck into the kitchen tent and made breakfast before anyone but Francis Allard was up. By 8:00 it was clear we were in for a good storm,

plan ultimately of Chinese derivation. Allard's and Erdenebaatar's teams have mapped the entire valley, but so far excavated only the arc of burials lying east of the large mound. These graves are probably court retainers and officials related to the person in the large mound. Another similar mound burial, Gol Mod-I, has been excavated by the French under the direction of Jean-Paul Des-Roches. Some of the Gol Mod-1 finds were exhibited in the art museum in UB last year—beautiful bronzes, silk garments, and other material. The Russians excavated similar Xiongnu mounds south of Lake Baikal. Their burial chambers are as much as 8-16 meters deep, layered above with rocks and timbers, making it dangerous to excavate without stepping the excavation back for a hundred meters to keep the loose sand walls from collapsing on the excavators, as seems to have happened to some looters who died when their pits collapsed upon them. (12 July 2005)

Gol Mod-1 Xiongnu Royal Cemetery ca. 200 BCE-200 CE, in Khanuy Valley, and map. (graphic: J. Bayarsaikhan)

Jargalant Deer Stone site KYR-119. Slab/Square burial feature excavated by Volkov and Sanjmyatav, observed on 9 June 2006, before restoration by Bayarsaikhan and Turbat; Allard and Erdenbaatar (2005) illustration of Jargalant DS 1-5 installation and associated structures.

Jargalant Am

A kilometer east of Urt Bulagiin is the huge Jargalant Am (KYR-119, N48°10.343' E101°5.606') deer stone site in Undur-Ulaan suum, Khuvsgul Aimag, only slightly smaller than Uushigiin Uvör site on the Delger Murun River west of Murun. Its original investigations were done by Volkov, who mapped the site and documented many of its 28 deer stones. Only three were standing when we visited the site in 2006, and we scanned these and photographed most of the stones on or embedded in the ground. Since then, Jargalant has been mapped, excavated, partially reconstructed, and reported by Turbot and Bayarsaikhan (2011) with support from a U.S. Ambassador's grant. Most of the site's deer stones were taken down and used as 'logs' to reinforce the excavation pits of several Slab Burial Culture graves that were constructed immediately following the DSK period. Several slab burials were excavated by Volkov and Sanjmyatav, who found sheep and bovid heads around the sides of the tombs and horse bones in the middle, and along with human bones, bronze arrowheads, pottery, and other implements.

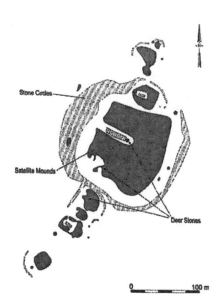

Deer Stone Project survey and research locations in northern and western Mongolia, 2001-2012.

9. Following the Volkov Trail: The Darkhad Valley

Following our initial research in Khuvsgul and the Arkhangai region dedicated to establishing a framework for our deer stone project and the major issues we wished to explore, we returned to the northern Darkhad Valley to begin a more systematic survey and excavation program. A major objective was to refine the chronology of the deer stone phenomena and hopefully identify its origin, developmental stages, and ending. We also wanted to explore the spatial and functional characteristics of deer stone sites through more expansive excavations, to inventory the artistic elements and symbolism of deer stone art, its regional variation, and hopefully to refine or clarify relationships between Volkov's three deer stone classification

types: Mongolian, Sayan-Altai, and Eurasian. We began with work in the northern Darkhad and over several years worked our way south into central Mongolia. We also began to explore the far western extension of the deer stone phenomena in the mountainous Altai region of western Mongolia, although these studies are not reported here. We began by working at sites in the Shishged River Valley north of Lake Tsaaganuur, the remnant of a great postglacial lake that was created when Pleistocene glaciers dammed the Shishged and its Yenesei River drainage.

What follows is a description of the field activities, sites, deer stones and other finds, documented during a decade of researching deer stone sites in Northern Mongolia. More information is available on the analysis of deer stone art in Bayarsaikhan's companion volume, *Deer Stones of Northern Mongolia* (2017 in Mongolian, and 2022 in English). Systematic

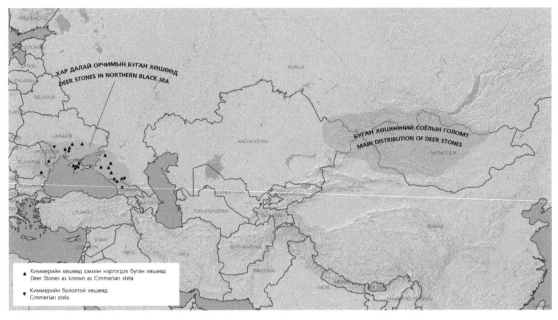

Eastern and western distribution of deer stones. (credit: JB 2022)

documentation on site lists, finds, horse heads, archaeofauna, deer stone graphics, and radiocarbon dates can be found in Bayarsaikhan's appendices. A journal article on the results of excavations at Khyadag East and Zunii Gol sites appeared in the Russian journal *Vestnik* (Fitzhugh and Bayarsaikhan 2021)

Shishged Surveys

In June 2006 we continued our earlier surveys along the north side of the Shishged River, recording a variety of sites, including petroglyphs and a looted Turkic period burial where we found an ornamented bone plaque. The Shishged flows north and west out of Lake Tsaaganuur, leaving the Mongolian steppe and entering the Russian taiga forest heading for the Yenesei drainage. Its sister river, the Selinge, flows south from Lake Khövsgöl and then turns east and north to Lake Baikal; both are major travel routes between Russia and Mongolia.

Exploring a looted Turkic grave north of the Shishged River, and an ornamented bone plaque found in the spoil pile.

The lands around these rivers have been occupied by the Dukha/Tsaatan and Buryats, both being non-Mongol reindeer herding peoples.

The Darkhad Mongols

In the Khuvsgul Lake area, the Darkhad Mongols are the dominant group. They are ethnic Mongolian pastoralists who trace their ancestry back to the time of Chinghis Khan. They are semi-migratory, and their movements range across the Darkhad Valley in summer to the margins of Khuvsgul Lake in winter. The Tsaatan (Dukha) by comparison, occupy the marginal northern mountain reaches surrounding the northern Darkhad Valley. They are Tuvan culturally and linguistically but were separated from their northern relatives when the Russians closed the Mongolian border in 1991. They interact with the Darkhad along the lower slopes of the Altai-Sayan range and along the shores of the Tengis and Shishged Rivers…

Between the Darkhad peoples and the Tsaatan/Dukha, interaction takes place on several levels, including ethnobotany and shamanism… Darkhad and Tsaatan have intermarried—the couples I spoke to said they had met at school; thus some Tsaatan live more or less permanently in Tsaagannuur, while some Darkhad live in the mountains with their Tsaatan partners and families. They maintain other ties as well. The Tsaatan pack out various plant and animal products for their family's use or for exchange or sale in Tsaaganuur and Murun. On my trip 'out', the Tsaatan packed, on their horses and reindeer, hand-sawn cutting boards, branches of juniper bundled in plastic sheeting, and reindeer milk in plastic bottles left behind by tourists. Tsaatan hunters provide skins for the Darkhad shamans' drums and hides and furs for clothing. (Marilyn Walker 2006:99)

The murunkhur (horse head fiddle), the instrumental backbone of traditional Mongolian music, which is dominated by the cadence of hoof beats, carries forward symbols of the Bronze Age Mongolian deer and Pazyryk Iron Age horse. Shaman Odkhuu Darjhat displays her drum used for many rituals still being practiced.

Ikh Davaa

We learned that one of the deer stone localities north of the Shishged is called Ikh Davaa (Broad Pass, N51° 27.387', E99° 21.799') and that the single deer stone there was moved to its present location in the middle of the pass by Batsuur, a herder who had a farm nearby and wanted to create an attraction for his small-scale tourist business. We met Batsuur one day while we were surveying. According to Batsuur, he found the deer stone lying fallen on the upper part of the south side of the pass about 200m from the forest edge. After moving and erecting it, he turned it into an ovoo by adding horse heads and a teepee of sticks festooned with silk sashes. Hoping to find charcoal or a horse head, we excavated the original location, recovering charcoal, a horse tooth, burned bone, sheep vertebrae, and several chert microblades, but no deer stone foundation pit, horse mounds, or hearth rings (Fitzhugh and Bayarsaikhan 2010:12, 92). We concluded that this was probably not the original deer stone site and never ran the dating samples. Near this location we met a local ranger named Daavaajav who told us about a group of deer stones at another place called Avtiin (N51°28.010', E99° 21.910') northeast of the Shishged ferry, where he said he once stopped local people from excavating. This location is also called Tsagaan Us, meaning 'white water pass'. Here we found a 'mother and babies' deer stone site: two miniature stones and one large deer stone with diagonal face slash marks, tools, and sun circles. We excavated three features, finding charcoal and calcined bone fragments in Feature 3 but no horse head.

On 11 June, 2007, we returned to Ikh Davaa, finding the deer stone ovoo more elaborately decorated than last year. Several dead conifers had been propped up and decorated with prayer ribbons and horse, sheep and other skulls. The transformation of a deer stone into an ovoo was garish and unpleasant to see. I wondered if this had been done to accommodate tourists coming to visit the West Taiga Tsaatan, or whether our surveys had inspired local people to honor (or possibly protect) the

Ikh Davaa deer stone, moved and made into an ovoo by Batsuur; Ranger Daavaajav and Byarsaikhan.

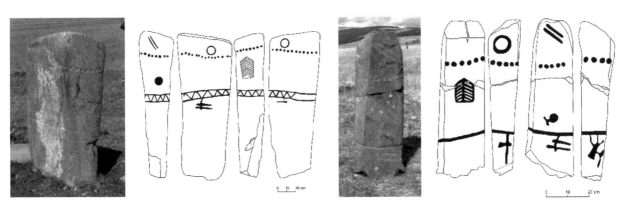

Avt Mod DS4, excavated and re-set (photo: C. Leece), and DS2, of dark granite with broken top. (photo: WF; graphics: JB)

site. Another deer stone we saw between here and the Hort Azuur deer stone site last summer had also been 'decorated'. This ovoo stone had a circle, belt, and a well-formed dagger and some other difficult-to-decipher implements due to erosive bird excrement. We noticed several clusters of rocks around the stone, confirming it is in primary position and had not been moved, as we suspected last year, so we thought we might get some horse head dating material.

part of a deer stone without any visible markings. *Deer Stone 4* has a rounded top, a row of necklace pits, two slashes (\\) on the face, and earring circles on the south and north sides. The front torso has a mirror disc, a belt with zig-zag decoration. We erected this incorrectly last year, turning the "face" side south when it should have been to the east. Looking closely at the pecking, it seemed like the delicate work must have been carved with a metal chisel,

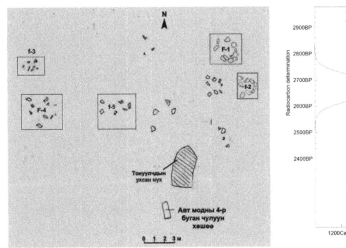 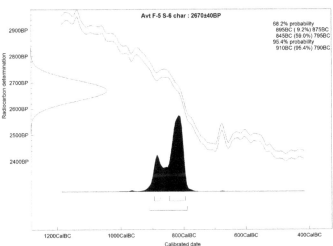

Avt Mod excavation map of DS4, and radiocarbon date from Avt Mod Feature 5 charcoal. (map: J. Bayarsaikhan)

We found the four Avt Mod deer stones (N51°28.010', E99°21.906') as we left them last summer, including the large stone (DS1) we excavated last year from a looter spoil pit and erected. *Deer Stone 1* is a very small deer stone of dark granite with many symbols, including a two face slashes, side earrings, a chevron with a vertical bar through it, a rectangular quiver, and several other implements. It is broken in half and was found in the looter pit last year. *Deer Stone 2*, of grey granite, has a flat top that slopes back to the rear (west) side, a row of pits and double slashes (\\) on the face, a single grooved belt with a suspended pick-ax and dagger, earring grooves on the north and south sides, and is broken 60cm from the top. *Deer Stone 3* is

so fine and thin were the lines. While we inspected the deer stones the rest of the team excavated Features 4 and 5, which turned out to be hearths with calcined bone fragments, although Feature 5 produced some charcoal and a bit of unburned bone. We found no sign of horse heads. The excavation showed that these deer stones had been trimmed into shape using percussion to remove spalls and chunks lying nearby.

After lunch on 12 June we returned to Avt Mod. Soon, Elaine Ling, a Canadian public health doctor famous for her world-wide travels and professional photography and who was travelling with us in 2007, arrived, happy with her visit to Khort Uzuur to see the 'tiger stone'

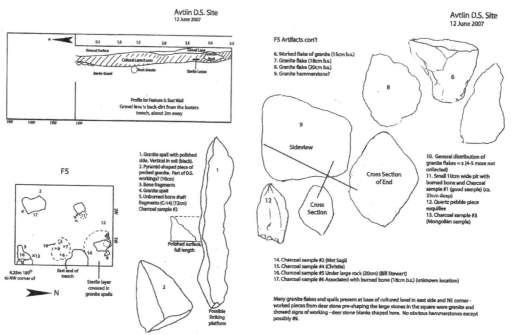

Avt Mod Deer Stone site, Feature 5. Excavations details and east wall profile; granite spalls from percussion flaking during deer stone production.

(see below). We had prepared a fake horse head 'find' for her arrival, as she had been desperate to photograph such a discovery. Since our excavations had not panned out, we placed a modern horse skull in the back dirt, saying we had dug it up while she was away. We did not convince her. "You wouldn't have NOT saved it in the ground for me," she laughed.

A Shishged Rock Art Panel

East of Avtiin on the south side of a north-south ridge at N 51°26.613'/E 99°24.299' we visited a rock art panel with a large carving of a Mongolian deer surrounded by many other animals. Bayaraa found the site when we were surveying the hill overlooking Lake Tsagaanuur. We had heard about this 'picture stone' from Ranger Daavaajav when he visited us at Avtiin, and what a stone it is!—the largest rock art

display in the Shishged region. Most of the rock art in the northern Darkhad are small single carvings pecked into the basalt blocks that outcrop along the northern bank of the river. By contrast, this was a monster, carved into a 4x1m southwest-facing block resting on the side of the hill, showing scores of animals, and in the center, the figure of the classic Mongolian deer 8-10 times larger than the other animal carvings.

On 11 June, 2007, we returned to document the panel. Only the front half of the large "Mongolian" deer, is finished; its rump and legs are not shown, perhaps because a goat was drawn there first, and the deer looks less weathered than the goats, ibex, and other animals. There is no lichen on the rock except on the lower portion, suggesting it may have been 'cleaned' in the recent past to be more visible to tourists, and some of the images have red paint traces, also perhaps recent additions. But red paint has been noted in many Mongolian rock carvings, and even on deer stones (Esin et al. 2017). The missing hind quarters makes the big deer look more bird-like than in other renderings, due to its rounded bird head and large round eye. None of the other animals cross or crowd the deer, making it the primary element of the composition, giving the impression of a "master spirit" presiding over its subjects. Bayaraa and Sasha drew the composition on a large sheet of plastic and excavated to see if artifacts or charcoal could be found at its base, but the ground was rocky and nothing was found.

This dominating deer recalled a similar image of huge Mongolian deer surrounded by smaller animals recorded by photographer Gary Tepfer and Esther Jacobson from the Altai region of Western Mongolia (Jacobsen 2001). In these scenes we have a strong indication of the role of the "mother deer goddess", the master spirit presiding over other animals as argued by Jacobson (1993). It does not stretch the imagination much to believe this spirit also protected humans as tattooed images in life, and after, in death—as representations on deer stones.

Shishged-Khogorgo Rock Art

Crossing back toward the southwest and the north bank of the Shishged, we located quite a few khirigsuurs and had a real surprise: Sasha found rock art pecked into the smooth face of a basalt/lava block. One carving at N51°24.841', E99°17.015' illustrated 3-4 animals, while a second at E51°24.836', E99°17.078' has a geometric grid with a human figure in the middle. There were also rocks with modern graffiti. This country is quite interesting, with level ground broken up by low ridges of east-west oriented lava and basalt outcrops whose smooth, lichen-free exposures tempted ancient artists. When we rejoined the group, we found Dennis and Betsy had also discovered rock art on the lava outcrops on the south side of the hill west of the Khogorgo River, facing the Shishged. Bayaraa, Od, and Sasha made a tracing of the images, which included deer, ibex, and mountain sheep. Sasha said it was all Bronze Age material. There was some modern graffiti present indicating local knowledge of the art, and the ferry operator said there are more images for the next 20 km east along the river. This is all new material not previously reported. (1 July, 2005)

Fitzhugh points out the 'master spirit' Mongolian deer image on the East Ridge rock art site. The carvings have the appearance of recent tracing. (photos: C. Leece, WF)

Petroglyph at the Avtiin Hill East site on the north side of the Shishged River show many animals including standing elk/marals with upright, 'realistic' antlers.

Kholboo Tolgoi-1

This site, translated as "Paired Hill" (N51° 24.908', E99°26.630'), has some fine rock art on ledge outcrops above a set of khirigsuurs in a valley south of the small bridge west of the Shishged bend, and southeast of a 'sand dune' valley. At Kholboo Tolgoi one of the rock art panels has three Mongolian deer stacked one on top of the other with extended legs and detailed hind quarters and withers. There are also simple carvings of Iron Age animals. Along the base of the hill below we found 10-12 khirigsuurs of various forms and sizes. The Iron Age art looks much younger, showing white pecking marks compared to the much darker, and usually more elaborate, Bronze Age carvings. We interpreted these carvings with the assistance of Dr. Richard Kortum, who was with our field team at the time.

Kholboo Tolgoi 1. Mongolian deer are carved into these rocks above Kholboo Tolgoi khirigsuur sites.

Kholboo Tolgoi-2

A second site (N51º 25.291', E99º 26.086') nearby has beautiful Mongolian deer carvings with a superimposed horse and rider, ibex, and other figures. The figures are on a clean slab of basalt some of which had been lost to spalling and breakage around the edges. The figures are only a few feet above the steppe grass. A deer and horse and rider and a couple other figures are on the largest, lowest panel, and two or three others are on the panel above it, and several more on a third above that. There are both khirigsuurs and circular pavement burials along the southwest side of the hill, making this a fourth location where we have found petroglyphs of Mongolian deer associated with khirigsuurs. These deer were in a very unusual arrangement, facing in different directions and only partially complete, emphasizing the head mostly, with the rest of the bodies not shown,

any overlapping lines, i.e. a concept of super-position rarely seen in deer stone art. This new recognition of an association between Mongolian deer and khirigsuurs was a novel concept we had not considered previously, and we have Richard Kortum to thank for pointing it out. Perhaps the deer image being applied to rocks in the vicinity of khirigsuurs served a similar function as their presence on deer stones, and presumably as tattoos on the bodies of those the deer stones represented—to ensure protection in life and the spirit's safe passage in death to the upper world. So far, the deer image-khirig-suur association has been observed only in the northern Darkhad Valley. One might ask, could it also be present in rock art in other regions where khirigsuurs are found?

While passing through Tsagaanuur we visited the Tsaatan Culture Center housed in an attractive new building that Morgan Keay made possible through the efforts of the Itgel Foundation. The Center has a nice exhibit area and

Tracing Mongolian deer images associated with the Kholboo Tolgoi khirigsuur site in sugar on the rock and with a marker pen on a plastic sheet.

or shown only impressionably. We have never seen a composition like this before, with multiple figures in overlapping position, but without

meeting room. The exhibits are several panels in English and Mongolian on various subjects, with attractive photographs. A couple of cases

Shaman Odkhuu Darjhat displaying her drum and robe to Marilyn Walker during a visit to Renchinlhumbe.

held Tsaatan handicrafts and carvings that were for sale. A panel by the front door introduces visitors to Tsaatan customs and proper behavior when visiting their field camps, providing rules about photography, waste disposal, food, and gifts (no alcohol!). All arrangements for visits are made through the center and not with individual Tsaatan. A Tsaatan herder was tending the center while its manager was away. He recognized me as one of the 'Ed Nef' crew and was one of those who received a horse from Ed during our 2001 visit. It sounds like that effort made a huge difference in his life. I asked about the "1000 reindeer festival" to be held later this summer, but he said it was not yet scheduled. The Tsaatan went from about 975 reindeer to over 1000 this spring—a milestone given the nadir of their numbers in the 1990s; the number is an official Mongolian government target inherited from the Soviet period.

Wayne Paulsen, who had been conducting anthropological studies for several years in Renchinlkhumbe, introduced us to one of the local shamans. During our meeting, shaman Odkhuu Darjhat showed us her paraphernalia and sang several songs and incantations. During the Soviet era shamanism had to be practiced secretly, but since Mongolian independence, it has resurfaced and is an important part of

Darkhad Mongol culture, as we had also found during our visits to the West and North Taiga Dukha reindeer herders. During our meeting we learned about rituals that were customarily held on Ongon Tolgoi (Shaman Hill) located west of town (N51°22.548°/ E099°34.988°). We visited the location and found the ground full of old stone features, khirigsuurs, and modern wooden platforms and other structures indicating active use.

Power of Smoke: Fragrance, Medicine, and Ritual

Plants can be used to restore a severed or compromised relationship or to maintain a mutual and reciprocal one, a relationship that my exist on the mundane and the metaphysical levels simultaneously. This relationship is most apparent in the use of plants for burning or 'smudging.' The smoke of certain plants is said to be one of the elements of a shaman's toolkit that can permeate the thin membrane between this world and the spirit world. Through such offerings, and the right intent on the part of the petitioner, spirits may be entreated to assist with worldly problems…

The smoke is used for ritual cleansing, to please the good spirits and draw them near, and to dispel bad spirits or negative influences. In shaman-

ic ritual, it cleanses the space, the shaman, the other participants in the ritual, and the shaman's paraphernalia. Very often the shaman's drum is held directly over the smoke to purify and cleanse it before it is played… The preferred plant for burning in the Khuvsgul Lake area is juniper which is scarce in the Darkhad Valley, so Darkhad people ask Tsaatan to bring it down to them from the taiga where it is plentiful. (Walker 2006:102)

Zeerdegchingiin Khushuu

This site, translated as 'mountain corner stone', north of Tsaaganuur, is a large double khirigsuur complex (both looted) with round fences, an oval stone enclosure with two internal features, and two rock mounds without fences. The site was mapped by Laura Short and Francis Allard, who were with us at the time, and designated DK1-2. Ranger Daavaajav said his mother told him the mounds had been looted by Buddhist monks in 1912. Christie and I excavated a ring feature at the western khirigsuur mound (N51°25.227', E99°21.839'), and Bayaraa excavated a horse mound southeast of the mound that contained a horse head oriented 111° and accompanied by six cervical, one thorasic, one atlas vertebra, and 2 hooves.

Targan Nuur

Several years after our 2009 season, Bayarsaikhan learned of a new deer stone site at Targan Nuur in the Shishged River region north of Tsaaganuur, not far from Khort Uzuur. This site has three deer stones. DS1 and 3 are normal 'simple' stones that would be classified as Eurasian types, with back-sloping tops, headbands, pendant earrings on its broad sides, two slashes \\ for a face on the east side, and sketchy weapons and tools (rein hook, axes, knives) on their

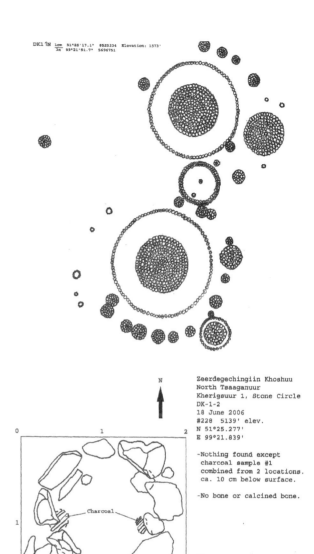

A map of the Zeerdegchingiin Khushuu khirigsuurs 1 and 2, and excavation of a hearth circle at K2. (graphics: Short and Allard; Leece and Fitzhugh)

belts, and no animal figures. DS2 had the same normal markings: a beaded necklace made of shallow pits, back-sloping top, and a belt groove with an ax, dagger, knife, a whetstone, quiver, and bow. However, the necklace was unusual in having a larger pit in the center of the east and west sides. Most unusual was a series of four

Mongolian deer stacked horizontally directly on top of each other, wrapping around the four sides, but in a form we have never seen elsewhere. Each deer carries the distinctive peaked withers above the shoulders, the rounded haunches, and the head of a bird with an open beak. But the heads and beaks are tiny rather than elongated; the sweeping antlers consist of a single straight line running above the back without curled tines; and there is a nucleated

Sortiin Denj

One other deer stone site stands out as anomalous in the normal run of deer stones. Sortiin Denj, located in Burentogtokh near the Delger Murun River, has two deer stones that do not fall into the normal classifications. DS1 has pendant earrings and necklace pits on its south, east, and north sides, and a single large necklace pit on its west side. Its east side has

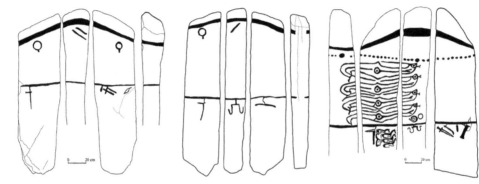

Targan Nuur Deer Stones 1, 2, 3. (graphics: JB)

circle in the chest area beneath the withers. The strange deer images suggest either a prototype, a degenerate, or a crudely executed form, while all other aspects of the composition are normal DSK emblems seen on Eurasian type deer stones. Another feature suggests this stone may date late in the DSK era: the broad headband and a group of five tiny horses below the belt on the south side of the stone. Horses are usually found only on 'late' deer stones. The stylistics suggest a similar date for the three stones. Our radiocarbon sample from a horse tooth in Feature 1 did not produce an acceptable date, so the age of the Targon Nuur deer stone remains a mystery.

two back slashes \\, a curled feline, above two vertical fish, a spoked wheel, and a belt with a knife and whetstone. Its south side has a coiled spiral above three vertical left-ascending horses. Its north side has a dagger, an ax, and a mirror floating above a belt with a bow and quiver. The west side is clear (or unreadable) except for an eight-chevron shield. DS2 follows the normal deer stone structure with pitted necklace (with one larger pit—a large bead?—and a broad belt band. However, the side with two \\ slashes that should be the east (face) side has an 8-bar chevron which would normally be on the west side. The south side has a coiled feline below the necklace and above two small vertical deer facing each other, being chased by two predators. Belt tools include an axe, sword, and dagger.

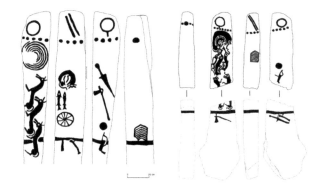

Sortiin Denj DS1 and 2. (graphics: JB)

Like Targon Nuur, the Sortiin Denj deer stones suggest later chronology or western influences from Scythian/Saka Iron Age culture. Coiled felines, chariot wheels, and spirals are common Scythian-Saka motifs, and horses and 'floating' tools do not appear in early DSK deer stones. It seems likely that the Sortiin Denj deer stones represent a blend of late DSK and early

Khort Azuur

Today (18 June 2006) we visited Khort Azuur ("Poison Corner") in the Tavh Hills north of Renchinlkhumbe (N 51°25.850', E 99°35.550'). We learned about the site from Tsog, our driver, who discovered it while escorting Japanese tourists. Its only standing stone has a design on the top but no other marks. During this visit we only had time to pace out a sketch map, identifying four groups of deer stones in the usual north-south alignment and noticed that one of the fallen stones (DS3) had a spotted feline and two deer on one of its sides. The entire series of stones points toward Rinchinlkhumbe's Ongon Tolgoi, due south, bearing187°M.

In 2007 we returned to map and excavate other features at Khort Azuur. DS1 was made of fine-grained, black-speckled white granite, and rises 120 cm above ground. At the top of the

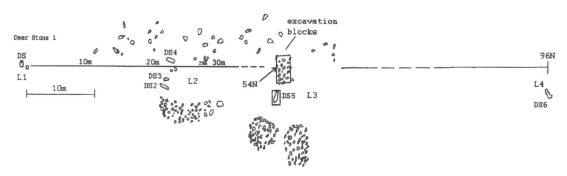

Map of Loci 1-4 at Khort Azuur showing locations of deer stones and cobble pavements east of L3. North is to the right. (graphic: Tsomoo and Adiya Namkhai)

Iron Age forms infiltrating the late DSK culture area, producing a blend of Sayan Altai and Eurasian deer stone elements, but still clearly within the DSK context, except for the misplaced shield ornament. Neither of these stelae have radiocarbon dates, so future researchers should investigate the site for possible horse sacrifices or other dating materials.

south side is a two-pendant circle groove; no belt is obvious, and there are a few obscure marks near the base. Nothing could be seen on the other sides. DS2, lying exposed on the ground, had an angled top, and is 122 cm long. It has a grooved earring at the top of the exposed broad side, face slashes \\ on the thin side; a necklace of pits ringing the top of the stone, and a sword with a hilt hung from a belt mid-way down the stone. DS3 is the 'tiger' stone, 159 cm long with a thin top and a broad base. The tiger/feline and deer are present on the broad side. This stone is unusual for its tiger image, for its larger deer having outstretched legs and its placement crossing the belt groove. DS4 has a belt all around and a grooved earring on one side. DS5 was broken in half (see field notes below). DS6 is 126cm long, has an exposed upper side and is badly eroded because it is made of large crystal granite. There is a belt and a possible ring at the top which we found on the side turned down into the earth, where it had better preservation.

Sanjmyatav tracing the spotted feline on fallen DS3 at Khort Azuur; a crew lunch break!

We inspected other flat slabs that might be deer stones, but all were un-worked. By 8pm we finished excavating what turned out to be four circular features adjacent to each other along

the east side of DS2, 3, and 4. Before excavation, the features appeared to be a continuous 8x3 m cobble pavement aligned north and south, but after clearing the turf we recognized four separate rings and had high hopes for horse heads, given their eastern position and boulder settings. Instead, we were rewarded with chert and chalcedony flakes, a biface base, and a few microblades from the northern and southern features F4, F3, and F1. There was also a dense concentration of chalcedony and brown/black chert flakes in the western wall of F2, but few diagnostic tools.

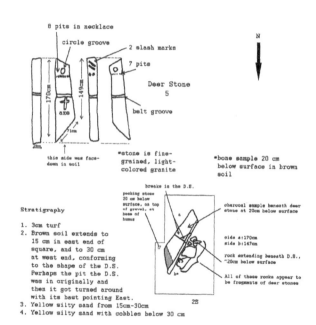

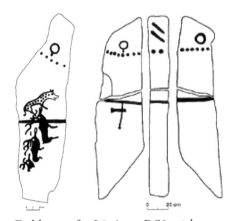

Field notes for L3 Area, DS3 with spotted feline, and DS5 graphic. (J.Bayarsaikhan)

This was disconcerting because we had never found so much flaked stone in a Late Bronze Age site. It turned out the flakes were coming from the lower brown loess soil and the upper tan sand and gravel. Some charcoal was present in the upper brown soil, and at first we discounted its association with the stone mounds, thinking it might be intrusive from squirrel holes; but the later were few. Some flakes and tools were found inside the rings, but most were outside, suggesting they are part of a Neolithic occupation pre-dating the circular pavements. Charcoal recovered from the brown/tan interface may substantiate this, but we never submitted the samples because the association with deer stone features was uncertain. Otherwise, excavation of the pavements was singularly unproductive, and we found nothing except in one case, outside F5, a small amount of burned bone—but no horse head burials or any sign of subsurface digging or pits. So, once again, the Darkhad deer stone contexts are different from those south of Oliin Davaa, and we need some believable dates to see why. The Khort Azuur circular features are not horse head graves or circular hearth rings known from more southern sites because they are fully paved and contained no horse or animal remains or calcined bone. Most likely they were sacrificial platforms related to those we identified at several other sites constructed on top of a Neolithic habitation site.

Zuun Shuregtei

While traveling south from the northern Darkhad in 2006 we visited a looted deer stone site at Zuun Shuuregbei (N50°58.617', E99°22.441') in Ulaan-Uul sum, Khuvsgul Aimag, finding a single deer stone in the bottom of a looter's pit mixed with recent charcoal and garbage from a campfire. The stone is ornate by Darkhad standards. One side has four deer, a ring circle with a triangular pendant, and a necklace of pits. Another side had an earring circle without pendants, next to a smaller circle/moon. The surrounding stone features did not look promising as horse head features. This deer stone looks more like the fancy southern deer stones than the simpler Darkhad stones.

On 25 June we accompanied Francis Allard and Adiya while they were conducting interviews about horses with herder families in the hills north of the ravine northwest of Ulaan Tolgoi. We were amazed to find Arctic pingoes in the ravine. Pingos are a type of Arctic geological formation that occur when ground water encounters permafrost and freezes, over time, thrusting the earth up into a cone-shaped mound. In summer, the ice near the surface thaws (see p. xx) and the mound subsides, making it appear as though the earth is going through a seasonal breathing cycle. In this ravine permafrost exists as deep as 15 meters, so

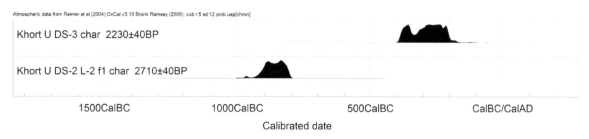

Atmospheric data from Reimer et al (2004);OxCal v3.10 Bronk Ramsey (2005); cub r:5 sd:12 prob usp[chron]

Khort U DS-3 char 2230±40BP

Khort U DS-2 L-2 f1 char 2710±40BP

1500CalBC   1000CalBC   500CalBC   CalBC/CalAD

Calibrated date

Radiocarbon dates from Khort Azuur.

wells can't be used in winter and animals get water by eating snow. According to the families we spoke to, when their horses die or are killed, they take their heads to the top of the hills east of their camp and place them where they receive the rays of the rising sun. We frequently found recent horse skulls in such locations. One of the herders received prizes in the Soviet period for animal productivity and recently had won a raffle for a new jeep! "Will your grandchildren grow up to be herders," I asked. "I have no idea," he said. "Perhaps if they get good marks in school they'll become professionals."

visited us at Khushuutiin Devseg. The location is unusual in being on a high ridge rather than in a flat valley, and the view also is restricted; one can see only a small section of the valley, so few could see it from below, and from the hills above it would not stand out either. Tomst is named for a plant that has an onion-shaped bulb used to make flour.

The three Tomst deer stones are all made of coarse pink granite that have fared poorly from erosion, making its markings almost impossible to decipher, but in any case, they appear to have been minimally carved. Only one stone was

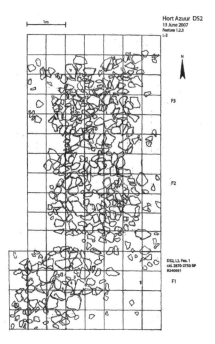

Khort Azuur L2 boulder Features 1, 2, and 3 east of Locus 3's DS2, 3, 4, looking north.

Tomst

Tomst is located on a ridge on the east side of the valley east of the Murun-Hotgol road at N49°53.482', E100°03.862' in Alag-Erdene suum, Khuvsgul Aimag. When we visited the site, the valley below had 10-12 families in residence, so it must be good pasture at this time of year. We learned of the site from a herder who

standing; its broad sides faces north and south and are split by fissures. This stone has a slightly angled top and a belt groove about one-third the way up from the bottom with an axe hanging from it. No circles or necklace are present. The east (narrow) side has three back slashes \\\. Two other granite stones were lying on the surface and appear to have been removed from depressions 2 m west of the standing stone, and another 8 m south of the standing stone. Both have narrow belt and necklace grooves, and the larger stone (DS2, 150 x 36w x 20t cm) has three slashes \\\ on it narrow original east side. It is roughly prepared but has a rectangular cross-section. The smaller fallen stone (DS3) has a dagger or knife on its belt. Dimensions are 112 x 30w x 25t cm. The lack of horse mounds standing stones in both sites are made of coarse granite that had lost details from weathering. Unlike most other sites, Khyadag East and West sites were not accompanied by khirigsuurs, and Khyadag East had few hearth circles. Khyadag East has been documented in several ASC Mongolian field reports and in Fitzhugh and Bayarsaikhan (2021).

  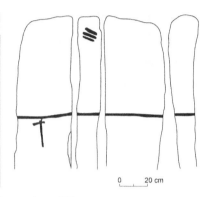

Tomst deer stone site excavation; DS1 and its marks. (photos: HRB, JB; graphics: JB)

and ornamentation suggests Tomst people were too poor to sacrifice horses or decorate deer stones for their honored leaders.

Khyadag East

Khyadag is located in a grassy plain midway between Murun and Lake Erkhel and has two deer stone sites a few hundred meters apart. Khyadag West (N49°48,876', E99°53,946') has four deer stones, three of which were standing in 2006. Khyadag East (N49°48.900', E99°54.042') has nineteen, only two of which were standing in 2007, and one of these (DS2) is broken in half with its top on the ground nearby. The large DS3 is badly weathered. Its most distinctive marking are two circled felines on its south side. This motif is a Pazyryk Early Bronze Age design and may have been carved a hundred years after the stone was erected. The

Khyadag East has two standing deer stones, one about one meter tall and the second, an imposing 1.98 meters. They stand in the middle of a complex of cobblestone features that includes a rectangular cobble pavement east of the deer stones. Two unusual features stood out as we made our initial inspection—the absence of the usual horse head sacrificial features and small circular hearths found at most deer stone sites. Soon after our arrival, Sanjmyatav noticed several small vertical slabs broken off just above the surface of the ground in a rough north-south alignment north of the tall DS3. Some of these broken slabs had horizontal grooves similar to belt grooves on deer stones. When we excavated this area, we found the upper portions of these slabs had circle grooves and necklace pits and realized we had discovered a new class of miniature deer stones, 30 to 60 cm in height, having characteristic deer stone markings (belt, necklace, and earrings) but not the images of deer and weapons seen on large stones. We

Khyadag East deer stone site southwest of Erkhel Lake, view NE.

identified these small stones as Deer Stones 2, 5, 6, 7, 8, 9, and 10. Our excavations provided no clue as to the meaning or function of these miniature monuments. One of the interesting problems at Khyadag East, in addition to the function of the tiny deer stones, is why so many of the small and larger stones were broken off just above the surface. Unlike larger deer stones that suffer damage from lightning and animal

rubbing, did this result from ancient vandalism or purposeful destruction? All the top fragments were found in the Bronze Age cultural layer 10-15cm below the surface, so this was not due to recent activity. It must be significant that the minimal marks on these stones correspond to Volkov's Eurasian Deer Stone type, except that the Khyadag stones are smaller and less finished and are made on slabs only a few cms thick.

Khyadag East Area 2 excavation showing small deer stone broken bases, view west.
Khyadag East A2 with mini-DSs with belts, broken from their bases.

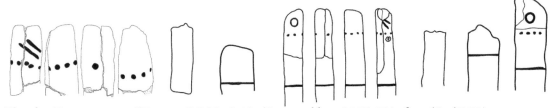

Khyadag East miniature "Eurasian" DS2, 5-10. (Bayarsaikhan 2017:281, figs. 45, 47-52)

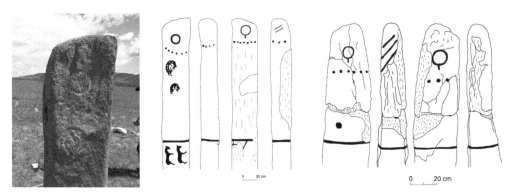

Khyadag East. (a, b) DS3, (c) DS1. (graphics: JB)

The larger stones follow the same style as the miniature ones, having earrings, pitted necklaces, and belt grooves but rarely tools or animals. DS1 (JB 2017:pl.43) is 105 cm high and is badly broken and spalled. Its east side has three forward slashes /// on the face and a belt groove around all four sides. The north side has a circle with a pendant at the top and three necklace pits. The south side has a similar pendant earring, six necklace pits, and a belt groove. The west side is illegible due to spalling. The site's huge standing DS3 (JB fig. 44), is 198 cm tall and has the same markings with the addition of an unidentifiable implement on the north side belt. Other marks may have been present but have been lost to spalling. However, its south side has two east-facing upright horses below the belt and two coiled felines below a necklace of pits. DS4 (JB 2017:pl.46), one of the fallen and excavated stones, is similar to DS1, 105 cm high with circle earrings, necklace pits, and a belt groove. Deer stones 16-19 have similar markings. Deer Stones 2, 5-10, and 16-19 (JB figs. 45, 47-56), when not eroded, have earrings, necklace pits, and belt grooves and no other distinguishable marks, except DS6 which has backward \\ face slashes, and DS16 which has two forward slashes // and an axe on its belt. The larger deer stones, DS1, 3, 4, 16, 17 (JB figs.43, 44, 46, 53-54), ca. 1.0-1.5m tall, were found below the surface when we excavated north of the standing stones. These stones have the same rudimentary markings seen on other deer stones at the site.

Deer Stone Area Excavations

Because no horse mounds were obvious, we began excavating a 6x3m boulder pavement designated as Area 1 east of DS3. This pavement resembled boulder pavements that Volkov found at several of his large deer stone sites, including Uushigiin Uvör. Subsoil was close to the surface, and we found sheep/goat leg bone fragments on the cobblestone surface.

Khyadag East site excavations showing miniature deer stones north of the large ones. Excavated cobble pavement is on the right (east) side of the photo. View N.

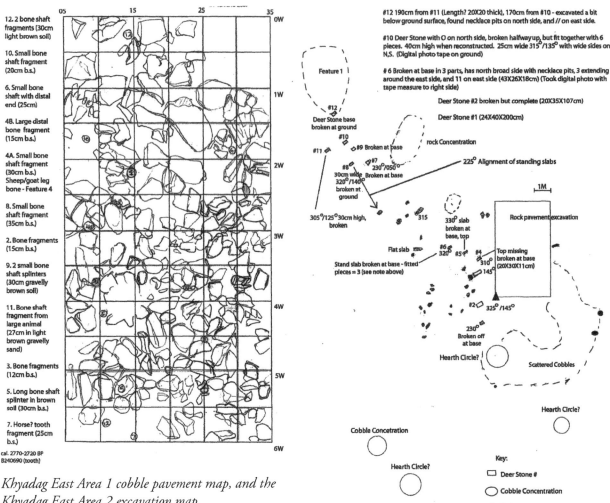

Area 1 labels (left side)

12. 2 bone shaft fragments (30cm light brown soil)

10. Small bone shaft fragment (20cm b.s.)

6. Small bone shaft with distal end (25cm)

4B. Large distal bone fragment (15cm b.s.)

4A. Small bone shaft fragment (30cm b.s.) Sheep/goat leg bone - Feature 4

8. Small bone shaft fragment (35cm b.s.)

2. Bone fragments (15cm b.s.)

9. 2 small bone shaft splinters (30cm gravelly brown soil)

11. Bone shaft fragment from large animal (27cm in light brown gravelly sand)

3. Bone fragments (12cm b.s.)

5. Long bone shaft splinter in brown soil (30cm b.s.)

7. Horse? tooth fragment (25cm b.s.)

cal. 2770-2720 BP
B240690 (tooth)

Area 2 labels (right side)

#12 190cm from #11 (Length? 20X20 thick), 170cm from #10 - excavated a bit below ground surface, found necklace pits on north side, and // on east side.

#10 Deer Stone with O on north side, broken halfway up, but fit together with 6 pieces. 40cm high when reconstructed. 25cm wide 315°/135° with wide sides on N,S. (Digital photo tape on ground)

6 Broken at base in 3 parts, has north broad side with necklace pits, 3 extending around the east side, and 11 on east side (43X26X18cm) (Took digital photo with tape measure to right side)

Deer Stone #2 broken but complete (20X35X107cm)

Deer Stone #1 (24X40X200cm)

Feature 1

#12
Deer Stone base broken at ground

#11   #10

#9 Broken at base

#8
30cm wide
320°/140°
broken at ground

#7
230°/050°
Broken at base

rock Concentration

225° Alignment of standing slabs

305°/125° 30cm high, broken

315

330° slab broken at base, top

1M

Rock pavement excavation

Flat slab

Stand slab broken at base - fitted pieces = 3 (see note above)

#6
320°   #5

#4
310°
145

Top missing broken at base (20X30X11cm)

#2   325°/145°

230°
Broken off at base

Hearth Circle?

Scattered Cobbles

Hearth Circle?

Cobble Concetration

Hearth Circle?

Key:
☐ Deer Stone #
◯ Cobble Concentration
● Rock

Khyadag East Area 1 cobble pavement map, and the Khyadag East Area 2 excavation map.

When we returned to Khyadag East in 2008 we opened a large trench (Area 2) northeast of DS1 to see what we could learn about the small deer stones we found last year rather than just search for horse head dating material. We laid out a 30x8 m area and started clearing a 5x8 m block around the small slabs. As soon as the sod came off, we found two medium size fallen deer stones of granite, so eroded we were not certain we could extract them and decipher the carvings. Some nice boulder features also appeared. Feature 1 was cluster of large rocks in a roughly circular arrangement with several of the largest in the outer ring. Beneath one we found four poorly preserved young horse teeth, probably the remains of a single mandible, 30 cm below the surface. An ashy deposit was at this level at the base of the tan gravelly soil and the white carbonate deposits, but no charcoal, bone, or other signs of cultural material. Feature 2 was a roughly lenticular-shaped boulder feature made of fist- to head-size rocks with nothing beneath them. Feature 3 had a weathered deer stone lying head to the south with its broken end 50 cm SW of its above-ground broken base, still in place. This stone (JAB 2017:pl.53) has an inclined top, necklace pits, circle earrings, a belt groove with one axe and two // slashes on the face. Feature 4 (JAB 2017:pl.46) is another deer stone with an eroded surface lying beneath the turf, showing circle earrings, a belt groove, and necklace pits.

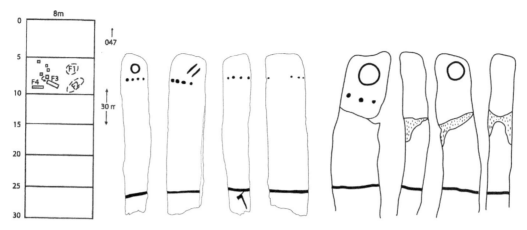

Khyadag East Area A excavation grid with broken small deer stone stubs, full-size deer stones and boulder Features 1 and 2; DS16; and DS4. (graphics: JB)

The afternoon was uneventful, except that we found another deer stone (DS5, JAB 2017:pl.48) in the excavation block east of the previous one, a fairly large and well-preserved stone with belt groove, shield/chevron motif with a concave disc, two slashes, pits, and circles. The stone fits on its base still fixed in the ground but is still missing the top above the necklace. Another interesting find was Sasha's discovery of a small deposit of burned bones lying a few centimeters from one of the small broken deer stone bases 18 cm below the surface, perhaps the remains of a ritual offering.

Khyadag East in mid-excavation showing exhumed and re-erected large and miniature DSs, View NE.

Visitors Arrive

During dinner a fierce storm nearly blew the cook tent down and filled our bowls and cups with dust, grass, and animal dung. We had to raise the lower tent walls to let the wind through to keep the tent from blowing down. That night we put the sheep we had bought for 70,000 tugriks each (ca. $8) in Khataa's van to protect them from the dogs that were lurking around the camp margin.

About 11 A.M. a van came roaring up to the site, but it was not Khataa. It was Bruno and Tugsoo, who arrived from UB yesterday and are in the middle of setting up their camp in the same riverside location next to the Delger Murun river. They came up via Erdenet and had a good trip. They have a smaller team this year and will be working on mounds south of us and across the river near the suum center. Bruno had never seen anything like the plate slag/metal we've been finding and suspects it's a by-product of metal production- but what metal? It makes a nice scratch in brass but did not mark his hard steel knife. He and Tugsoo and their driver stayed for a khuushuur lunch and potato salad and then went off to select some khirigsuurs to dig. Some just southeast of our camp have become endangered by a phosphate mining operation. The Institute of

Archaeology may be contracted for big $, in which case the sites may be off-limits for research to others. Lots of mining deals are being made with the Institute these days, with probable special deals that never quite get made public.

The breeze was from the north again, and we weathered a short cloudburst of icy rain just before supper, one of the few rainstorms when the rain actually reached the ground, so dry is the air. Dinner was the remains of the sheep. It simply does not seem possible for Mongolians to live without meat for lunch and dinner, even though it is only cut into tiny pieces and used as garnish for pasta, soups, and stew. Bruno is talking about getting a refrigerator into his camp to keep his meat fresh more than two days – maybe his conditions are different by the river than here, but ours lasts 5-6 days in the open.

The storm was gone by morning, and after some overall photos of the second excavation block, we began working on the new deer stone area, finding black earth mixed with charcoal overlying a rocky layer where we started finding broken metal-like objects that seemed more rock than metal and would not attract a compass needle or scratch steel. Then some pottery started showing up, and a piece of rib bone—all around the base of the deer stones. This is the first time we have seen slag-like materials at deer stone sites, although pottery was found at Erkhel DS4 and Khushugiin Devseg. This time there seems to be pyrotechnic operations going on, and this was finally confirmed by a piece of slag. We also began finding pieces of shiny flat metal-like fragments that may be some kind of cast metal. After lunch we exposed the slag/

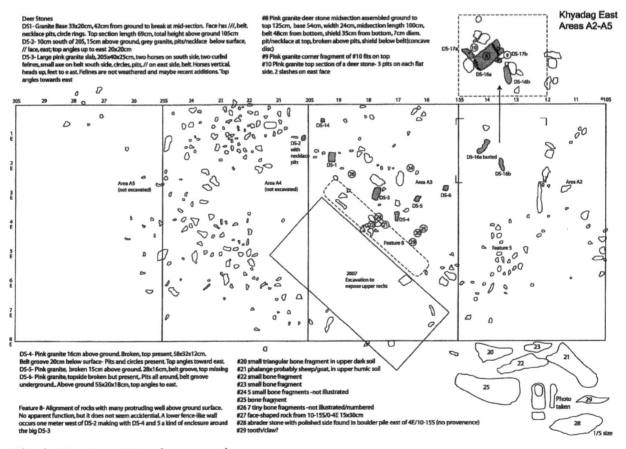

Khyadag East Areas 5-7 surface map and notes.

Khyadag East Area 2 excavations. Prying up one of the buried deer stones; excavation showing stubs of miniature deer stones in northwest Area 2 and the excavated DS erected on its in situ *base. View to north.*

Amaraa and Khataa cooking dinner; our cordless 'refrigerator'; and the team enjoying our last Khyadag supper.

charcoal cultural level that turned out to be about 2cm thick with slag at the bottom of the brown/gravely soil and on top of a very fine humic silt/loess soil, and then, deeper, sterile gravelly sand. Slag was quite widespread throughout the deer stone area. Sasha found a large plate of material with a constant 3-4mm thickness and a curve like the wall of a vessel exhibiting melted areas. At first I thought it was part of a broken (sacrificed?) metal vessel related to deer stone ritual, but it was too hard to be scratched by a knife. Breaking some of these pieces revealed a granular texture with some glassy areas, so even though they seemed like metal plate, they must be copper slag. This was later confirmed by Smithsonian laboratory studies (see Appendix 2;

Watson, Goodman, and Speakman 2009). Also present with these plate-like pieces were charcoal and true slag, as well as pieces of pottery and clay with slag deposits on one side and orange-fired matrix on the other, perhaps being clay furnace lining material. These deposits ran throughout the area, but test pits showed it did not extend beyond the big stone pile to the east, or further north. Its relation to the buried deer stone is uncertain. Two visiting herders who looked at the plates, tapped them and responded, "tumor?" (iron?). Subsequent dating of charcoal from the slag horizon produced dates of ca. 22-2400 BCE, suggesting a post-deer stone metallurgical event.

DS 7a/b - 157cm (above ground) x 27 x 23. Pink granite. Broken at ground level above belt. Badly preserved. Belt groove only present. Top angles forward East
DS 8 - 10 cm (above ground) x 29 x 12. Top missing. Eroded. Only belt groove present
DS 9 - 19 cm (above ground) x 23 x 15. Pink granite. Eroded. Top missing. Belt groove present, one belt appendage (rectangular shape) on North side.
DS10 - 40 cm (above ground) x 26 x 14. Pink granite. Top broken above pits, but present. South's side top spalled off but present. Circle, belt and bow (on North side). // on East
DS 11 - small possible DS base broken below ground surface. No marks. 18 x 18 cm
DS 12 - 35 cm (above ground) x 25 x 20. Pink granite. Top missing. Belt groove at ground level. North side badly spalled.
DS 13 - 13 cm (above ground) x 24 x 10. No marks. Eroded. Not excavated. Pink granite
DS 14 - (in A3) Underground - rounded top appears intact. 18 x 13 (Lw). Pink granite. Possible DS

① Bone pieces F2 - 20cm
② Charcoal piece - 25cm F2
③ Black flint utilized flake
④ 4 young horse (?) teeth - 30 cm F1
⑤ Deer Stone F3
⑥ Deer Stone F4
⑦ Small calcined bone fragments - 18 cm
   5 cm SW of DS in grey sandy soil

Box-like setting of small Deer Stones in A-2? What purpose/pattern for this arrangement?
Deer Stones 9, 10, 7a align N-S: DS 12 rightangle
with DS-10; DS-11 N/S with DS12-
This area inside box Sasha excavated to 25-30 cm below surface
The rest of Area 1 was excavated only to -10, except for F1, and F2

ⓧ small pieces of broken bone 15cm deep

11. rib bone, -25cm, between rocks, with charcoal
12. ceramic fragment, charred, -25
13. ceramic fragment, charred, -25
14. ceramic fragment, charred, -25
15. slag from -25cm with inclusions
16. bone piece, -25cm in dark sandy/gravelly soil
17. ceramic fragments - ? or smelter liner clay (fired)
    with orange interior and black slag-like exterior
18. slag "plate" resembling vesse, -19cm in black soil
19. Thick slag/fired clay pieces, below rocks
19A. sheep bone from base of rockpile. Feature 5, -28cm
    below surface

Feature 7 is at Northern end of the F2 rockpile.
North of F5. Surface rocks did not identify
the buried circular arrangement of inclined
slabs, slanting into a 50x50cm space on
sterile sandy gravel. Nothing was found in
this feature, which may have held perishable
deposits. Similar inclined slabs were found
in F5

Excellent charcoal samples collected from beneath rocks with slag

Slag/charcoal layer present throughout 10-15S/0-4E. However, it was most
concentrated in areas where rocks were present.   Generally, this level is only 2-3
cm thick, or less

Excavated block 10-15S/1-4E is sterile soil that was generally 20-30cm below
surface, and was deepest between 2-3F/15S. 20 symbols record depth to sterile

Fired clay with open side having a slaggy surface and the other side fired to an
orange color were present in several areas, but mostly were isolated finds. 19
was largest piece. These may be clay furnace linings - but if so, why are there not
more?

If this is a smelter (for bronze?), where is the furnace area? There is so far no
indication, and our finds seem more like water deposits, not metal, more like a
middle than a furnace area.

What is the association with deer stones? The slag/charcoal seems to be directly
associated with the deer stones and the boulder pavements. Some boulders in
pavement apear fire cracked, but not enough to be furnace floors, and slag &
charcoal are not found between the rocks, but except in their lowest levels

Khyadag East, Areas A1, 2, and 6 excavation map; Khyadag East Area 2 excavation map with slag features.

Site work advanced to clearing the Area 2 floor and removing all the rocks by lunchtime. Lots of charcoal turned up beneath the rocks, so we will have more than enough for dating the slag level. But we still need a horse to date the deer stones. I began wondering if our smelting operation might be using the mineral deposits that miners have recently identified in this valley, but it turned out it was to be a phosphate mine. A storm struck after lunch, making it difficult to collect charcoal as the wind kept whisking our samples from under our noses. We managed to clear Block 2, prepare profiles, and begin turfing Block 3 that contained the two standing deer stones. It's still a mystery why there is a slag midden with no obvious furnace structure. The presence of slag and charcoal directly under the lower level rocks suggests they are related, but the deer stones are not so easily linked to either. And it still leaves open the link with the upper level rocks, which we have assumed are related to deer stone activity. The slag level lies on sterile gravelly sand 25-30cm below the surface, and we generally assume the DS level is 10-15cm below surface. What time is represented by 15-20cm of sterile humic soil? Again, we don't have good answers and will have to see what results come from the C14 dates. (Two dates on charcoal from the slag level both came in between cal. 2700-2400 BCE, while a tooth date from Area 3 Feature 32 produced a similar date range, which is at the late end of most deer stone horse dates.)

Charcoal, ash, and slag level at Khyadag East; and fragment of copper slag.

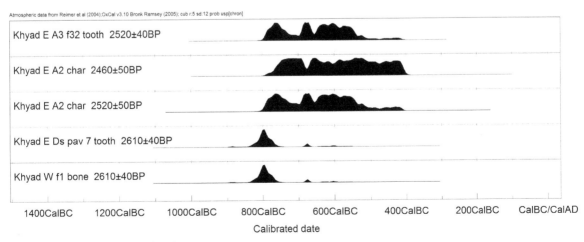

Atmospheric data from Reimer et al (2004);OxCal v3.10 Bronk Ramsey (2005); cub r:5 sd:12 prob usp[chron]

Khyad E A3 f32 tooth 2520±40BP	
Khyad E A2 char 2460±50BP	
Khyad E A2 char 2520±50BP	
Khyad E Ds pav 7 tooth 2610±40BP	
Khyad W f1 bone 2610±40BP	

1400CalBC 1200CalBC 1000CalBC 800CalBC 600CalBC 400CalBC 200CalBC CalBC/CalAD

Calibrated date

Radiocarbon dates from Khyadag East.

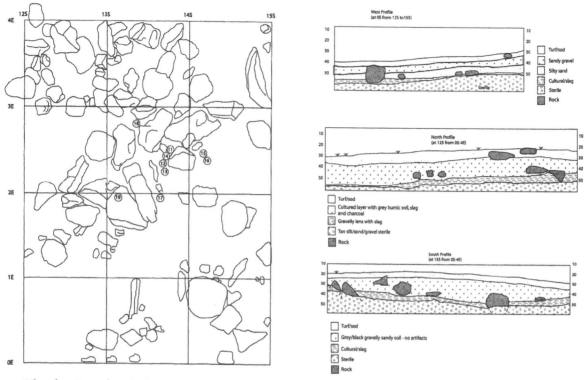

Khyadag East, detail of Area 2 finds map, and Khyadag East Area 2 soil profiles.

Area 3 The next afternoon we got into the upper layer of Area 3 and immediately started finding bones of sheep/goat and larger animals, most of them broken for cooking. There were also a few pieces of slag and horse teeth, most looking like young animals, and more fragmented pieces of deer stones. One of the horse teeth produced a date of cal. 2740-2470 BP, in line with the charcoal dates from Area 2. Area 3 revealed that the slag horizon is only weakly present in the northern part of the block. Instead, we found broken horse teeth and processed food bone of sheep/goats and larger animals, some chewed by dogs. There is no apparent pattern to their distribution–they mostly cluster around the big deer stone, from just under the sod to 15-20cm deep on sterile gravel. They seem to be the remains of meals associated with the deer stones. We found similar deposits in the excavation block east of the standing deer stones last year. Their depths and preservation are all the same, suggesting a single deposition dating to the deer stones.

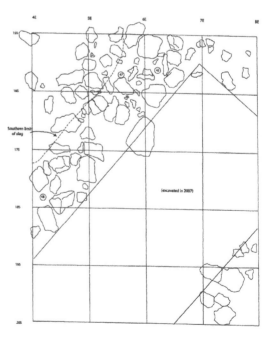

Khyadag East Area 3 excavation map showing Area 1 2007 boulder pavement and eastern limit of slag finds.

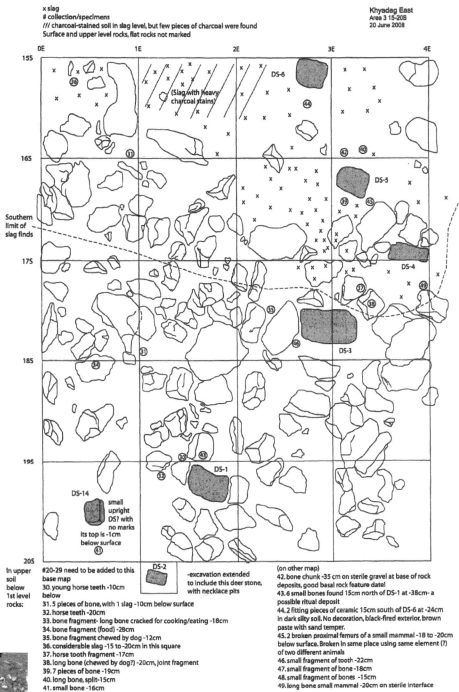

x slag
collection/specimens
/// charcoal-stained soil in slag level, but few pieces of charcoal were found
Surface and upper level rocks, flat rocks not marked

Khyadag East
Area 3 15-20S
20 June 2008

Southern limit of slag finds

(Slag with heavy charcoal stains)

DS-6
DS-5
DS-4
DS-3
DS-1
DS-14

small upright DS? with no marks its top is -1cm below surface

DS-2

-excavation extended to include this deer stone, with necklace pits

In upper soil below 1st level rocks:

#20-29 need to be added to this base map
30. young horse teeth -10cm below
31. 5 pieces of bone, with 1 slag -10cm below surface
32. horse teeth -20cm
33. bone fragment- long bone cracked for cooking/eating -18cm
34. bone fragment (food) -28cm
35. bone fragment chewed by dog -12cm
36. considerable slag -15 to -20cm in this square
37. horse tooth fragment -17cm
38. long bone (chewed by dog?) -20cm, joint fragment
39. 7 pieces of bone -19cm
40. long bone, split -15cm
41. small bone -16cm

(on other map)
42. bone chunk -35 cm on sterile gravel at base of rock deposits, good basal rock feature date!
43. 6 small bones found 15cm north of DS-1 at -38cm- a possible ritual deposit
44. 2 fitting pieces of ceramic 15cm south of DS-6 at -24cm in dark silty soil. No decoration, black-fired exterior, brown paste with sand temper.
45. 2 broken proximal femurs of a small mammal -18 to -20cm below surface. Broken in same place using same element (?) of two different animals
46. small fragment of tooth -22cm
47. small fragment of bone -18cm
48. small fragment of bones -15cm
49. long bone small mammal -20cm on sterile interface

Khyadag East Area 3, units 0-4E/15-20S map with slag finds. Photo, view north; finds map; list of finds for map.

2008 excavation team at Khyadag East, L to R: Sodoo, Kyle, Amaraa, Sasha, Nasaa, Khadaa, Tseeree, Ayush, Bayaraa, and Mogi.

One surprise was finding flat slabs around some of the small deer stones and near some boulder features, as though there were small areas of pavement around the base of the deer stones. Digging below the slabs around DS1, 5, and 6 we found small deposits of broken bones and bone splinters, and in DS-5 were two snapped femurs of some small mammal we could not identify, and in DS-6 was a piece of ceramic pot. Last year Sasha found small calcined bones at the south side of miniature DS-12, so maybe we have evidence of small ritual deposits at the bases of deer stones. Whatever it is, it is quite simple and has not been found before. We found more slag, but only along the A2/3 border, and little charcoal. There were also two barrier-like linear constructions, one of large, stacked rocks east of the large deer stone, paralleling the 2007 excavation block, and the other consisting of two vertically positioned rectangular rocks west of the DS3. Our travel schedule made it impossible to investigate these features.

Excavating large areas around Khyadag East produced new knowledge of its complicated history: (1) a classic deer stone site with two standing deer stones; (2) discovery of several broken and buried "regular" deer stones; (3) finding miniature (perhaps purposefully destroyed?) deer stone slabs with characteristic markings surrounded by small pavements and ritual animal bone deposits; (4) a pavement or 'killing floor" on the east side of the monument site; (5) the conversion of the site at the end of the deer stone period into a bronze production site; and (6) around 2400 BP, the addition of a Scythian coiled animal motif to the west side of DS 1. To acknowledge the obvious, expanding the footprint of excavations at deer stone sites adds importantly to understanding the complex behavior that produced them, and how they were used over time. (see also WF and JB 2021)

Khyadag West

With only a few days remaining in the field, we turned to Khyadag West, located about 400 m west of Khyadag East at N49°48,876', E99°53,946' in Burentogtokh suum, Khuvsgul Aimag. By this time, we had noticed both similarities and differences between the two Khyadag deer stone sites from surface observations. Both were surrounded by a ring of boulder features but had different styles of deer stone art. There were no miniature or broken deer stones at Khyadag West, and Khyadag East lacked hearth circles.

Khyadag West DS1-3 (right to left) with Khyadag East in background. View east.

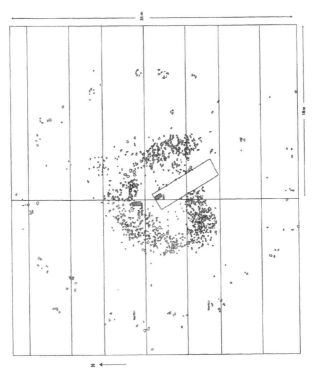

Surface map of Khyadag West showing deer stones, inner cobble features, outer circle hearths, and excavation trench.

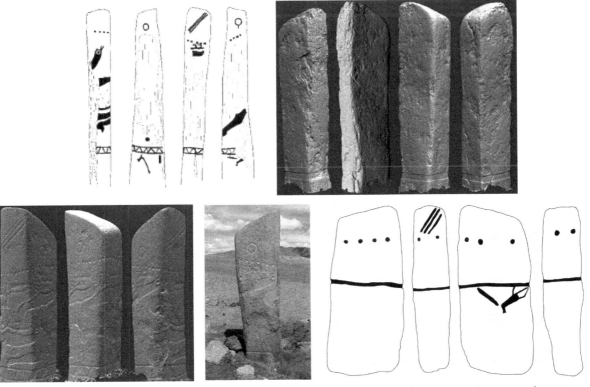

Khyadag East DS1-4: DS1 graphic; DS2, 3 scans and color; DS4 graphic. (photo: WF; others JB and HFB et al.)

Khyadag West Deer Stones

The deer stones from this site share characteristics with Khyadag East, but have a greater tendency toward full decoration, although this is difficult to assess because spalling due to poor stone quality has resulted in the loss of image detail, as seen in DS1 (JAB 2017:pl.39). This 3 m tall stone has /// slashes on the face, the remnants of several deer images lost to erosion, pendant earrings, a pitted necklace, a mirror, and a belt band with zig-zag decoration, an axe, whetstone, knife and quiver. DS2 (JAB 2017:pl.40) is too eroded to show more than earrings and a broad belt band. DS3 (JAB 2017:pl.41) is the best preserved of the group and shows a /// slash face, earrings with pendants, necklace pits, three deer wrapping around its four sides, and a belt decorated with a zig-zag design.

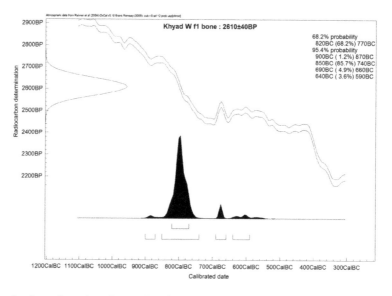

Radiocarbon date from Khyadag West.

Khyadag West trench showing Feature 1 in foreground; and excavated. View north.

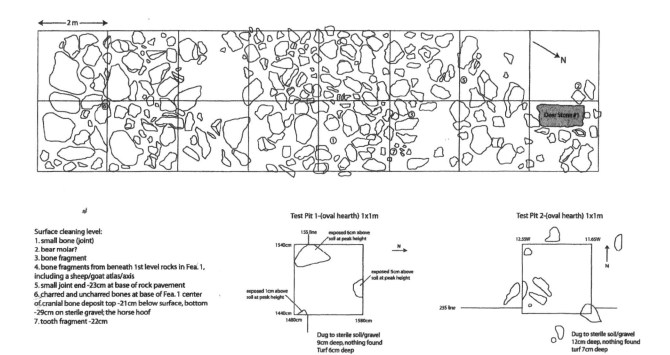

Surface cleaning level:
1. small bone (joint)
2. bear molar?
3. bone fragment
4. bone fragments from beneath 1st level rocks in Fea. 1, including a sheep/goat atlas/axis
5. small joint end -23cm at base of rock pavement
6. charred and uncharred bones at base of Fea. 1 center of cranial bone deposit top -21cm below surface, bottom -29cm on sterile gravel; the horse hoof
7. tooth fragment -22cm

Test Pit 1-(oval hearth) 1x1m

155 line
1540cm
exposed 6cm above soil at peak height
exposed 5cm above soil at peak height
exposed 1cm above soil at peak height
1440cm
1480cm
1580cm

Dug to sterile soil/gravel
9cm deep, nothing found
Turf 6cm deep

Test Pit 2-(oval hearth) 1x1m

12.55W
11.65W
25S line

Dug to sterile soil/gravel
12cm deep, nothing found
turf 7cm deep

Khyadag West trench upper level rocks with Feature 1 at south (left) end.

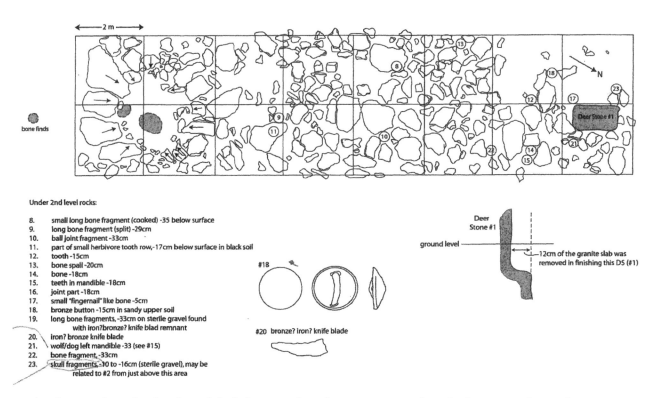

bone finds

Under 2nd level rocks:

8. small long bone fragment (cooked) -35 below surface
9. long bone fragment (split) -29cm
10. ball joint fragment -33cm
11. part of small herbivore tooth row, -17cm below surface in black soil
12. tooth -15cm
13. bone spall -20cm
14. bone -18cm
15. teeth in mandible -18cm
16. joint part -18cm
17. small "fingernail" like bone -5cm
18. bronze button -15cm in sandy upper soil
19. long bone fragments, -33cm on sterile gravel found with iron?bronze? knife blad remnant
20. iron? bronze knife blade
21. wolf/dog left mandible -33 (see #15)
22. bone fragment, -33cm
23. skull fragments, -10 to -16cm (sterile gravel), may be related to #2 from just above this area

#18

#20 bronze? iron? knife blade

Deer Stone #1
ground level
12cm of the granite slab was removed in finishing this DS (#1)

Khyadag West lower level rocks and finds from trench and Feature 1 mound south of DS1. North to right.

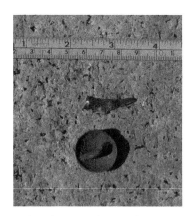

Khyadag West bronze button, metal knife blade remnant, and canid remains found at the base of DS1.

DS4 (JAB 2017:pl.42), 95cm long, was lying on the surface and has a /// face, necklace pits, a belt groove, a bow in a quiver, and an unidentifiable tool.

We did not have time to excavate north of the deer stones to see if this site has small broken deer stones, but the design similarities suggest this might be the case. For this reason, we were interested in obtaining a date from some of the stone features surrounding Khyadag West.

We set up a grid and lined out a trench from DS1 to the outer edge of the boulder apron extending six meters to the south, reaching Feature 1, a circular rock feature that looked like a possible horse head burial. Sasha found a portion of a large carnivore jaw or maxillary fragment near the base of DS1, and Moogi found burned and unburned sheep remains beneath Feature 1 including skull fragments, but no horse remains. This feature was constructed with large flat rocks slanting down into its center. After clearing the second level rocks from the trench we found more of Sasha's carnivore—a wolf or dog—and a tiny metal blade of bronze or iron, used to exhaustion, and on the south side of the deer stone a bronze button with a loop attachment. So, once again, the immediate vicinity of deer stones seems to have attracted idiosyncratic deposits. In this case we

were not certain whether the knife or button date to the deer stone or were later additions. The rest of the trench yielded more splintered or broken bone fragments, evidence of cooking, but no artifacts. This concluded our work at Khyadag, unfortunately with little clarity for Khyadag West other than a date on bone from Feature 1: cal. 2870-2750 BP, toward the end of the deer stone period, a bit earlier than dates from Khyadag East, and finds of a button and knife blade.

A lighter moment: digging DS1 with goats.

DS1 and 2 at the Tugsoo khirigsuur site north of Uushigiin Uvör. These DSs are set inside the fence, which is unusual in central Mongolia. However, they were reportedly re-erected by Tugsoo and may not be in original position, and they are not properly set facing east; A ger camp in the eroded grantite knobs west of Khyadag.

Tugsoo Site

At the beginning of the 2009 season, traveling north from Murun, we stopped briefly at N49°52.065', E099°46.852' to inspect a large round-fenced khirigsuur that Bruno Frohlich's assistant, Tugsoo, had mentioned had two deer stones. The site is halfway between Uushigiin Uvör and Murun. Stones had been taken recently from the top of the mound for construction, and two small deer stones were standing inside the fence in the northern part of the khirigsuur plaza. Both were granite and had earrings on opposite sides, and two face slashes on the original east sides of the stones. As currently but incorrectly set, DS1 had circles on its north and south sides and two back-slash \\ marks on its west side. It's dimensions:

58(h), 23(w), 18(t). DS2 had a beaded necklace around all four sides, a mirror in the middle of the necklace on the current east side, circular earring grooves on the south and north sides, with the south side circle having a pendant triangle suspended below the circle; and two back-slanting face \\ slash marks on the west side. A belt may be present below ground surface. Dimensions: 35(t), 25(w). Both stones had been re-set by Tugsoo, and both lacked carvings typical of Uushigiin Uvör style deer stones and would fall into Volkov's Eurasian or Sayan-Altai categories. Deer stone-size blocks of rectangular pink granite around the base of DS1 suggest that there may have been other deer stones present. We planned to excavate the khirigsuur's horse mounds to obtain a date but never found an opportunity to return.

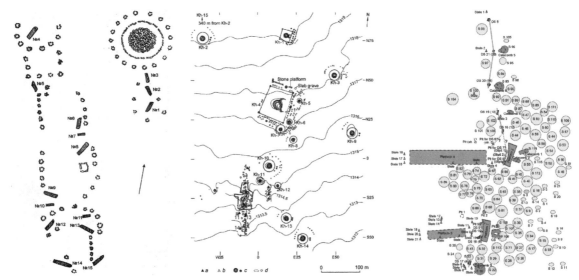

Uushigiin Uvör site maps by Volkov 1981; Taka-hama and Shu 2006; and Kovalev et al. 2016.

10. Following the Volkov Trail: The Northern Steppe

Uushigiin Uvör is the largest deer stone site north of the Delger Murun River, having at least 15 known deer stones associated with an array of khirigsuurs between 'Lung Mountain' and the river, a few kms west of Murun. It was initially studied and published by Volkov, and more recently, archaeological research has been conducted by Takahama et al. (2006) and Kovalev et al. 2016), who excavated a large khirigsuur

and a large area around the deer stone installations. We are concerned here with its deer stones, which stand in three north-south rows surrounded by hundreds of small stone rings and mounds, as well as one or more rectangular boulder pavements. All the deer stones de-

scribed below were documented with laser scans which are illustrated in JAB 2017: pl. 25-38.

The 14 Uushigiin Uvör deer stones presently standing have most recently been described by Bayarsaikhan 2017 and from a conservation perspective by Beaubien et al. (2008:86-95), who discovered the missing Deer Stone 15 in a storeroom of the Murun Police Station after it had been recovered from thieves. Probably all of these deer stones have been reset during the past several decades, and fragments of others found recently indicate that more probably were standing during the DSK period.

Volkov documented fifteen deer stones at Uushigiin Uvör. We visited the site several times since it was on our route north to the Darkhad, and our laser scanning team of conservators spent several days scanning several of its stones, including DS14, the most famous stone with a beautifully modeled face. This was the stone that Paul Rhymer and Carolyn Thome had made a latex mold of to fabricate two replicas, one for the Smithsonian and one for the Mongolia National Museum. The latter one became the centerpiece of the MNM's main display hall for many years. Then in the 2006-7 seasons, Harriet F. Beaubien, Basiliki Vicky Karass, and Leslie G. Weber produced laser scans of all the Uushigiin Uvör deer stones and many from several other sites we studied. Laser scan files were used to illustrate the carvings on the selection of Uushigiin Uvör deer stones described below:

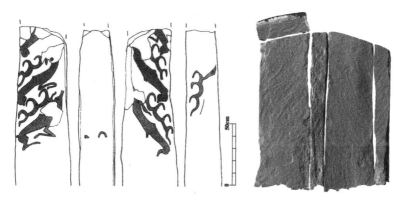

Uushigiin Uvör DS1, graphic and laser scan. (graphic JB; scan: H.F. Beaubien et al) Deer Stone 1 (JAB 2017:pl. 24, 24a) has a broken top and three ascending deer on its north and south sides and eroded images on its east and west sides.

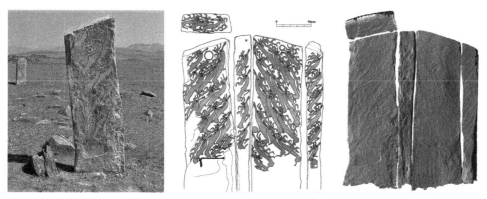

Uushigiin Uvör DS2 showing severe surface deterioration in 2002; graphic markings; and laser scan. (photo: WF; graphic, JB; scan: HFB et al.) Deer Stone 2 (JAB 2017:pl.25, 25a) displays one of the densest concentrations of Mongolian deer on any deer stone in Mongolia. Its original south side has 16 deer ascending right, an earring, and an ax. Its east side has four deer ascending right and its west side has six deer ascending right over a seven-bar chevron shield. No belt or necklace is present.

Uushigiin Uvör DS3 3 graphic, and laser scan. (graphic: JB; scan: HFB et al.) Deer Stone 3 (ibid. pl.26, 26a) displays four right ascending deer, an earring, and a zig-zag /\/\/\/ double belt on its south side and four left ascending deer on its north side with an earring, a mirror, and a double /\/\/\ belt with a hanging knife. Its narrow east side is blank, and its narrow west side has part of a deer image and a 17-bar chevron—the greatest number of chevrons of any deer stone in Mongolia.

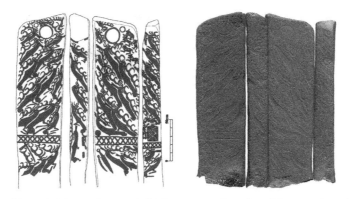

Uushigiin Uvör DS4, graphic, and (b) laser scan. (graphic: JB; scan: Beaubien et al.) Deer Stone 4 (ibid. pl.27, 27a), like DS2, is tightly packed with deer images. Its south side has 16 deer, three of which are below a cross-hatched belt with a hanging ax, with large and small ('sun and moon') earrings at the top. The north face has three deer below the belt with a sword and knife, and above the belt, a mirror and nine left-ascending deer, one small right-descending deer, a large and small ring at the top and four feline predators chasing a horse below the rings. The narrow west side shows two right-ascending deer below the belt, and five left-ascending deer above, with four small left-ascending deer on the left side of the panel. This side also has an elaborate multi-facetted diamond design for its shield ornament.

Deer Stones 5 thru 13 and 15 have similar designs that vary in numbers of deer depending on the side and shape of the stone. Most have belts with different styles of decoration (probably based on embroidery). A few have hanging tools, earrings, and chevrons.

Uushigiin Uvör deer stones stand out because of their large number, their settings in three parallel north-south lines, their lack of necklaces (except DSs 7 and 14), their different styles of belt ornamentation, and extreme 'packing' of deer images on the stones. These features seem to distinguish an Uushigiin Uvör style linking a long lineage, or perhaps three different chiefly lineages (one line for each)—of local or regional leaders. If the three deer stone lines represent clan lineages, then Uushigiin Uvör had a very long initial 'reign' of six leaders, followed by a second lineage line of six, and a third lineage of only three leaders.

Uushigiin Uvör Deer Stone 14 graphic, and (laser scan. (graphic: JB; scan: H.F. Beaubien et al.) Only DS7 and DS14 at Uushigiin Uvör have necklaces.

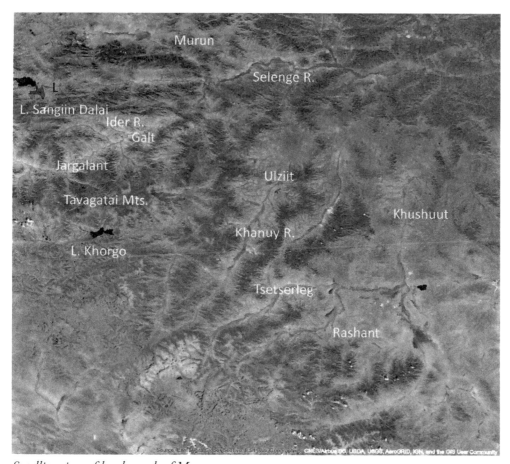

Satellite view of lands south of Murun.

179

Bor Khujiriin Gol-1 Feature 2, view east.

Bor Khujiriin Gol

We began our 2008 project with a study of the large Tsagaan Uul Bogd Mountain site named Bor Khujiriin Gol-1 (N49°44.269', E98° 17.826') described by Volkov (1981). Sasha had worked with him here in 1971 but says they did not excavate. The site has five standing stones, one lying on the surface and one with its corner protruding from the ground, all accompanied by what seemed like horse features and hearth circles. We gridded some features out, and Nasaa started mapping while Sasha traced out the art on the stones with chalk so they could be photographed and drawn. The two big hills to the south of us are Big Bogd (in Buddhist terminology, "prince/king") to the east, and Little Bogd to the west. DS1 facing 126°, 165h, 41w, 28t; DS2: 115°, 133h, 34w, 32t; DS3: 110°, 234h, 50w, 28t; DS4: 115°, 164.5h, 27w, 33t; DS5: 115°, 165h, 34w, 30t; DS6: lying down NW of DS4, 196h, 34w, 22t; DS7: buried between DS4 & 5. Our first excavation produced a small charcoal sample (S1) 32 cm below the surface under a large rock in the southeast quadrant of Feature 1. Feature 2 west of DS4 and DS5 was a small stone pile with small cobble rocks. Here we found a poorly preserved skull of a 1-year-old horse oriented 135° 15 cm below the surface under a flat slab. Deer Stone 7 has an axe or knife; with no circles or pits and is 93 cm tall.

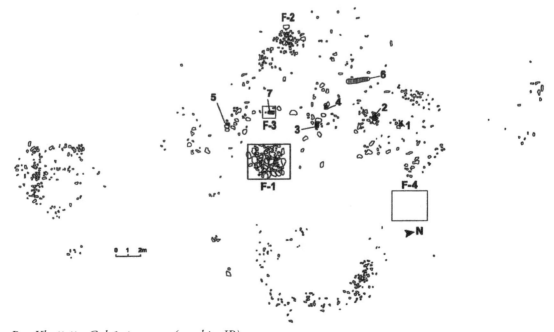

Bor Khujiriin Gol-1 site map. (graphic: JB)

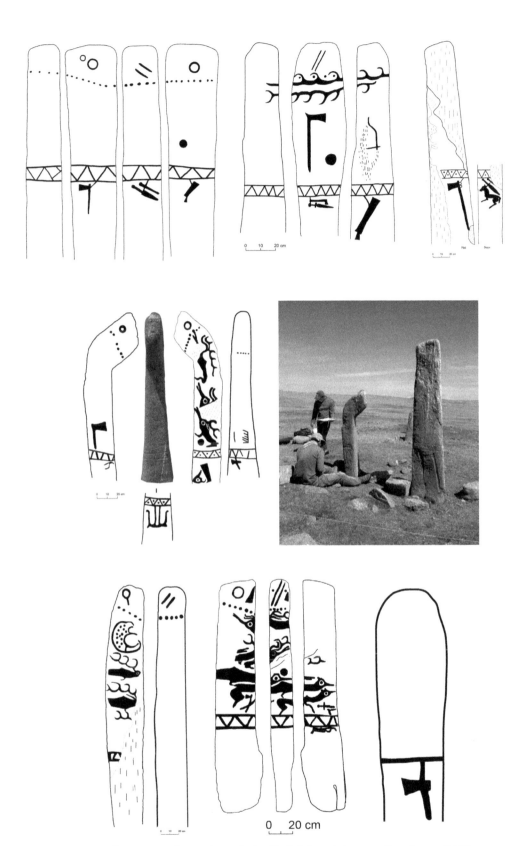

Bor Khujiriin Gol-1, DS1-7 (a-h; d/e DS4 with human face facing DS3).
(graphics and photos: JB, WF)

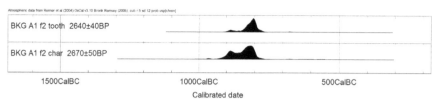

Atmospheric data from Reimer et al (2004);OxCal v3.10 Bronk Ramsey (2005); cub r:5 sd:12 prob usp[chron]

BKG A1 f2 tooth 2640±40BP	
BKG A1 f2 char 2670±50BP	

1500CalBC   1000CalBC   500CalBC

Calibrated date

Bor Khujiriin Area 1 Feature 2 radiocarbon dates on horse tooth and charcoal.

After lunch we opened Feature 4, potentially a "horse" feature, east of DS1, but it was empty. A pit Kyle, Sasha, and I dug at the partially buried DS7 turned out to be a fallen "baby" deer stone less than a meter long whose only marks were a belt line and a small knife. We have no idea what these small stones represent—children, lesser figures, or something else? It's hard to see how they would be valiant warriors or leaders.

Some general thoughts on Bor Khujiriin Gol, which is one of the larger deer stone sites not damaged by earlier explorations: Volkov visited it but illustrated only the unusual DS4 face stone with its crooked neck, seemingly placed as if speaking to DS3, one meter to the east and the tallest of all the stones at this site. Might this represent a shaman counseling a leader? Many of the deer stones have complicated images, with multiple deer, a horse, and a spotted feline. The southern stones all have belts decorated with pendant triangles with pits in their centers. Most stones have // face slashes and circle earrings and two have triangles to the right of the circles, bow and arrows, axes, a beautiful dagger, and other implements. Some deer have antlers and no bodies, and some bodies have no antlers. The 'baby' deer stone has only a belt groove and an axe. The deer stones are aligned at 011°, and all face east/southeast at 110°-126°.

There are many rocks around the stones that may be horse burials, but those we excavated east of the deer stones were empty and had charcoal that we considered untrustworthy. The one feature excavated to the west of the deer stone line contained a one-year old horse skull. Overall, the stones are slender, all of granite, and except for one, have tops angling down away from the front/east side. Magnetite crystals embedded in the granite in DS2 made it difficult to get a consistent compass reading. Many of the stones had spalled areas that made it impossible to trace carvings, and DS3, the tallest stone, is riddled with cracks, and chunks have fallen away from the edges. We only have

Bor Khujiriin Gol horse Feature 1 west of the deer stones, viewed to east; Feature 2 horse remains; Feature 3 horse head feature.

one horse sample (F2) and from F4 a chunk of charcoal and a piece of unburned food bone from 8-10 cm below the surface. Like the Khyadag sites, Bor Khujiriin Gol-1 has no associated khirigsuurs, which is not the case with BH-2,3, and 4 which are smaller deer stone sites with nearby khirigsuurs.

Tsagaan Uul officials visit our camp at Bor Khujiriin Gol.

Official Visitors Arrive

As we finished lunch a green UNICEF Jeep drove up and spent a while looking at the site. They did not look like tourists and turned out – as suspected – to be Tsagaan Uul sum officials: a uniformed police fellow, the warden we looked for the other day, and a couple others. They'd come to check us out, asked for our permit papers (thank goodness we had been able to add this suum to our list). After some talk, we invited them for lunch and tea. We showed them the horse head, photos, and last year's report, and gradually we got around to discussing their interest in getting an inventory of sites and GPS positions. The Mongolian Cultural Heritage Center has asked the suums to organize inventories but has given them no guidance, and they of course have no archaeological knowledge at all. It does not seem they have done their homework, although they did get a big grant from the Japanese Ambassador for inventory work. Before leaving, they came to Bor Khujiriin Gol-2, saw us working, and had lots of questions. (9 June 2008)

Bor Khujiriin Gol-2

In 2008 we documented three other sites at Tsagaan Uul Bogd Mountain area, and two are deer stone sites west of Bor Khujiriin Gol-1. Bor Khujiriin Gol-2 has two standing stones, one large (ca. 2 m) and one small (ca. 1 m). The small stone is 1 m east of large stone and slants towards it. Both are square/rectangular granite and well-finished. The large one has a top that angles away from its east/front side. There are six circle hearths and five or six probable horse features.

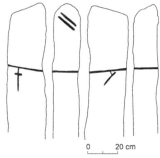

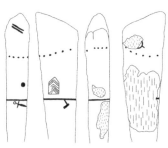

Bor Khujiriin Gol-2. DS1 (large), and DS2.

Bor Khujiriin Gol-2 Feature 1 excavation, and surface map. (photo and map: JB)

Bor Khujiriin-3

Bor Khujiriin Gol-3 is next to two Turkic burial structures at N49°46.078', E98°17.469' and has two granite standing deer stones. DS1 measures 97(l), 28(w), and 24(t) and has deer, a necklace, and earrings on its north and east sides, but no slashes for a face; its necklace 'beads' change from round pits to rhombus shape. The stone is circled by rock features 6-10

m away. DS2 is 215(l) and 46(w) and is lying 2 m north of DS1. A chevron motif with 10-12 bars is on the original west side. Its original position would have been in north-south alignment with DS1. No excavation was conducted at either stone. A Turkic structure four meters southeast of the standing deer stone had been looted or excavated; a second was 20 m to the southwest and had a long line of balbals extending to the east.

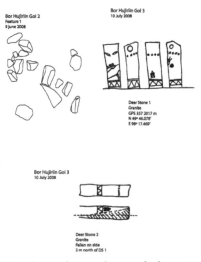

Bor Khujiriin Gol-3, DS1, Standing, and DS2 lying beyond. (graphics and photo: JB)

Bor Khujiriin-4

Bor Khujiriin Gol-4, N49°48.638', E98°18.693', has two deer stones. DS1 is 170 cm tall and has a belt groove. DS2, about the same height, is east of DS1, poorly preserved, but has a belt and a suspended tool or weapon. Neither have associated rock features. These monuments are associated with a group of 20-30 khirigsuurs positioned at the base of the nearby hill, and some of these monuments extend up the lower sides of the hill. Most have square fences with corner mounds. We were not able to trace carvings on the deer stones.

Bor Khujiriin Gol-4 Deer Stones 1, 2.

Khushuugiin Gol-1

One of the largest deer stone sites in north-central Mongolia is Khushuugiin Gol-1, located in the steppe south of Murun at N49°42.261', E98°35.708'. The site was studied by Volkov and Sanjmyatav who unearthed, mapped, recorded, and erected many of its 13 deer stones. Khushuugiin Gol appears to have been constructed in three parts, probably in three time periods. I imagined the first people to use the site erected deer stones in Area 1, the southernmost part of the terrace where the largest number of deer stones, pavements, hearth circles, and horse mounds are found. This was a time of highly professional deer stone carvers who used granite and had excellent skills for cutting and polishing stone. The only pecking marks showing are in peripheral areas. I imagined that Areas 2 and 3 were later creations judging from the use of bluestone rather than granite and the more rudimentary nature of the carvings. The society that produced A2 and A3 was not interested in artistic perfection as in the classic era represented by Area 1. Their interest seems to have been to follow the general belief system, ritual, and social norms, but with less concern for artistic proficiency and investment in the hardest, more durable materials like granite and basalt. Another observation supports this preliminary analysis: The number of ritual features per area follows a sequence of A1 (many), A3 (fewer), and A2 (fewest) which may provide a clue to site chronology. The larger depictions of deer and tools, seen especially in Areas 2 and 3 are more like deer stone art in western Mongolia than in central Mongolia, where horse depictions are rare. These differences may also be indicators of chronology or geographic stylistic variation.

We spent only two days at Khushuugiin Gol-1, intending just to verify Volkov's work and prepare new maps, photograph and record deer stones, and find and excavate horse head features. Area 1 has seven deer stones, all made of white or pink granite carved with great skill, its lines looking like machine cuts, and many surfaces are carefully smoothed—certainly the work of highly skilled craftsmen. Area 2 has two deer stones, both of bluestone; its DS8 has a highly polished silica sheen, and DS9 has been broken from its base. Area 3 has five deer stones all made of bluestone, including one uncarved standing stone. In contrast with Area 1, the carvings on Area 2 and Area 3 stones are shallow, barely cut into the stone, almost just scratched on the bluestone.

We set out a 305°M baseline through the crest of the hillock from the southern and largest group (Area 1) north to a small central group (Area 2) having three rock features but only two deer stones at its southern end, to the northern group (Area 3). (On some of our field notes these were labelled as Areas A, B, C.) We photographed the two large fallen stones (DS1,

a painted portrait of the deer stone's namesake. Some years after this observation, Esin et al. (2019) confirmed the presence of red pigment on the underside of fallen deer stones that had been protected from the elements.

This site is important for its fine deer stone carving; but what we were most interested in was the site layout with three clusters of deer stones. This suggested the possibility that the three clusters might document chronological change during the tenure of leaders from three lineages or clans. The presence of horse-themed DS7 as the northernmost DS in Area I suggest-

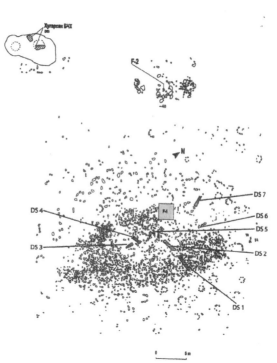

Khushuugiin Gol-1, Area A map showing locations of DS 1-7 and Features 1 and 2 excavations. (graphic: JB)

2) uncovered by Volkov and laid out a 2.5 m square unit at a possible horse feature (Feature 1) 2 m west of DS-5, which is one meter south of the baseline. Looking at the southern deer stones, I noticed none had the standard slashes // on the face and that their east-facing surfaces are finely polished compared to the rest of the stone, suggesting these areas might have carried

ed this might be the latest leader in that particular lineage. Unfortunately, many of the DS in Area 1 had fallen, but their original locations could be surmised by the adjacent pits. We hoped that Feature 1 west of DS7 would provide a horse skull, but the feature was empty. We returned later to excavate Features 5 and 6, but both of these were empty.

Khushuugiin Gol Area 1, the southern deer stone area showing two sides of DS1 (a, c) viewed to north.

This site is important for its fine deer stone carving; but what we were most interested in was the site layout with three clusters of deer stones. This suggested the possibility that the three clusters might document chronological change during the tenure of leaders from three lineages or clans. The presence of horse-themed DS7 as the northernmost DS in Area I suggested this might be the latest leader in that particular lineage. Unfortunately, many of the DS in Area 1 had fallen, but their original locations could be surmised by the adjacent pits. We hoped that Feature 1 west of DS7 would provide a horse skull, but the feature was empty. We returned later to excavate Features 5 and 6, but both of these were empty.

Deer Stone 1 was lying on the surface when Volkov and Sanjmyatav recorded it. Its original east side has a highly polished face area, a beaded necklace, two right ascending deer, and a belt with alternating triangle decoration above a suspended dagger. The south side has an earring/sun with a smaller moon ring and two right ascending deer. The west side has portions of a wrapped deer, a 9-chevron shield, and a tool hanging from the belt. The north side has a small moon circle over three right ascending deer and an ax on the belt.

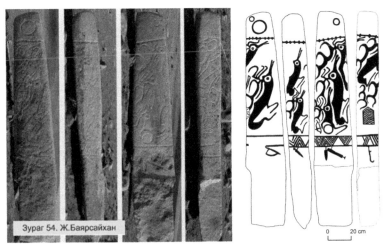

Khushuugiin Gol-1, Area A-1, DS1. (photo and graphic: JB)

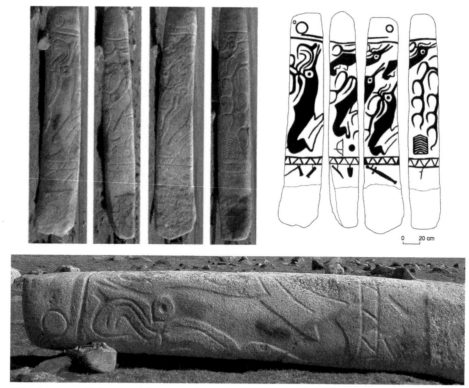

Khushuugiin Gol DS2. (photos and graphic WF, JB).

Deer Stone 2, also found fallen and exposed on the ground as it was in Volkov's time, displays very large, bold images of five deer. The east side has a polished face panel, a double necklace groove above the wrapped bodies of two right ascending deer, above a bow and mirror, and a \/\/\/ zig-zag ornamented belt with an attached knife and whetstone. The south side has an earring/sun and moon circle, and a single large deer image over a belt with an ax and quiver. The west side has a wrapped deer head and double antlers, an 8-chevron shield, and a suspended knife. The north side has a moon circle, parts of four wrapped deer, and a suspended sword.

Deer Stones 3-6 are fragmented and/or eroded, providing little information on their carving, but have the same style belt ornamentation as other Khushuutiin Gol-1 deer stones, perhaps indicating local lineage continuity.

Deer Stone 7 displays a dramatic departure from the iconic deer-bird spirit or god-figure by introducing horses as the dominant theme. The profusion of horse images leaves little doubt that this leader was banking on a new economic, political, and spiritual regime. Its east side has a single broad forward / face slash, a pitted necklace above six galloping horses, a mirror, and an inverted triangle belt with a suspended bow. The south side has earring/sun and moon circles above five horses, a belt, another horse below the belt, and suspended weapons. The west side has four horses above the belt, one below the belt, and three predators, two at the top and one in the middle of the torso, and a fifth horse and an ax below the belt. The north side has six horses and two suspended weapons. Horses were crammed into every tiny empty space. What happened to the Mongolian deer? At least for this leader, who seems to have been

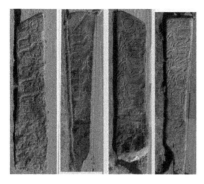

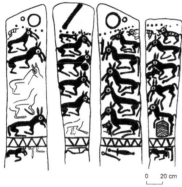

Khushuugiin Gol Area 1, DS7.
(photo and graphic: JB)

banking on a very different future than his contemporaries, horses had replaced the Mongolian stag as a personal guardian spirit or purveyor of power. A few centuries later, by Pazyryk times, the transition from the deer spirit ideology to a horse-powered future was complete.

This stone also announces another shift in Deer Stone culture—a change in artistic sensibility as evidenced by the rather crude rendition of the horse images. Compared with the elegant deer image, these horses are treated in a very cursory way, stylistically, capturing only their characteristic elements, their long ears and snout. One deer is draped inelegantly over the shield, and the whole herd can be interpreted as running from predators, likely wolves, thus introducing Scytho-Saka predation and narrative themes into this composition. The introduction of horses in DS7 suggests that this stone marks a chronological transition from the deer-theme stones of the Area 1 group and the

more Altai-like deer stones in Area 2. Despite the introduction of the horse into deer stone iconography, there is no hint of human aggression or social interaction either with animals or other humans.

We excavated several mound/hearth features at Khushuugiin Gol-1. Feature 1 is at 0E/N21.5; F2's unit coordinates are N41/W0.5, N44.5/W0.5, N44.5/E2.6, N41/E2.6; and F3's coordinates are 66N/3.5 and 5.5 W, and 68.5N/3.5 and 5.5 W. Feature 1 west of DS7 turned out to be 'dry', with no horse head or reliable charcoal, so we laid out Feature 2 in Area 2 and Feature 3 in Area 3 for excavation.

Khushuugiin Gol-1, Area 1, Feature 1.
Nothing found.

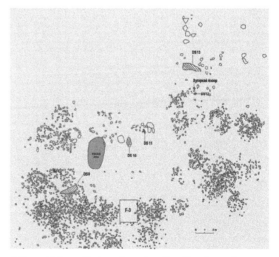

Map of Area-2 showing the distribution of surface boulders, DS 8-13, and excavated Feature-3. (photo and graphic: JB)

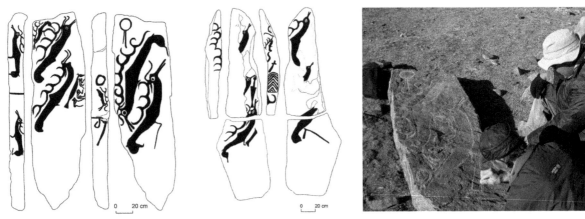

Khushuugiin Gol-1 Area 2, DS8 and DS9 made from thin unfinished slabs of bluestone; Sasha and Bayaraa tracing figures on DS9. (graphics: JB)

Deer Stone 8 is the southernmost DS in Area 2 and was found in two pieces. It is a stelae made of bluestone that is unusual because it does not follow normal DS protocol; it has an irregular shape and has not been trimmed to a square or rectangularly cross-section, has no belt, necklace, earrings, or face slashes, and its animals and tools (ax, dagger) float unattached. Its south and north sides each have three right ascending deer and there is an 8-bar shield on the west side.

Deer Stone 9, also of bluestone, is stylistically similar to DS8, with images barely scratched into the stone, and was found partially buried and not found by Volkov. Its north and south flat sides have two deer each, ascending right on one, with a floating dagger and three possible tiny predator figures, and one ascending and one descending on the other, which also has a tasseled earring. The face side has no slashes but has a belt-line with an ax and hook, and possibly a mirror. The back (west) side has two left-facing upright deer and a belt line.

The blue granite used in Areas 2 and 3 seems to have been nearly impervious to Bronze Age tooling. The images are barely scratched onto the surface, removing the dark patina and revealing a pale blue interior that is very attrac-

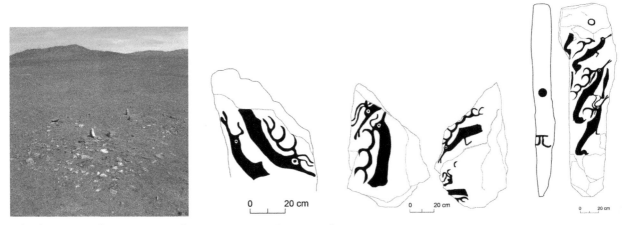

Khushuugiin Gol-1, Area 3, with DS 10, 11, 13. View north.

tive; even the necklace pits are barely excavated. These stones are not only technologically and materially different; they have swords or daggers floating in the main part of the stones and often don't have belts with hanging tools. One stone (DS9) has three felines carved in a very crude manner compared to the beautiful work on the deer on this stone, making one wonder if they were later additions. The deer of these stones are also very large and run up and down more than across the stone and sometimes have no antlers. Such stones are more like the Sayan-Altai deer stone type than the classic Mongolian style.

horse cranium. The atlas vertebra was in loose gravel 20 cm away and two hooves were on either side of the snout. The mandible was missing. By the end of the day, we found the cervical vertebrae along the north side of the skull, which was pointing SE (115°). The herders observed that the horse was a male about 20 years old. A storm struck before we could complete the excavation, so we extracted the canine from the F3 horse to ensure local people would not take it during the night, and covered the head with dirt. (Nadaam festival horse races were approaching, and riders use horse canines as

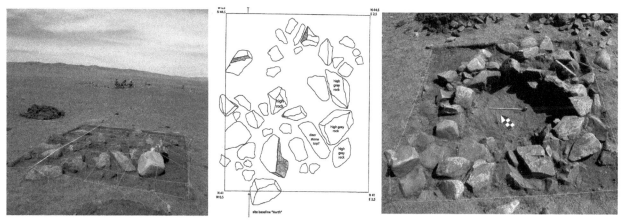

Khushuugiin Gol-1 Area 2, Feature 2 surface rocks, map, and excavated horse mandible. Area 3, Feature 3 is seen being excavated in the distance north of F2.

However, we are finding horse graves with these stones and do not find them in Altai Mongolia. These differences suggest a later date for Areas 2 and 3 than for Area 1 with its highly styled carvings conforming closely to the classic Mongolian deer stone style.

Later in the day herders dropped by to see what we were finding. By this time, we actually had something to show them. Feature 3 upper stones were made of rounded river cobbles. Below this we found an outer ring of rounded stones around a ring of vertical flat slabs inclined toward the center of the feature. Under a large, flat center rock we found the top of a

charms; they especially value ancient horse canines, believing they must have been powerful and fast to have been selected for burial.)

While we worked on Feature 3 the Mongolian team uncovered Feature 2, finding a mandible without a skull, just the reverse of the F3 find. The jaw looked as though it had weathered before burial, but it was still solid. Sometime during the day, Sasha lost his gold ring which was engraved with animal carvings. Some of the Mongolian students thought the lost ring and violent weather were retribution for disturbing ancient horse graves.

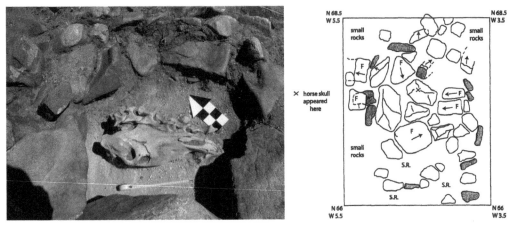

Khushuugiin Gol-1, Area 3, Feature 3, contained a southeast facing horse head (sans mandible), vertebrae, and two hooves from a ca. 20-year-old horse; excavation map of A3, F3 upper layer rocks. (graphic: JB)

Excavation of Feature 4 produced nothing at all–not even charcoal, so we began a new feature southeast of the outer rock features in Area 1, seeing this as our last chance for finding a horse date for this most important Area 1 part of the site. While we back-filled Feature 4, Nasaa continued rock-by-rock mapping of this complex area. Turning over DS4, we found new carvings. Feature 5 was another 'dry hole', and Feature 6 had the same outcome, although it produced a well-buried charcoal sample (undated). Perhaps the Area 1 residents had better ideas about what to put in their carefully prepared features than horses, like something organic that has not been preserved; or did not have the horses to spare but went through the motions just the same. This seemed odd considering the high quality of the deer stone art and horse-featured DS7.

While Bayaraa and Kyle worked on the Area 3 map, Nasaa finished Area 1. I drew sketches of most of the DS at the site and will be interested to see how they compare with Volkov's illustrations. Sasha has been a real expert at interpreting the eroded marks, maybe because he is doing it for the second time after his work here with Volkov! The pits where he and Volkov excavated fallen deer stones are still hollows today, so you can see where most of the stones were originally standing. Some broken deer stone fragments are still missing and must be buried nearby. I include below a couple of pages from my field notes to provide a sense of our field observations and methods. While I sketched and annotated, Bayaraa's team make detailed DS recordings and photos. Following fieldwork, Bayarsaikhan and his students used their field notes and photos to create the final illustrations and maps used in his 2017 thesis and in this report.

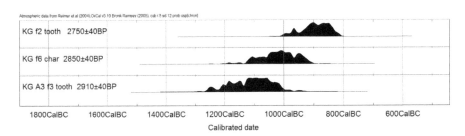

Radiocarbon dates from Khushuugiin Gol.

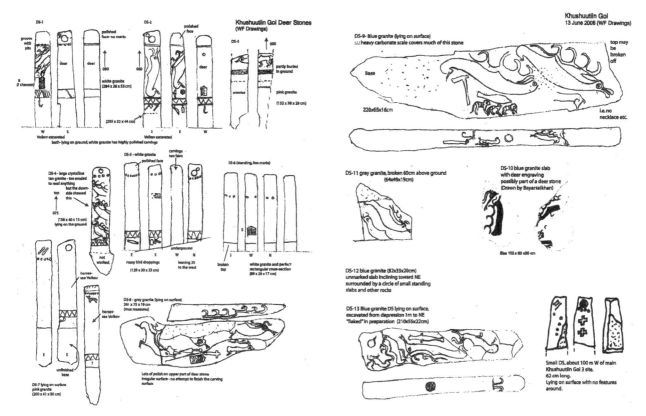

My field notes on Khushuugiin Gol-1 deer stones. Deer Stones 1-8; Deer Stones 9-13.

My supposition about site chronology was not borne out by the radiocarbon dates. One of the two charcoal samples from Area 1 (Feature 6) produced a date of cal. 3070-2860 BP, about one hundred years later than the horse tooth date from Area 3 Feature 3 (cal. 3210-2940 BP), quite the opposite of our hypothetical reconstruction based on art and site spatial/geographic patterning. If these dates reflect reality, my suggested site chronology is wrong. On the other hand, two dates, especially one on charcoal, can only be seen as tentative and is not sufficient for firm conclusions.

Khushuugiin Gol-2 and 3

Khushuugiin Gol-2 (N49°42.190', E98°35.514') is a single granite deer stone resembling those in KG-1, surrounded by a few features in a disturbed area with modern garbage. We designated this site as KG-2 but numbered its deer stones in the KG-1 series, thus becoming DS14. Only the upper portion of the stone could be seen, protruding from ground slanting up toward north. Its southeast side has a 'polished' face with no marks, and it has necklace beads and earrings on the south and north sides, and several large deer carvings around its four sides. Ten meters to the east is a 4 m diameter circular feature. Khushuugiin Gol-3 (N48°42.140', E98°35.361') is a 62 cm long, greenish granite deer stone fragment,

27(w), 18(t) that had been broken from its base, found on the surface south of KG-2 with no associated features. Its deer stone is also assigned in the KG-1 series as DS15. An earring, necklace pits, and two swords or daggers are on the original south side of the stone, while the east face side has three /// forward slashes and a descending line of pits. The floating swords and lack of other features make this unique among the usual inventory of deer stone design and similar to the Eurasian form.

a belt with a /\/\/\ design. All four stones are in north-south alignment and have six associated horse features (one bordered by quartz stones) south and east of the deer stones. Several hearth rings lie to the north. The surrounding vicinity has many khirigsuurs clustering around the east and south sides of the nearby hill. Most khirigsuurs have square fences with eastern orientations of 100°-130°M that follow the curved base of the hill rather than adhering to a single fixed (eastern) cardinal direction.

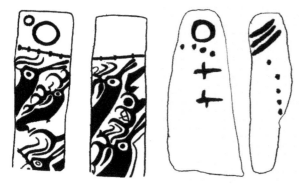

Deer stones from Khushuugiin Gol-2 DS14, and KG-3 DS15. (graphics: JB)

Buyant Gol

This site at (N49°42.935', E98°35.077') has three damaged deer stones standing and a fourth lying on the surface with only its top showing. DS1, the southernmost, is a broken granite stone with a chevron shield on its west side. DS2, the middle stone, is grey granite and shows part of a deer on its northeast side. DS3, the northernmost, has three slashes ///, five pits, and part of a deer image on its east side. The south side has an earring, four necklace pits and

Buyant Gol, a small deer stone site 1 km. north of Khushuugiin Gol, and its DS2. (photos: JB)

The unusual Zunii Gol-1 DS10 (see below for description).

11. Following the Volkov Trail: Arkhangai

The final year of the Smithsonian-Mongolian Deer Stone Project in northern Mongolia was conducted from 30 May to 1 July 2009. We planned to complete field studies in Khuvsgul and Arkhangai regions of northern Mongolia. Work began with a short foray into the Darkhad Valley to work further at sites visited in 2006-8 like Khyadag. However, most work concentrated on excavations and mapping south of the Delger Murun River between Murun and the Khanuy Valley where Volkov had worked but needed more recording and dating, such as Zunii Gol, Khushuugiin Am, and other sites around Galt. We also mapped and recorded sites in the Ikh Tamir and Tuul River valleys west of Ulaanbaatar. The Darkhad work was conducted in collaboration with Richard Kortum of East Tennessee State University, who brought petroglyphic expertise to our Darkhad work (as reported above) for the first time.

As in previous years, our goal was to record, date, and determine the archaeological context and stylistic variability of deer stone monuments. Our previous research had concluded that most deer stones in this region dated within a 500-year period between cal. 3200-2700 B.P. and conformed to a 'classic Mongolian' type with tool belts, images of the iconic Mongolian deer (MD) with swept-back antlers, and a set of standardized motifs including earrings, beaded necklaces, pentagonal 'shields', mirror discs, and a variety of tools. However, Volkov identified two other types of Mongolian deer stones he called Sayan-Altai and Eurasian. The former, known in small numbers in northern Mongolia but a dominant type in Western Mongolia and the Altai, depicted belts and necklaces, but its deer were less stylized and more variable in

Julia, Uuganaa, Barbara, and Bayaraa relaxing, with horses, at Khanuy River near Rashaant. (photos: WF, B. Betz)

form, and its tools were frequently displayed 'floating' on the stone monument rather than attached to the warrior belt. Volkov believed these monuments were prototypes of the later 'classic' style stones. The much simpler Eurasian stones had only grooved lines for belts, earrings and necklaces and were thought to be post-classic deer stones.

Our previous research had shown that the classic, Sayan-Altai, and European deer stone types could be found in the same sites in northern Mongolia. However, dating the smaller Sayan-Altai and European deer stones had been difficult, and there was some evidence from Khyadag East, north of Murun, where they occurred together in a single site and might post-date the classic deer stones by

200-300 years. Our work in 2009 attempted to obtain better dating for Sayan-Altai stones and see if they were culturally and chronologically distinct from the classic deer stone sites. We also hoped to refine the styles and chronology of the classic deer stone types. With such information we might then be able to tackle the question of the origin and spread of the deer stone phenomenon and its relation to earlier and later cultures, including the Scythian culture developments that took place immediately after the deer stone period in Central and Western Asia. Some of the sites reported above, like Khyadag East, Khushuugiin Gol-1, and Zunii Gol shed light on these stylistic and chronological problems.

Badrakhiin Ovoo

Following a brief excursion to the northern Darkhad where we found Mongolian deer images carved into the rocks surrounding khirigsuurs at the Kholboo Tolgoi south of the Shishgid River, we headed south into Arbulag sum, north of Murun, looking for Volkov's Badrakhiin Ovoo site (N49° 47.745', E99°27.429'), which we found in a grassy valley filled with knobby granite outcrops. While searching for the site we came across ger homesteads scattered between granite rock outcrops. Some of these camps were poor while others had shiny land cruisers parked nearby—the new Murun elite. The site has three small deer stones. We gridded it into 50 cm blocks for mapping and opened two features that seemed likely to produce horse heads.

We puzzled over the deer stone art, finding it unusual in a number of respects. DS1 (JAB 2017:pl.14) is an irregular stone with no visible marks other than a belt with a dagger and two forward slashes // on its face side. DS2 and 3 have unusual deer images. DS 2 (JAB 2017:pl.15) has a necklace and belt groove. It has two Mongolian deer on its original south side, with an earring and a belt axe. Its north side has a single deer, as does its east side, and this deer has a double let of antlers (perhaps the artist's recognition of perspective?). Volkov's drawing of these two stones are poor representations. DS3 (JAB 2017:pl.16) has earrings, two slashes (\\) on the face side, necklace pits, and rudimentary Mongolian deer on each side of the stone, and an eight-bar chevron on the original north (rather than the usual west) side of the stone. This stone had fallen and was erected recently by local people who painted it white, leaving the earrings to stand out clearly, and painted the necklace beads red—perhaps a bourgeois touch for a Murun 'suburb' attempting to attract tourists. Neither of the two horse features excavated east of the stones produced horse remains. The deer images show a combination of crudely done Mongolian deer (DS2) and ones with extended legs (DS3), suggesting they are late DSK creations.

Badrakhiin Ovoo deer stone site, with DS1, 2, and 3 seen left to right, viewed to north; and Bayaraa records Badrakhiin Ovoo Deer Stone 2.

Badrakhin Ovoo deer stones. (a) DS1, (b) DS2, and (c) DS3. (graphics: JB)

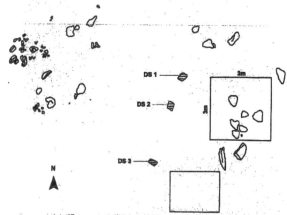

Badrakhin Ovoo site photo and map (b) showing DS1-3 and Feature 2 (foreground) and F1 upper right, to the north. (photo and map: JB)

Mongolia's Achilles Heel: Summer Water

Despite the scenic countryside giving the appearance of excellent grazing capacity, there is a serious problem: lack of water and dependence on snowmelt and rainfall. We searched for a water source but found none, and as a result could not have breakfast when we left the next morning. The large lake next to the nearby town is salty, so you need to have a vehicle to get water from a distant source. This is a major problem for the entire suum; even Arbulag, the suum center, is supplied by a central well that does not provide much volume. After taking refuge from a passing storm, we returned to finish the two features we had opened east of the deer stones. Both had nice rock features, but they both were empty; whatever may have been buried was no longer present. Perhaps LBA people found this a difficult environment, like today, accounting for the small size of their deer stones and lack of sacrificed horses.

South of Arbulag we drove up a large conical hill whose top was covered with a huge ovoo complex dedicated to Chingunjav, a Mongolian hero from Arbulag whose resistance to the Qing (Manchu) Chinese ended in the defeat of his forces and his subsequent torture and death in Beijing in 1752.

Zunii Gol

From Murun we drove south over the mountain, and after an hour reached Zunii Gol (N49º 18.562', E99º 50.984'), a large deer stone site investigated by Volkov having many deer stones and several large khirigsuurs, one of which he excavated and left un-filled. The site is in a broad valley on the northern side of a river—mostly dry now—but during our visit the surroundings had lots of green grass from recent rain. Volkov made a sketch map of the khirigsuurs and deer stones, but he missed some of the smaller deer stones. The site was too large for us to map in detail during our 5-day visit, but we were able to improve on his map and made more accurate drawings of the deer stones.

The giant ovoo for the Mongolian hero Chingunjav on a hilltop south of Arbulag (photo: B.Betz).

Zunii Gol was noted by Volkov as being unusual, and it is in several respects. The deer stones are not granite but made from green-stone schist. Most seem to have no belts and frequently no head features. Tools are floating free as in the Sayan-Altai stones, though they tend to be near the bottom of the stone. Many of the stones have been broken off or smashed (resembling Altai deer stone sites like Tsagaan Asgat), and you can see evidence of the damaging blows on the stones. Perhaps most unusual are the feature associations: here, deer stones act like khirigsuurs and have horse mounds to their east (as at Khushuugiin Am), and there is a rectangular pavement on the north side of one deer stone group. Khirigsuurs are present nearby—large ones—and some deer stone lines (north-south at about 040°M) have mounds 3-4 times larger than the usual horse mounds, resembling small khirigsuur central mounds. These seem to be part of the complex and not later additions—could they be for sacrificed persons as well as horses? We did not excavate any of these large features.

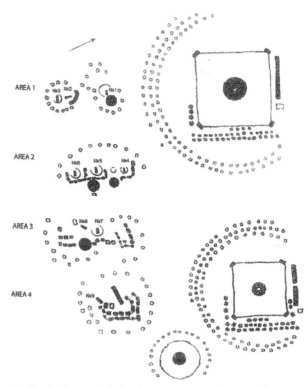

Volkov's Zunii Gol sketch map (2002: fig. 80) showing the four deer stone concentrations and associated khirigsuurs.

Zunii Gol deer stone site, showing deer stone alignment with horse features on its east side, view north; and Areas 1 and 2 viewed to the southwest.

Volkov produced sketch maps of the Zunii Gol site and described the seven deer stones that were standing or on the ground during his visit. Our work amplifies and adds to his descriptions.

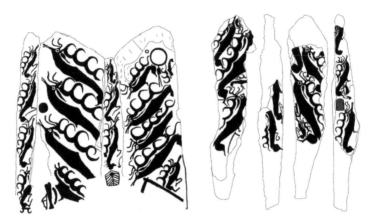

Zunii Gol-1 DS1 photo and graphic; and DS2. (graphics: JB) Deer Stone 1 is 161 cm tall and has five right ascending deer and a tasseled earring with a small 'moon' circle and an axe on its south, broad face, and four left ascending deer, a dagger, bow, and a mirror on its north face. Four right-ascending deer are on its narrow east face, and three deer ascend to the right on its west face above a shield motif. No belt or necklace is present. *Deer Stone 2* at 242 cm tall is fragmented but shows two and three right-ascending deer on its broad sides, two ascending on its east face and three ascending with a shield on its west face; again, no belt or necklace.

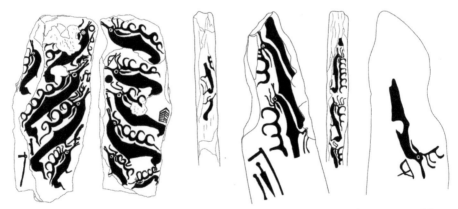

Zuni Gol-1 DS3 and DS4. (graphics: JB) Deer Stone 3, 202 cm above ground has four large left-ascending deer above two small deer at the bottom, and a mirror and shield on one broad face, and five right-ascending deer and a floating axe and rein hook on the other broad face, with no belt, necklace, or earring circles. *Deer Stone 4* is an irregular stone 108 cm tall with three ascending deer and an axe, dagger, and knife on one broad face, and a single descending deer and bow on the other broad face. Two and three ascending deer are on the narrow sides; no belt or necklace is present, and the tools float.

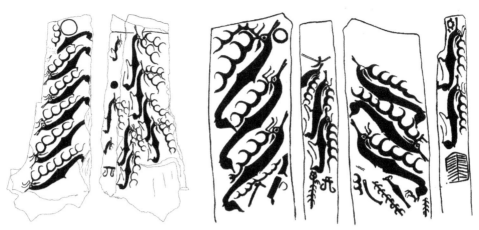

Zunii Gol-1 DS 5 and 6. (graphics: JB) Deer Stone 5 is very elaborate: one broad face has six left-descending deer and an earring, and the other has four large and three small left-ascending deer, and a necklace groove. A narrow side has a rein hook, a mirror, and three left-ascending deer. *Deer Stone 6* has three large and one small right-ascending deer, an earring, axe, and quiver on one broad face, and three large left-ascending deer and a dagger, knife, two barbed feather-like motifs, and two small animals on the other. Its narrow sides have a necklace with a boar tooth pendant, a rein hook, a barbed motif, and three left-ascending deer on the east face, and two left-ascending deer and a shield on the west face.

Zunii Gol-1 DS 7 graphic and photo; and DS8. (graphics: JB) Deer Stone 7 has a steeply angled top with five left-ascending deer, a mirror, dagger, and rein hook on its north side, and four right-ascending deer, an axe, quiver, and bow on the south side; its narrow east side has five left-ascending deer, and its narrow west face has three left-ascending deer above a shield. The absence of belts, free-floating implements, and rare earrings and necklaces are notable features of these Zunii Gol deer stones. *Deer Stone 8* While working here we uncovered and recorded several buried stones that were not known to Volkov. DS8 had fallen and has broken sides and is missing its top. It has four right-ascending deer on one broad side and two deer on the other side, one ascending left and the other descending right.

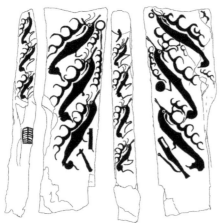

Zunii Gol-1 DS9 graphic, and an un-numbered broken DS base whose top may be below ground nearby. (graphic: JB) Deer Stone 9 has three deer ascending right on one broad side, a pendant earring, an ax, and a quiver on one side. The other side has a small 'moon' ring at the top, three left ascending deer, a mirror, a quiver and bow, and a small horse at upper right. The face side of this stone has a boar's tooth suspended on a necklace groove, a rare motif also found on DS6 and the newly discovered DS10, discussed below.

We began work on Deer Stone Group 3 (second from east) and chose a well-formed 'horse' mound east of Volkov's DS7. We excavated down along the base of a broken-off grey granite deer stone whose top is probably to be found nearby, but found no carvings on its base. Then we began excavating a greenstone deer stone (DS10, see below) whose corner was just showing on the surface. DS10 also was not known to Volkov, and it had very unusual carvings.

Prying Zunii Gol DS10 from its pit and views of its frog and salt-encrusted ibisbill sides.

A young herder grazing his sheep around the site was curious about what we were up to. He had been grazing sheep here for years but had no idea there were pictures on the stones, or even that they were called deer stones. With timber levers we lifted the new deer stone out of the ground and found new and amazing images on the bottom side: at the top, an image of an ibisbill bird with its wings outstretched and a long down-curved bill presiding over Mongolian deer while tigers were confronting cows and pigs.

Zunii Gol-1 Deer Stone 10, the 'frog-ibisbill' stone, showing "narrative-style" Scythian-Saka artistic elements, a significant departure from all other deer stone art; and its ibisbill side. (graphic: JB)

Our understanding of this unusual stone progressed the next morning. The broad side with the ibisbill had a rack of eight pigs on the lower left side. Two pigs and cows occupy the middle of the stone, confronted by two tigers, and presiding over all, the ibisbill with its long down-curved bill and outstretched wings. Five

Mongolian deer ascending left are found at the lower right part of the stone and there is a chevron shield and ax at the bottom. According to deer stone practice, this should be the west-facing side of the stone when erected. On the other broad side, which would have been the east-facing side when erected, three tigers whose claws and teeth are emphasized occupy the center field, over two Mongolian deer, and a bow and a dagger are carved below. At the top, a boar's tusk is suspended on a necklace and above the necklace is the striking image of a frog, an 'imperial' animal in Mongol belief as far back as Genghis Khan's time, and—apparently—honored also in the Bronze Age. Normally this would be the 'face' side of the stone, but here there is no face area indicated in the usual manner by showing backward or forward slash marks (\\, //). One narrow edge of the stone has a circular earring, and below that a toothy beast, a disc/mirror, a quiver, rein hook, and two more quivers. Rather than a traditional 'deer stone,' this monument seems to be telling stories, not just illustrating the static image of an iconic warrior-leader!

The chalky white calcite deposit on the underside easily dissolved in water, but this surface of the stone is soft and flaked off easily and had areas that were illegible due to eroded surfaces and spalling. The diverse subject matter, the excellent carving, absence of some usual motifs like a patterned belt and necklace pits, and presence of a mirror, rein hook, finely made 'floating' tool images and chevron, the unusual use of greenstone, and the roughly shaped block all make DS10 and some others at Zunii Gol distinctive. But this particular stone is of special importance, being so unlike all others we have seen at DSK sites in northern Mongolia. It is a great pity that we were unable, for lack of time, to excavate a larger area around this stone to find an associated dating sample.

Zuni Gol DS7, excavation of a poorly preserved horse cranium but sound mandible and vertebrae. (photos: WF, JB)

Zunii Gol Horse Head and Areal Excavations

In addition to deer stone documentation, we needed to search for dating materials from among the hundreds of small mound features associated with the Zunii Gol deer stones and khirigsuurs. We began with a mound feature associated with DS7.

The next day, June 14, Julia, Barbara, and I began digging a small horse mound, Feature 3, in Area 1, southwest of the northernmost standing deer stone. This feature was surrounded by

a ring of angular blocks, and its center was full of stream cobbles all the way down to the horse head, which we found off-center in the eastern side of the feature. The preservation of the upper part of the skull was poor because it was only 38 cm below the surface; its base was at 50 cm. But the lower portions were fine, and we found six vertebrae touching the skull, with the atlas vertebra between the mandible branches. The four hoofs were all in the correct four corner locations.

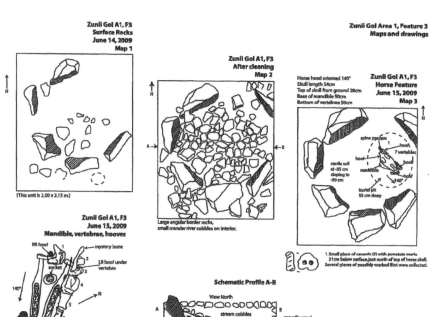

Zunii Gol, Area 1, Feature 3 horse mound excavation with Julia Clark and Barbara Betz; Zunii Gol Area 1, Feature 3 horsehead.

Area 3 During the late afternoon we finished mapping Area 3, including its 105 stone rings around the north, east, and especially the south side of the deer stone area. They were so densely packed, sometimes having less than a meter between them, that they could not all have been used at one time. Also, we found that some—but not many—had been cannibalized, presumably for preparing other hearths. We also found that many stones could not be interpreted as hearths or other features when you get close to the south border of Area 3. All the hearths mapped here are clearly associated with this area of activity. The single burial mound in this area is peculiar in being surrounded by horse head mounds rather than a stone fence. For this reason and the presence of the unusual DS10 found here, Area 3 should receive further archaeological attention since it appears to represent significant culture change in the latter part of the deer stone era. Detailed info on the Area 3 map include: DS7 standing, greenstone, mapped by Volkov; DS8, fallen, on surface, greenstone, excavated by Volkov, notched on both edges in an attempt to break it in half; DS10 (see main text description); DS11: stub of its base showing, dark speckled granite, no markings; DS12: another greenstone stub broken just above ground. Most hearth circles have 9-10 stones.

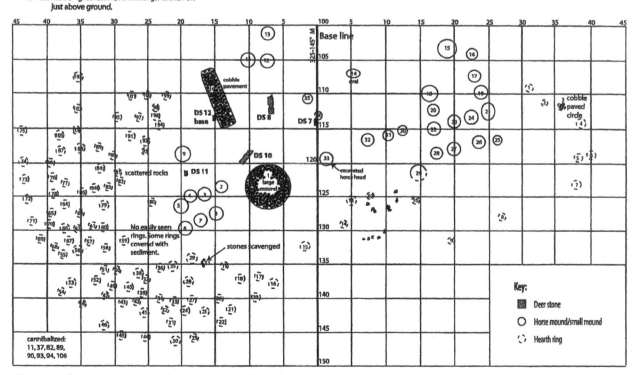

Deer Stones
7. Standing, mapped by Volkov, greenstone
8. Fallen, excavated by Volkov, on surface, greenstone notched on both edges from attempt to break in half.
10. Side Ridge showing in sod, excavated and recorded for first time, greenstone. A most important new discovery.
11. Stub of base showing above ground. No markings. Speckled granite (dark).
12. Possible DS - greenstone, no markings. Broken off just above ground.

Most hearth features have 9-10 stones.
Except in SE sector, all seem to be visible.
In SE, many close to inner area may be buried, and some probably were cannibalized. There is more soil build-up in this area, covering these rocks. Many rocks are visible here, but their patterns were not discernable.

Zunii Gol Area 3
June 13, 2009
Surveyed by William Fitzhugh,
Barbara Betz, and Julia Clark

Zunii Gol Area 3 map (graphic: B. Betz and J. Clark)

Bayaraa spent the day tracing DS1 art and one of the deer stones in Area 2. Good light conditions allowed him to see a belt and a rein hook on DS9. In the evening, members of our crew went off to visit 'the yogurt family' and spent the evening drinking milk tea and watching a reality show on their battery-powered satellite television featuring a well-known Mongolian actor. This family has 600 sheep and goats.

Area 4 Greenstone and grey schist slabs were showing on the surface of Area 4 where we found another fallen deer stone, and fragments were concentrated between 15 cm and the base of the brown silty soil. Below that I encountered a grey flint end-scraper, the only diagnostic artifact present and certainly not associated with the deer stones. The north face of the stone (when properly erected) was worked to a rough but flat surface by pecking and chiseling. Its length is 174 cm, cleavage face is 21-14 cm wide, and the stone has a roughly square-cross-section. We excavated around the stone and reached sterile gravel at 19 cm. Barbara, Julia, and I excavated the stubs of greenstone slabs in Area 4 that seemed like possible deer

stones, but most were not and had served some other purpose; one Julia excavated had small Mongolian deer and axes on it. This piece had been broken off purposefully, and the upper part must be buried near it. We also mapped the horse mounds and general features of Area 4.

Our second horse head—this one from Area 2—and a third, from Area 3, were picked up this afternoon. The Mongolian team began work on one of the four inner fence horse mounds at the big khirigsuur north of Area 1, and after having done all the hard work of pedestaling the Area 2 horse, Bayaraa had the women do the detailed cleaning for photography. I worked on a possible deer stone in Area 4 that turned out to be a preform, a small stone that was roughly finished but not carved.

A Surprise Visit

It started to get cloudier and cold about 7:30, so we returned to camp and found a butchered 70,000 tugrik lamb hanging from the roof of the tent and Tsogoo tending a huge steaming pot of organ meat. The liver and blood sausage came out first, then kidneys, gall bladder, and finally the whole stomach full of cooked blood. Bayaraa served as master of ceremonies and did the cutting and distribution, along with pickles and potatos— the great-tasting yellow Mongolian variety we were always careful to choose from the vegetable lady at

Zunii Gol, Area 4, Feature 1 deer stone construction slabs.

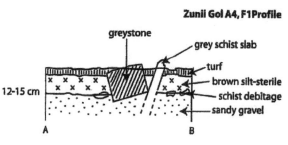

the market in Murun. There was much discussion when we ate the stomach-muscle meat, which is a sandwich of meat, tough tissue, and fat. Mongols say if you eat too much of this and go outside without enough clothes, or you drink cold liquids, the fat and stomach tissue congeal and stop your digestive system and you will die. Fortunately, we did not have the right weather or means to test this theory. Rice soup and yogurt finished the meal, and just as we were almost done an old Jeep came chugging up the hill and six people piled out—a large heavy-set man who looked perfect for a Genghis Khan movie role, his wife, their 5-year old son, another woman, and three young men who were their herding assistants.

Tsogoo's friends from across the valley arrive for breakfast at Zunii Gol; and the next day comes the boy who brings yogurt.

Other than a brief "ah-sain-bain-o" on both sides, no one said anything for several minutes because we were busy eating. But then conversation began, and the silence was replaced with a lively exchange facilitated by candy we had on hand for such occasions. The little boy, after giving his name, launched into a memorized poem or ditty about a little bird, much to his parents' delight. Their dress indicated they were not well-off, and they eagerly took the milk tea and rice Amaraa prepared for them. I asked about the weather and animals, and the father said it was a good winter without deep snow and enough water to make grass this spring. He said there are about twenty families in this part of the valley and the average number of sheep and goats owned by a family was about 500. His family has 400, and some families have 1000. When you have 1000 the government gives you a prize of money. Bayaraa says Chinese and Koreans living in UB are starting to migrate to the countryside, working as assistant herders for others or on their own if they have the money to buy animals and start a flock. As a result, some areas are getting over-grazed, which can be a big problem in a bad year. If you have many animals, a bad year can be a worse disaster than one for owners of a small herd; you are more likely to lose them all because it's more difficult to share hay among a large herd than provide for a small one. (The government stockpiles hay for such disasters and distributes equally to all.) There is no sanction or limits to herd size and available pasture. You can go anywhere you want with your animals in the summer. In winter you are confined to the environs of your winter camp. The kind of care you give the herd and how energetic you are cutting hay for winter is a major factor—other than weather—in herd survival and growth. When some family has a disaster, all give help and animals to get them started again. The 1000-animal owners have a special obligation to give animals away, sometimes hundreds of new-born animals. There was lots of discussion about our guests after they left, as is always the case with surprise visits by those you don't know. They come from the camp directly across the valley from us.

We spent two days mapping the khirigsuur and surrounding rock features in Area 4, as shown below:

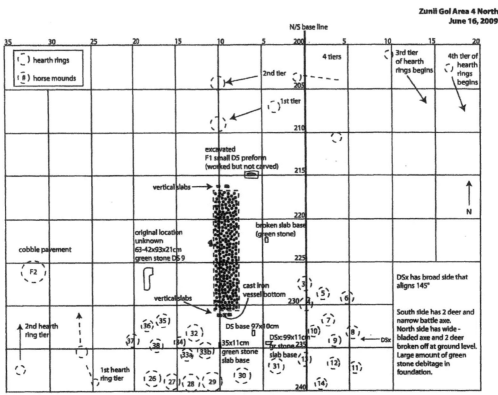

Zunii Gol Area 4 North map. This map joins the two ZG A4 South maps, by matching grid #s.

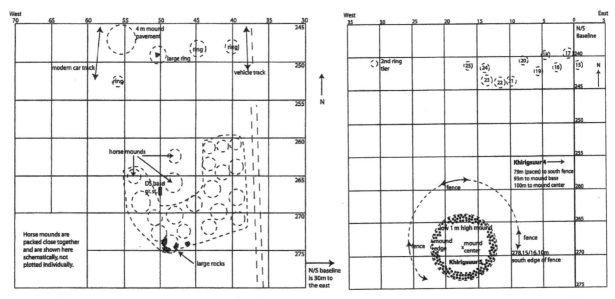

Zunii Gol Area 4 South map, 245-280m south. These two maps join the map above, according to the grid #s.

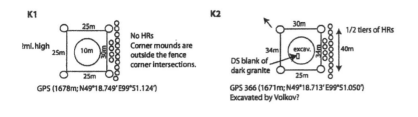

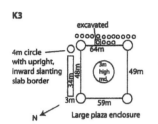

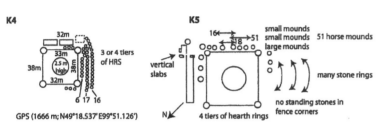

Khirigsuur 3 (Horse mound excavated)

GPS (1696m; N49°18.640' E99°51.302')

Square khirigsuur with corner mounds but without standing stones.
4 east fence horse mounds (northern one excavated).
2nd and 3rd tier of horse mounds on east and south sides.
Rectangular 3m wide pavement with two upright slabs,
marker at east and west ends, outside north fence.
Hearth rings around entire khirigsuur in 2/3 tiers.

Zunii Gol has five large square khirigsuurs in Area 4 (K1-5), one of which, K2, Volkov excavated and is seen in this photo. View west.

Khirigsuur 1 (N49º 18.749', E99º 51.124') is the northernmost khirigsuur at Zunii Gol and is a square monument with a central mound 10 m in diameter and 2 m high. Its corner mounds lie outside the intersection of the fence lines, and the north, west, and south fences are 25 m long, and the east fence is 30 m. Four horse mounds are centered on the east fence with eleven horse mounds in a second row outside these four. No hearth rings are present.

Khirigsuur 2 (N49º18.713', E99º 51.050') is another square khirigsuur, and this one has had its central mound excavated completely, probably by Volkov. Its fence has corner mounds, and its north fence is 30 m, its east fence 40 m, its south fence 25 m, and its west fence 34 m. A dark granite deer stone is lying in the southwestern part of the excavation pit, perhaps

having been part of the khirigsuur. Four horse mounds are centered outside the eastern fence, and a second row of about ten horse mounds lie beyond these. One, and in some places, two tiers of hearth rings surround the khirigsuur.

Khirigsuur 3 (N49º 18.640', E99º 51.302'), the site of one of our horse mound excavations, is a square khirigsuur with corner mounds with no standing stones. The central mound is ca. 3 m high. The east fence is 64 m long, south fence 49 m, west 59 m, and north 48 m. There are four horse mounds outside the mid-point of the east fence, and in the northernmost mound we found a horse head oriented 103º. There is a second and third tier of horse mounds along the east and south fence lines. Parallel with and outside the north fence is a 3 m wide rectangular cobble pavement which has two small upright slabs at the corners of the pavement at its east and west ends. At the east end of the pavement is a 4 m diameter circle of inward-slanting slabs. Hearth rings are found in two or three tiers around the entire circumference of the khirigsuur.

Khirigsuur 4 (N49° 18.537', E99° 51.126') is a square structure with a 2.5 m high central mound and a fence with corner mounds. A 32 m long rectangular pavement with a gap in its center parallels the northern fence. Two vertical slabs mark the east end of the pavement, and east of this is a rectangular structure. The north fence is 33 m long, east 38 m, south 32 m, and west 38 m. Four horse mounds are centered outside the east fence. A second row of horse features has ten mounds; a third row has 17 mounds, and a fourth has 16. Six horse mounds are present along the north fence wall. Hearth rings are present in three or in some cases four tiers around and outside the pavement and horse mounds.

Khirigsuur 5 is another square construction with corner fence mounds, 18 large horse mounds around the north, east, and south sides of the fence, 51 smaller mounds in a second east-side tier, and another tier of 16 mounds. Like the other khirigsuurs, it has a stone pavement marked by upright slabs at its east and west ends, and four tiers of stone hearth surround the outskirts of the mound.

That the rectangular pavement in Area 4 is associated with deer stones suggests deer stones have something to do with death ritual, or at least horse death ritual. Similar pavements are found at two Zunii Gol khirigsuurs. At Khyadag East we excavated a rectangular pavement with butchered animal bones east of the deer stone group, so these slaughter places seem to be associated with deer stones as well as khirigsuurs. Zunii Gol deer stones do not have ornamented belts and only in a few cases have belt grooves. Many deer images have their legs extended, springing but not standing. Tools 'float' unattached as in West Mongolian Sayan-Altai deer stones. The tops of the standing deer stones are broken (lightning strikes? purposeful destruction?), and their missing pieces are probably to be found in the ground nearby. Earrings are sometimes present, but slashes for faces are not. A few necklace lines are present but have no beads. The two southern deer stones in Area 1 are made of dark hornblende-like rock and have irregular shape, and their carving style is reminiscent of the dark bluestones in Area 2 at Khushuugiin Gol.

Zunii Gol turned out to be a fascinating site. The frequent use of a soft schist-like greenstone is unique, as is the art on DS10, which seems likely to be later than art on other deer stones at Zunii Gol or other sites in Central

Zunii Gol Khirigsuur 3 Feature 1 horse head excavation in progress; cleared; and mandible and hoof cores, (photos: WF and JB)

Mongolia. It was therefore with keen anticipation that we awaited the dating results on our Zunii Gol horse heads. As shown below, the calibrated dates for horse heads associated with features in Area 1 and Area 3 are virtually identical, lying in the early part of the DSK chronology, while Khirigsuur 3 Feature 42 is the oldest of the four dates. Therefore, one could argue that the unusual features of Zunii Gol deer stones (absence of neck beads, wide, prominent textured belts with attached weapons, the presence of boar's tusks, 'floating' animals with extended legs, and absence of face slashes, could be a function of greater antiquity than the average Khuvsgul Aimag DSK deer stones. That is certainly the case with DS10, the frog-ibisbill stone for which we have no radiocarbon date.

deer stones (irregular slabs, partially extended legs, lack of ornamented belts, floating tools, lack of beaded necklaces, etc.) may result from regional variation in the DSK culture, rather than being a function of late DSK chronology. The undated Deer Stone 10, however, is certainly the exception, and must fall near the DSK-Square Burial transition as an example of western Pazyryk-Saka influence because its features all trend stylistically in the direction of Pazyryk/Scythian narrative style iconography, far from the classic DSK Mongolian standard and would be expected to date ca. cal. 2700-2500 or later.

Bayaraa found three deer stones across the stream on the other side of the valley with normal earrings along with khirigsuurs. This makes Zunii Gol almost as large a deer stone area as

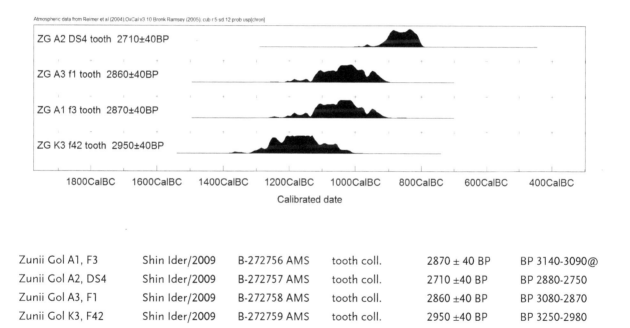

Zunii Gol A1, F3	Shin Ider/2009	B-272756 AMS	tooth coll.	2870 ± 40 BP	BP 3140-3090@
Zunii Gol A2, DS4	Shin Ider/2009	B-272757 AMS	tooth coll.	2710 ±40 BP	BP 2880-2750
Zunii Gol A3, F1	Shin Ider/2009	B-272758 AMS	tooth coll.	2860 ±40 BP	BP 3080-2870
Zunii Gol K3, F42	Shin Ider/2009	B-272759 AMS	tooth coll.	2950 ±40 BP	BP 3250-2980

@ B-272756 Zunii Gol A1, F3 has a second intercept at BP 3090-2870; Radiocarbon dates for Zunii Gol.

However, the dated stones, falling into the center of the DSK chronology, suggest that the 'new' features found in these 'central' Mongolia

Uushigiin Uvör. Just as we were finishing our work, we had a visit from suum center officials who arrived to inspect our papers and progress. This is the first archaeological work in their suum since Volkov's time, and they were very pleased with our results. One of the officials shot video of Bayaraa's tour and the suum Chairman, dressed in a suit and tie.

Visitng suum officials join our team for a photo at Zunii Gol.

Khushuugiin Am

In 2006 we had to have our archaeology permit signed by officials in each of the suum centers where we were working. All science projects, including botany, must have a local research permit. In return we are obliged to provide the officials a project monograph. As we approached Khushuugiin Am we lunched at a roadside "truck stop" having 6-7 tables backed by wide benches that doubled as seats and sleeping platforms, typical for restaurants on main routes where travelers would then lean back and nap at their tables.

That afternoon we visited the Khushuugiin Am site (N48°42.288', E99°53.669') in Galt suum, not far from Bayaraa's home town in Jargalant. Sanjmyatav worked at this site with Volkov and told us that when they arrived, all the deer stones were lying down and partly buried. They dug them out to draw them and erected them where they were found. Volkov's map shows the fallen deer stones giving a good sense of their usual north-south alignment between rows of rock features, horse mounds east of the deer stones and hearth circles to the west

in the same relative positions they are found at khirigsuurs.

We did not map or excavate in 2006, but in 2009 we spent a few days working here and in the vicinity. Today Khushuugiin Am has six large standing deer stones (most re-erected by Volkov), the southernmost at N48°42.237', E99°50.070' and the northernmost at N48°42.308', E99°50.002'. DS3 had been reset upside down. All are large stones with many deer images, some shown in vertical position. Few of the deer stone surfaces are carefully prepared; many have unmodified quarry surfaces,

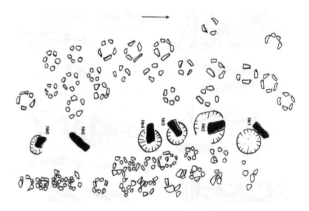

Khushuugiin Am: Volkov's map from 2002:Fig. 85; the site viewed to northwest during our visit with DS1 at far right, running south to DS6 in both images. (photo: H. Beaubien)

and some have spalled since erection, damaging the carvings, most of which are indistinct; even the best preserved are difficult to read. DS1-3 are dark granite, and DS4-6 are light-colored granite. We described the deer stones, excavated a horse head at DS6, prepared a site map, and traced carvings on three of the six stones. As a group they are all made of hard, dense granite and have a similar carving style and an absence of chevrons, necklaces, and other features that are typical of Khuvsgul stones. Their uniformity suggests production within a close-knit social group like a clan. Other deer stone regional styles probably represent social boundaries between clan groups rather than differences in chronology. Source material may also have influenced the form and degree of slab preparation, perhaps accounting for the relatively unfinished, irregularly shaped Galt area stones compared with the finely dressed stones of Murun and Khanuy Valley.

Khushuugiin Am site map with excavation Features 1-3 located. Horse mounds lie east of the deer stones and hearth circles to the west. (graphic: JB)

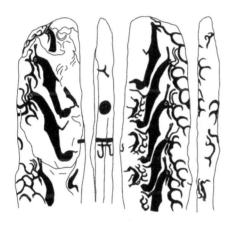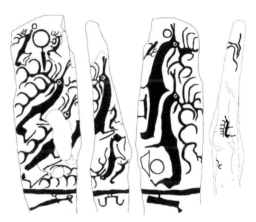

Khushuugiin Am DS1; and DS2 images. (graphics: J. Bayarsaikhan) Deer Stone 1 (JAB 2017: pl. 69) is of dark granite with a split in its wide cross-section, bearing104° measured on the south earring side. There is an earring circle on its south side with three large vertical deer and two small deer ascending left upside-down. There are deer antlers showing on both north and south sides. The east narrow side has a mirror and rein hook. The north (broad) side has five large vertical deer ascending vertical facing left and three small left-facing deer descending between the legs of the larger deer. The narrow west side shows antlers wrapping from the other sides and a tiny right-facing descending deer at the bottom. The top angles up toward the east (face) side. The carving is shallow, and the stone surface is lightly finished with no attempt to make it flat. *Deer Stone 2* is of dark granite, bearing115° measured on the south earring side and 107° on the north earring side. The south (broad) side shows an untextured belt band holding a dagger with an ibex hilt, two large vertical deer, two small deer on either side of a small 'moon' circle and an earring with a long pendant. The west side has one small deer and shows antlers from the north side. The north (broad) side belt has a quiver, bow, mirror, two large left-facing ascending deer, a small deer in upper left, and an earring. The east side has one large right-facing ascending deer at the top, a small descending deer at left bottom, and one small right ascending deer at lower right, and a rein hook on a belt band. The stone has an irregular shape with little finishing and very light carving, perhaps due to the hardness of the granite.

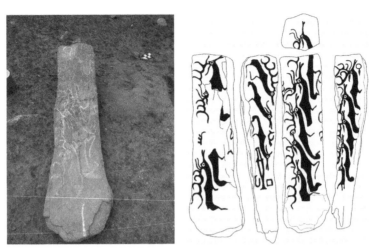

Khushuugiin Am DS3 which we excavated because it had been re-erected upside-down; and its graphic carvings. (graphic: JB) Deer Stone 3 (JAB 2017: pl.71) This stone has a broken top and had been reset upside down, and we re-excavated it to record it and set it up properly. This stone has 17 deer on all four sides. One narrow side shows three left-facing descending deer above a sheathed dagger with a U-hook to its left and a square figure to its right. The other narrow side has five right-facing ascending deer, one of which is a small deer at the bottom, and an earring with a pointed pendant. One broad side shows five right-facing ascending deer. The other broad side shows four right-facing ascending deer; the three upper deer are incomplete due to spalled surfaces.

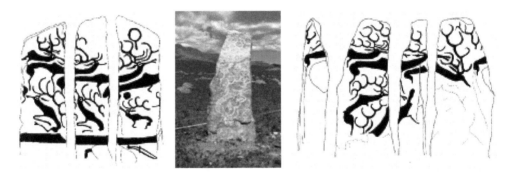

Khushuugiin Am DS4 and DS5. (graphics: JB) Deer Stone 4 is made of white granite with a square cross-section, bearing 048° on the east side and 045° on the west side and has little surface finishing of the original quarry surface. The north side has an 8-9 cm wide belt composed of two light grooves with no internal texture design, and has a suspended bent-handled knife, a horizontal left-facing running deer with a mirror above the antlers, and two right-facing horizontal deer, the upper one showing the head and body mid-section, and an earring with a pendant at the top, which angles up to the east side. The south side has a lower image of a left-ascending deer and an upper image of a right-facing deer head. The east side has a large right-facing deer head, and lower down a left-ascending deer, and a belt band. The west side has no legible carvings. *Deer Stone 5* is made of rough and irregular-shaped pink granite with a rectangular cross-section, bearing 042° on its north side; its other sides are irregular. The north (broad) side has two horizontal right-facing deer above a right ascending deer and a left-descending deer, and no belt or earrings. One narrow side has the neck and rear of two deer at the top. The other (narrow) side has antlers at the top over the rear half of a deer. The south side shows a deer head descending with double antlers and a right-ascending deer rump.

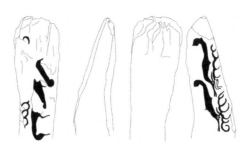

Khushuugiin Am DS6. (graphic: JB) & Khushuugiin Am Feature 1 horse mound in foreground east of DS6, viewed to northwest; F1 excavated, and horse cranium and vertebrae south of skull. (photos: WF and JB) is of hard pink granite, irregular in shape, with little surface preparation, and bears 110° on the south side and 185° on its west side. One side has three right-facing ascending deer, all partially lost to spalling. One other side has two left-facing descending deer; the other two sides are illegible. See JB 2017 or 2022 for DS6 illustration. *Feature 2* is a horse head 4 m east of DS4 where we found the mandible of a small horse oriented 089°. The top of the mandible was 12 cm below surface, the bottom at 21 cm. Max width between ramuses was 12cm; tooth row length (molars) was 16.7cm; max length of mandible was 34cm. The radiocarbon date was cal. 3150-2880 BP, in the middle of the DSK range.

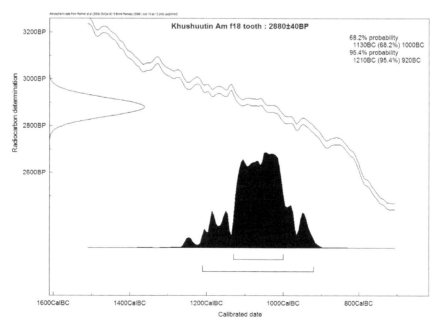

Radiocarbon age on a horse tooth from Feature 18 (F2).

Khushuugiin Am Feature 2 horse mound east of DS3 with DS1,2 in distance, view north-west; and (b) Feature 3 hearth ring west of DS5 that contained charcoal and calcined bone. (photos: WF, JB)

There were a few other features farther north that might have offered the possibility for chronological separation from Features 1 and 2 at the south end of the deer stone line, but those features were not so distinct and had less horse head potential, given our limited time at the site. In addition to excavating and resetting DS3, we excavated Feature 3, a hearth ring northwest of DS5, finding flecks of charcoal but not enough to date, and calcined bones of a small animal, perhaps a marmot, 18-22 cm below the surface. Khushuugiin Am maintained the pattern found in khirigsuurs, having horse mounds lying east of the deer stones and hearth circles to the west.

Galt Surveys

Our brief survey south of Galt in 2007 located a partially buried deer stone 0.5 km north of Khushuugiin Am next to a cluster of rock features east of the road. There was also a Turkic memorial and *balbal* site here. Further north on a terrace at the edge of the river lowland we excavated and drew three partly exposed deer stones arrayed in a northerly line. All were similar to Khushuugiin Am deer stones, being irregular-shaped plinths with large deer images and no fancy belts, face slashes, floating tools, necklaces, or chevrons, and only a few earring circles. We did not have time to search for associated features or make excavations or maps.

Students display an irregular shaped deer stone found on the surface north of Khushuugiin Am deer stone site; and Julia and Barbara take a break at the second DS site north of Khushuugiin Am, south of Galt, where we unearthed three buried deer stones.

Khuurain Bulangiin Tarkhi (Dry Corner)

We found a second deer stone site north of Khushuugiin Am on the south bank of the Ider River at N48º04.343', E99º10.500'. The stones had fallen in place in the usual north-south alignment, and we excavated, recorded, and re-erected them.

Deer Stone 1 has a broken top and irregular bottom and has deer images wrapping around all four sides. Its original south side has two right-facing deer descending with two small deer ascending to the left above and below the larger two, and a dagger at the bottom. The east side shows a deer midsection and a rein hook. The north side shows the head of a deer descending to the right with elaborate double antlers and a mirror, below the second deer midsection, two small deer ascending left at the top of the stone, and a single deer ascending left at the bottom. The west side shows small parts of the wrapped deer. There is no belt, necklace, or earrings.

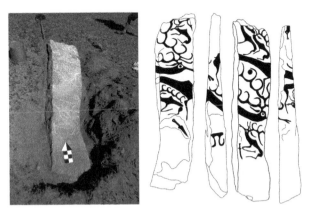

Khuurain Bulangiin Tarkhi DS1. (photo and graphic: JB)

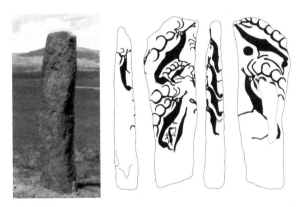

Khuurain Bulangiin Tarkhi DS2, DS3. (photo and graphic: JB)

Deer Stone 2 is too eroded to read many details. One narrow side has a deer hind-quarters above antlers and a right-facing deer midsection above a rein hook. Two earrings with pendants are also visible.

Deer Stone 3 has a broken, angled top. One broad side has two large right-ascending deer, two small deer nestled between the deer's legs, and a large sword-like image at lower right. There are four small ascending deer on one of the longer narrow sides and one deer on the other. Two large left-ascending deer and a mirror are on the other broad side (a large spall obscures the lower deer).

Several passers-by stopped as we were erecting the stones and assisted lifting them. It took about four hours to dig the three stones out, clean them, draw them in sugar, photograph each side, and erect them. At first, the surfaces looked nearly empty of illustrations, but when some forms began to emerge, others took form. Most distinctive are the antlers and parts of the bodies as their shape and position determine where the rest of the form should be. DS2 was too eroded to see anything. The unusual thing about these stones was their close proximity, less than one meter apart, and absence of belts and 'head' area motifs. This and the large-scale art might be called the 'Galt Style,' compared with, say, the Uushigiin Uvör or Murun style. The two sets of deer stones west of Galt at Nukhti-in Am also fit the Galt pattern. I suggested to Bayaraa that he try to find some money to erect signage and information at these sites with pictures of the now correctly shown art. They would be a great addition for local people and for visitors. An initial attempt at such signage was done at Uushigiin Uvör ca. 2008, but the panels were not large enough or weather-proof.

The newly erected deer stones at Khuurain Bulangiin Tarkhi north of Khushuugiin Am, and the site area, both to the northwest.

Khirigsuur Surveys on the West Side of Ider River at Khushuugiin Am

K1 N48º42.000', E99º54.117': Square khirigsuur eroding out of the bank; one horse mound outside the east fence, which is 24 m/200º; north fence 18.5 m/284º; south fence is eroded out at the bank. The center mound is 8 m in diameter, the fence is 32 m diameter, and there are no hearth rings.

K2 N48º42.192', E99º54.03': Circular khirigsuur with 8 horse mounds; 1.5 m high center mound; 12 m fence diameter; hearth rings occur in 2 or 3 tiers around the entire structure.

K3 N48º42.236', E99º51.005': Square khirigsuur with about 12 horse mounds outside east fence and several hearth rings outside west fence; east fence 20 m/010º; south fence 17 m/104º; west fence 17.5 m/191º; north fence 16.5 m/278º; center mound 11 m diameter and 1.2 m high.

K4 N48º42.326', E99º54.060': Small, possibly looted, circular khirigsuur with a scavenged fence; two eastern external horse mounds.

K5 N48º42.321', E99º54.040': Square khirigsuur 1.5 m high; 15 m mound diameter; north fence 241º/24 m; south fence 075º/28 m; east fence 149º/36 m; west fence 147º/31 m; several external features but no obvious horse mounds or hearth rings.

K6 N48º42.270', E99º53.004': Circular khirigsuur with 14 external horse mounds; central mound 1 m high, 12 m diameter; fence is only 2 m beyond the mound base.

K7 N48º 42.387', E99º53.771': Round khirigsuur with mound 1.7 m high, 12.5 m diameter; oriented 078º with a gap between #3, #4 external mounds, of which there are six; three hearth rings on west side; khirigsuur diameter 25 m.

K8 N48º42.422', E99º53.709': Mapped by students. Square khirigsuur 3 m high; 24 exterior mounds along east fence; pathway pavement from mound edge to east fence; four prominent horse mounds in first row, others beyond that tier; mound is 18 m diameter with many internal features; west fence 190º/50.5 m; east fence 009º/49.5 m; north fence 100º/34 m; south fence 099º/41 m; other than four horse mounds, external features look more like large hearth rings.

K9 N48º42.448', E99º53.707': Large round khirigsuur, 3 m high, 17 m diameter mound, 47 m fence diameter; some kind of east side pavement from mound to fence, oriented 105º; fence walls are two rocks wide; no hearth rings; 6-8 external mounds, but they merge and are hard to count.

K11 N48º42. 515', E99º53.070': Square khirigsuur with central mound about 4 m tall; part of east fence missing; about 44 external features (horse mounds or rings, cannot always tell which as large rings are present also); some features at base of mound's east and west sides; four big external mounds in center of east fence; south fence 288º/50 m; north fence 090º/ 46 m; east fence 005º/59 m; west fence 007º/50 m.

Turkic site 1 N48º39.607', E99º51.045': Several kilometers south of our site area we found three standing stones 50-60 cm high. The center stone has a good face, the left one an eroded face, the right stone, nothing.

Turkic site 2 N48º39.492', E99º51.364': One small uncarved standing stone on east side of a 3x2 m slab box; 080º balbal line.

Circular khirigsuur N48º39.872', E99º52.020': 25 horse mounds from the north to southeast side of mound, with four on the west side; there is a circular enclosure inside the fence.

Nukhtiin Am-1

Early in the 2006 season we encountered the Nukhtiin Am khirigsuur and deer stone sites in Galt suum on the plain north of the Ider River. Deer stones were found in three groups: Nukhtiin Am-1 (N48°49.057', E99°47.626') with nine deer stones, several lying flat and associated with a few stone features; Nukhtiin Am-2 with two deer stones; and Nukhtiin Am-3 at the Ider River Bridge. Our second

visit took place in 2009 when our task was to describe, draw, and photograph the images. This took almost four hours because we kept finding new deer stones that had fallen or were broken. The recording system works well now that our Mongolian students are trained in reading the art and drawing it in sugar before photographing each side. It's amazing what can be drawn out from a seemingly blank stone! Of course, most deer stone art is formulaic, and that helps in interpreting the figures. Just as we seemed done, we would discover a new set of finds.

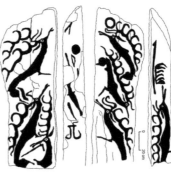

Students 'sugaring' Nukhtiin Am-1 DS1 north side; and DS1 graphic. (photo: WF; graphic: JB) Deer Stone 1 Nukhtiin Am-1 has nine deer stones, most of which are small, fragmented, and had fallen (Bayarsaikhan 2017:pl.58-66). Of the two standing, DS1 has three right-ascending deer on its broad south side, and two left-ascending deer and one right descending deer between the other two on its north side along with an earring circle. Its narrow east side has a rein hook, dagger, mirror, and bow, while its west has a right-facing ascending deer, a chevron emblem, and a spear.

Nukhtiin Am-1 DS2 south side; north side graphic; and DS6. (photo: WF; graphics: JB) Deer Stone 2 has lost a section of its north side. Its broad south side has three left-ascending deer, one right descending deer, and a pendant earring. The north side three left-ascending deer, a right-descending deer second from the bottom, and a mirror, while its west side has an 8-bar chevron shield, three deer, and two small horses. The other stones are too fragmented to reconstruct. Only DS6 has a belt with suspended weapons, in this case an ax and a dagger or sword.

Nukhtiin Am-2

This site at N48°49.150', E99°47.554' has two standing deer stones in north-south alignment. Both have an unusual style of carving, are surrounded by cobble features, and Deer Stone 1 has one side with a 'herd' of horses. Both deer stones are made of the same dark granite, have tops angling up toward the east face, and only DS2 shows a belt. Deer Stone 1 and 2 are 12.5m apart and align 030/210°.

Excavating Nukhtiin Am-2.

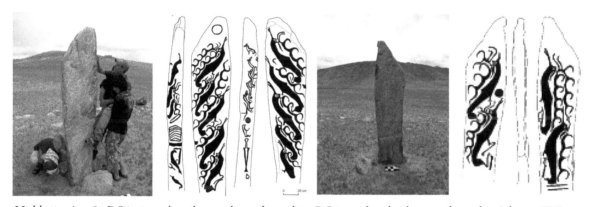

Nukhtiin Am-2. DS1 viewed to the north; and graphic; DS2 north-side photo and graphic (photos: WF; graphics: JB) Deer Stone 1 (JAB 2017:pl.67) This northern stone has a south side with five right-ascending deer and an earring circle at the top. The top deer shows both sets of antlers. The north side has five left-ascending deer. The west side has five small vertical deer facing left, and an oval image above a seven-bar chevron figure, above a belt band and a battle axe. The east (narrow) side shows one left-facing horse above four right-facing horses above a mirror, above a right-facing horse, above a sheathed dagger. Its broad sides are oriented 127/307°. *Deer Stone 2*, the southern stone, has a south side with two large, right-ascending deer with a mirror disc between them, and a bar-like implement (perhaps a club or arrow-straightened) at lower right. The north side has two left-facing ascending deer, a bow at middle left, a dagger or sword at lower left, and a suggestion of a double-grooved belt. Nothing is on the narrow west or east sides. Its south side is oriented at 128/308°.

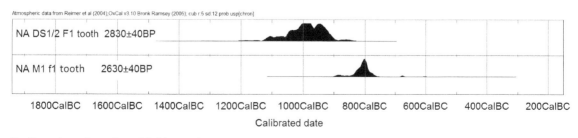

Atmospheric data from Reimer et al (2004);OxCal v3.10 Bronk Ramsey (2005); cub r:5 sd:12 prob usp[chron]										

NA DS1/2 F1 tooth 2830±40BP

NA M1 f1 tooth   2630±40BP

1800CalBC 1600CalBC 1400CalBC 1200CalBC 1000CalBC 800CalBC 600CalBC 400CalBC 200CalBC

Calibrated date

Radiocarbon dates from Nukhtiin Am.

The Nukhtiin Am-2 Feature 1 horse mound produced stone club heads and part of a horse head buried nearly a meter below the surface. Horse mound, Feature 1. One of many similar small mound features surrounding DS1 and 2, Feature 1 was three meters south of DS1 and produced horse remains dating cal. 3050-2850 BP beneath a deposit of rocks and slabs more than a meter deep. This horse feature was different from all others we have excavated because most contain near-surface remains and no artifacts. In addition to the fragmentary, dispersed location of the horse bones, we recovered a doughnut-shaped stone ring and a fragment of a second ring that may have been the heads of clubs used to kill the horse. *Khirigsuur 1.* Fifty meters south of the deer stones is a square khirigsuur with a cobble pavement outside of and parallel to the north fence with an intrusive slab burial at its east end. We mapped this mound and its associated hearth rings and horse head graves. One of the later, Feature 1, located next to the mid-point of the mound's east fence, produced a horse head oriented 120° with a broken mandible, seven vertebrae alongside the south side of the skull, and no hooves. The radiocarbon date of this horse is cal. 2790-2730 BP.

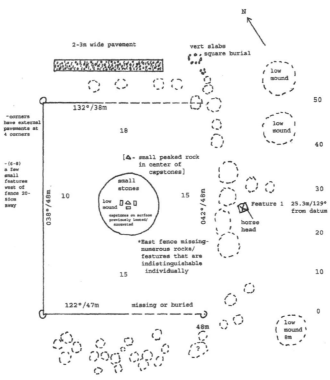

Nukhtiin Am Khirigsuur 1 and surrounding features, including the excavated horse head feature.

Satellite Mound
(C.Leece, Mendee,W.F.)
4 July 2006

N ↑

MAP 1

sr ↑ 2 1

sr

sr

*top rocks not plotted
but were photograohed,
except those shown
here; no pattern to them-
just a tightly-packed
jumble of stones.

sr

1

-sterile gravel
15-20cm below
surface

-upper soil is
sandy silt
with little or
no organic
content

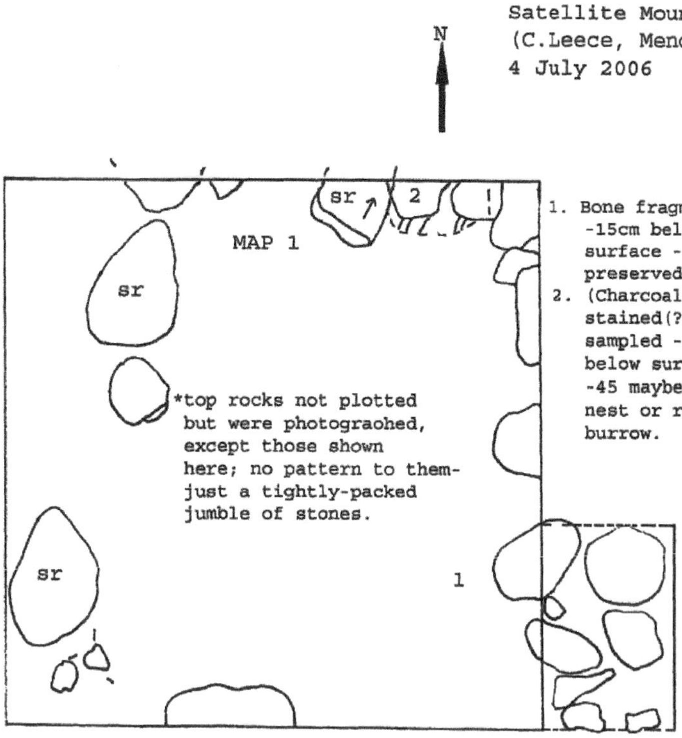

1. Bone fragments
   -15cm below
   surface - poorly
   preserved.
2. (Charcoal?)-
   stained(?) soil,
   sampled -38cm
   below surface to
   -45 maybe an ant
   nest or rodent
   burrow.

*these
rocks are
directly
above the
horsehead

Excavation fine silty sand from surface
to top of rock level. Below rocks fine
sand continued to sterile gravel level
at -30cm to -32cm below surface. Below
5cm of gravel, fine silty sand begins
again. So gravel level is probably
an erosion/lag surface.

Bone was first found in SE corner of
square near the wall, so we expanded
the square 50x75cm and found the front
teeth very poorly preserved because it
was only 10-15cm below the surface.
Cranium mostly just flakes of bone and
even the teeth are not very solid.
Vertebrae line is on south side of skull
with 4-5 verts present in very flaky condition.

MAP 2

120°

verts

-top of
remains 15cm
below surface

-50cm from
maxilla incisors
to end of skull

*Orientation of head
similar to N,S fences
of the Kherigsuur S=122,
N=132. Base of skull is
20cm below surface.

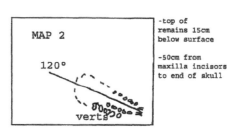

*this is a mystery bone: see photo (two bones, articulated)

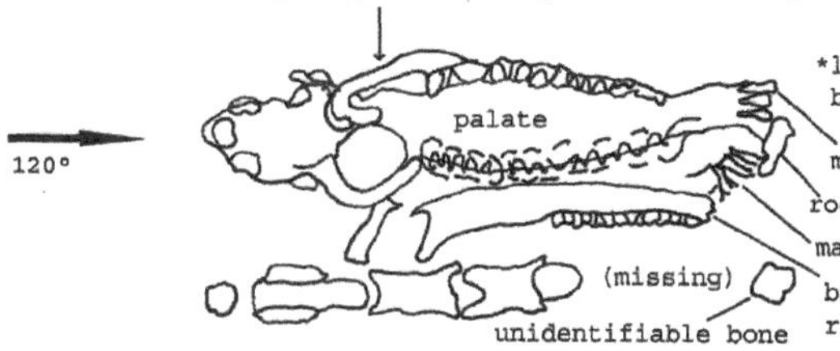

120°

palate

(missing)

unidentifiable bone

*left mandible is
beneath skull

maxillary incisors

rock

mandible incisors

broken distal end
right mandible

*No hooves found

50cm teeth to proximal end of skull

*Nukhtiin Am-1, Khirigsuur 1, Feature 1 horse head excavation:
(a) feature map, and (b) horse head. (graphics: WF and JB)*

Nukhtiin Am-3

(designated Nukhtiin Am-1 in JB 2017)

Our last work in 2009 was to record a set of deer stones at Nukhtiin Am 3, which had one standing stone with art and two lying down. Bayaraa dug one of these out, and it was a large stone which we recorded and erected. Bayarsaikhan grouped these deer stones in the series of Nukhtiin Am stelae in 2017.

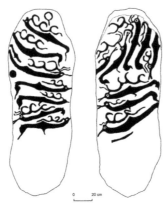

Nukhtiin Am-3 DS7 photo and graphic; and DS8. (photos: WF; graphics JB) Area 1 DS7 (N48o49.949', E99o47.440') is a fallen stone and a fragment near the west Ider River bank in a cluster of boulder features. One small deer stone, DS7, was white granite, lying on its broad side with seven deer facing both left and right on one side, a mirror, and a circle with earring pendant at the top. The other side has three left descending deer on the bottom above a knife-like form and five right-ascending deer at the top. No necklace or belt is shown. *Area 2 DS8* (N48o49.046', E99o47.626') has its top broken off and is made of black and white granite. One broad side has three right-ascending deer. The other broad side has a belt with a sword, below two left-ascending deer. One narrow side has a deer hind-quarters and another deer at the top.

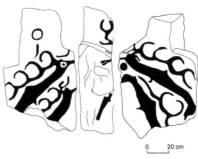

Nukhtiin Am 3, Area 3, DS9. (photo: WF; graphic JB) Area 3 DS9 (N48o49.013', E99o47.400') has one wide, unfinished broken top of a deer stone with a circle and pendant, a large deer ascending right on fine-grained white granite, and a second deer below, head and antlers ascending right. On the narrow side is a sheathed dagger, and on the other broad side are two deer and a mirror. *Area 4* (N48o49.046', E99o47.626') Here we found boulder clusters in a 49 m long north-south alignment, with three deer stones, each in a separate boulder feature. We were unable to document two of the stones lying in the ground but excavated and recorded the third, DS 8 (JAB 2017:pl.65). After we finished recording and were back-filling, a huge thunderstorm approached and we retreated, watching our sugared lines dissolve in the downpour.

Bayaraa's relatives' camp east of Jargalant, a khorkhog feast being prepared and with his grandmother at their Ide River camp. (photos: WF and B. Betz)

As we were back-filling, a huge thunderstorm approached and we retreated to our camp, watching our sugared lines dissolve in the downpour.

A Khorkhog Feast

West of Galt we visited the Banzai family, relatives of Bayarsaikhan, who invited us to camp in their compound and killed a sheep in our honor, to be cooked the old khorkhog way in metal milk container. It was a great night with a new moon, croaking frogs, and calling geese in the 'bayou' behind their house. The next morning preparations for the khorkhog began. The young man, the son of Bayaraa's aunt, saddled their grey stallion and got a bronco ride for about one minute—and did a good job of it. Watching the Banzai family from the sidelines, they seemed to have 1000 things to do to get the day started. In fact, I don't recall seeing anyone having "free" time at all other than the children, except when visitors came by and everyone sat around the ger chatting and drinking milk tea. Bayaraa's cousin was busy heating the rocks for the khorkhog, first in a tin stove he had outside, and then in an open fire with lots of wood, to get them really hot. Then a few were picked out of the fire with tongs and put in the bottom of the milk container with a bit of water. Then in went chunks of mutton on the bone, chopped onions, more hot rocks, more mutton and then lots of potatoes. The mass was already steaming and cooking by the time the lid was secured, with a rag between the can and its top as a kind of relief valve.

I filmed much of this process and then went for a walk along the river, where earlier in the morning one of the boys caught three large fish— one looking like a rainbow trout—destined for fish khuurshuurs. I thought there would be lots of time before the mutton was ready, but when I returned in thirty minutes the can was open and the crowd was already eating, with big, greasy grins! The meal was terrific, and the fat was as tasty as the meat. But perhaps it was the potatoes that were best, slightly charred and stewed in the oil and broth. The latter was the coup de grace, taken from the bottom of the can. Before the mutton was distributed, everyone got a 'hot rock' from the pot to pass around the circle, juggling it from hand to hand to avoid blisters. A khorkhag feast is supposed to promote good health, but one thing it certainly does is provide hospitality and friendship. The Mongolian national holiday, Naadam, was about to begin and we were delighted to see how race-horses were being groomed and beautified—a tradition reaching back to Bronze Age horsemanship and horse ceremony.

Another group of Bayaraa's extended family living east of Jargalant; Bayaraa and a decorated Naadam race-horse, a tradition handed down from at least the Iron Age.

Teeliin Am

Before reaching Jargalant, we veered off to the east up a valley to find Volkov's Teeliin deer stone site (N48° 36.579', E99° 28.087'), which we located just as a storm approached. We were shocked to find its two stones painted in garish colors, surrounded by the type of vertical stone box settings used in Turkic memorial sites. *Balbals* extended eastward from each, many from the southern stone, which was indeed a Turkic stone with a crude face and other carvings, while the northern one was a deer stone with a human face that had been re-used in a Turkic setting. The two granite stones were 1.5 m apart, aligned 243/060°, inside square slab boxes (1.9x1.6 m) with *balbals* extending toward

133°. The south stone was lightly fractured and eroded.

Deer Stone 1 The northern stone was in relatively good condition with deer stone art, a rectangular cross-section and a flat top. Its original north side has a small circle at the top above four right-ascending deer and a belt band. Its narrow east face has two right-facing vertical deer above the belt and a slightly cocked human face at the top. The south side has a large earring at the top, four deer ascending right, above a sword, a vertical deer head, and the belt band. The west side has two right-ascending deer and a horse at the bottom above a five-bar chevron shield. Two *balbals* extend east from this stone. The southern stone, a true Turkic monument with a crudely carved face, faces east and has six *balbals* visible to the east.

The Teeliin Am site, with two stones set in stone boxes, DS1 to the right; DS1 was re-purposed as a 7-8th C. Turkic memorial and recently received garish painting as a tourist attraction; graphic of DS1. (photos: WF; graphic: JB)

Shin Ider: A Family Visit and Town Meeting

The trip in June 2009 took us south through Shin Ider (New River) suum center, and past Zuun Nuur (East Lake). It rained for an hour early in the morning but cleared with a chilly east wind by breakfast time. The team took a while to get organized and packed for travel, but we got on the road about 10, stopping briefly at Tsogoo's friends to pay them for bringing us milk and yogurt for the past few days. Their ger was very neat, and the wife served us milk tea, dried curds, and a soft buttery-creamy cake-like milk substance – ummmm, good! This family is one of the wealthier ones in the valley, having more than 1000 sheep and goats. They were well supplied with home amenities, and the three children were watching a TV powered by a solar panel and satellite dish. Their winter place is nearby, so they can move everything by animals and a cart, the usual one-axel type.

We passed Zuun (East) Nuur, which I remembered from our route through here a couple years ago with its 'valley of many gers'. At Shin Ider suum center we stopped to get our papers signed by the officials. A meeting of four administrators was in progress, causing a delay. Their discussions were over issues relating to private and public land. Some people looked like herders, others like miners, westerners with paunches accompanied by a Mongolian driver in a fancy SUV. Lots of people were waiting in front of the building for the end of the meeting and its outcome. A couple Russian Jeeps belonging to leaders of other suums were parked nearby. The town square has five bronze sculptures on pedestals representing the traditional Mongol economy: camel, horse, yak, sheep, and goat. Around it are shops, an administrative building, a freshly painted Khan Bank, an unfinished two-story timber building, and a restaurant. The usual bunch of old warriors (old men in deels and fedoras) sat on a bench kibitzing outside the entrance of the administration. On the hill rising at the east end of town a Tibetan Buddhist script mantra written with white rocks read 'Om Mani Padme Hum.'

Tsokhiotiin Ovoo

This deer stone site is located southwest of Shin Ider one kilometer farther up the valley from the Duruljiin site. The site name comes from a prominent ovoo on the hillcrest northwest of the site. Volkov recorded the site and its three deer stones, two of which have horse mounds. In addition to two standing stones, there is a third that had fallen and was mostly buried at the southern end of the deer stone settings. Each stone had its group of east-side horse mounds or pavements, and some had hearth rings. As at Duruljiin Am, there is a large khirigsuur. Both Duruljiin and Tsokhiotiin have granite stones that have suffered varying amounts of erosion, some to the point of illegibility. The nearby hills are granite, and near Duruljiin Am there is a hill on the north side of the valley where granite occurs in linear slabs which may have been the quarry for local deer stone rock.

Bayaraa set out a huge meter square grid around the northernmost (and largest) stone, using up our entire supply of string, and Sodoo started mapping it in very cold and windy conditions. Barbara, Julia, and I spent all morning excavating Deer Stone 3, finding it lying with its upper end to the south and its top missing. A charming old herder stopped by while tending his horses. Then, a couple of young herders dropped by on motor bike on their way to town. I suppose we will soon have the suum officials now that our presence is known. What a cold summer this has been so far!

Bayaraa explains our research at Tsokhiotiin Ovoo to Shin Ider suum officials; Tsokhiotiin Ovoo site area with the ovoo on the near shoulder of the hill behind camp; Cold, snowy weather was taking a toll on our summer students!

The Ovoo

At the shoulder of the hill north of the deer stones is Tsokhiotiin Ovoo, the huge ritual stone mound that gives the site its name. Climbing the rocky slope, I encountered horse skulls on rocky outcrops and at the top found the huge ovoo made of sticks propped up in teepee shape 4.5 m tall. The construction had been sculpted by northern and western gales into a windswept configuration and was cupped in on the northwest side. Blue khadags were looped among the sticks, and various offerings had been placed on its eastern side, where most of the khadags were located. A deeply worn path circled the base where pilgrims had walked while intoning ritual chants. Small stones had been piled upon all the rock outcrops within hundreds of

feet of the ovoo. In fact, the whole top of the hill, which is free-standing and not connected to the nearby hills, was covered with small mini-ovoo piles made with small and tiny rocks, as many as could be balanced on any given rock protrusion. Bayaraa says this is the most famous sacred site for the Shin Ider region. In a few days there will be a festival and people will bring new sticks to the ovoo, make or renew the small stone piles, pray and make sacrifices, and afterwards, celebrate with wrestling, racing, and drinking.

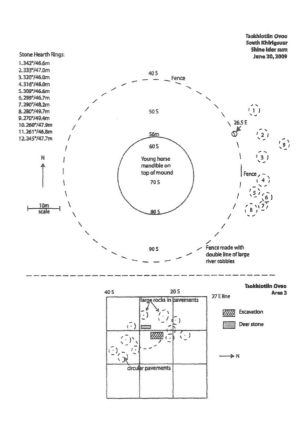

Tsokhiotiin Ovoo site maps. (upper right) The large south khirigsuur mound and fence with probable horse features east of the boulder fence; (lower right) the Area 3 deer stone and excavation trench. Site map (above) with deer stones and stone features. (graphics: B. Betz, J. Clzark, and WF; JB and Sodoo)

Tsokhiotiin Ovoo Deer Stone 1, excavated to reveal images and re-set, and graphic. (photo: WF; graphic: JB) Area 1, Deer Stone 1 is 225 cm long, made of greenstone with dark crystals, is beautifully finished, and has a necklace groove around all four sides. Its features include four large right-ascending deer and a small deer, an earring, and dagger on its original south side; three left-ascending deer, a quiver and a bow on its north side; three left-ascending deer on its east side; and on its west side, one deer ascending right (with doubled antlers) and another ascending left below a 12-chevron shield. Around the entire stone there is a zigzag (/\/\/\/\) ornamented belt. After Bayaraa dug it up to see if there were carvings below ground, we erected it with the chevron shield facing west.

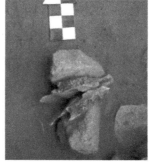

Tsokhiotiin Ovoo DS 1 and horse feature, view north toward the ovoo hill, and (b) a horse mandible supported between two rocks, possibly to keep the head upright. (Photo: W. Fitzhugh, J. Bayarsaikhan) Area 1 Feature 2. The second Area 1 mound produced a partial skull of a young horse oriented an unusual 010°, perhaps resulting from post-deposition disturbance. Only the lower jaw was preserved. This horse produced a date of cal. BP 2980-2790, once again, in the middle range of the DSK date range.

Most of the day was spent finishing the northern horse mound in Area 3, but it had a disappointing result–a sterile bottom. We could not even be sure it was a feature. As a result, we extended the excavation 150 cm south, but without result. The Mongolian team's first mound came up empty, like ours, so they started another. Digging conditions were terrible—windy and cold, and it snowed during our mid-day dinner.

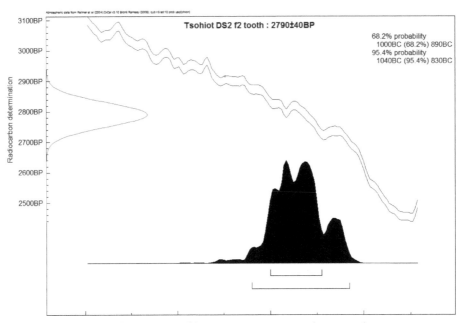

Radiocarbon date from Tsokhiotiin Ovoo DS2 F2 horse tooth.

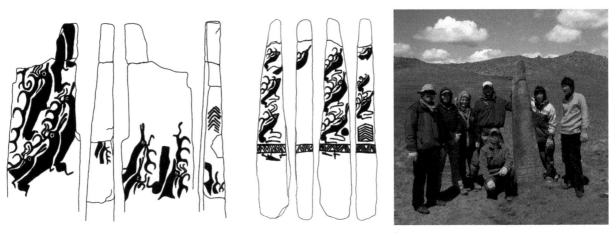

Tsokhiotiin Ovoo DS2, and DS3, excavated and reset. (graphics: JB, photo: WF)

Area 2, Deer Stone 2. I excavated below ground around this 145 cm high, badly fragmented, standing stone to reveal its buried carvings, finding a partly finished deer and a belt. Several pieces broken from the top of this stone were located nearby, some with the missing parts of deer images. One broad side has six right-ascending deer while the other side has four fragmented left-ascending deer. The original west side has a 9-bar chevron. No belt or necklace is present. *Area 3 Deer Stone 3* (N48°53.353', E99°18.740') Barbara, Julia, and I excavated this fallen stone, finding it lying with its upper end to the south and its top missing. This stone has a triple-lined zigzag /\/\/\/\ belt band with a suspended dagger, ax, and other tools, three right-ascending deer on the dagger side, and three right-ascending deer and a mirror on the other broad side. Despite the complex belt, earring circles and a necklace are absent. The west side has a seven-bar chevron.

Tsokhiotiin Ovoo produced a new deer stone find and a horse head date. Most of the deer stone art has gorgeous lines, more similar to Uushigiin Uvör than Zunii Gol. However, here we have no pitted necklaces–only lines, and no slashes for faces. There are belts with tools and weapons, and chevrons are found on all three stones. Bayaraa and the students climbed to the ovoo to take pictures of the valley. One wonders about all the ritual donations that have been contributed to this ovoo over many years and what archaeological treasure it will produce some day—although it's long use chronology will prove daunting to unravel. This ovoo reminds me of the Saami, and Russian Nenets and Iron Age sacred caches that also accumulate ritual donations over long periods of time.

A Freezing Summer

Last night after supper I walked to the large winter herder's camp at the head of the valley. It was one of the largest I've seen, with three or four sheep byres and several storage sheds. Storms were continuing to blow in from the north. The wind shifted today from northwest to north, and when I got to my tent, snow that fell during supper was still frozen on the fabric. This morning I unzipped the door and looked out to a white landscape, the wind still strong–not a howling gale or a blizzard, to be sure, but a very COLD wind, and while grass was showing, everything had a cast of white, except the clouds, which were dark grey separated by deceptively blue patches between the scattered, streaking clouds. To the north, another deep grey band was approaching. Mongolians are very surprised to see this kind of weather in mid-June. While the pasture lowlands are clear, even the lower parts of the hills now have snow, and their tops are all white. Yesterday the plateau north of Shin Ider was solidly blanketed. I hope some of our students have enough clothing. The Americans are

okay by sharing stuff, and Bayaraa has been wearing his father's quilted deel for the past two days. This morning I noticed the horse that had been alternately lying and browsing near our dig was still there, on its feet. There's no water around here and we suspect it's not well–it's not a good time to be sick. The idea of large animals surviving on hay stalks sticking through the snow all winter out in the storms and gales at -40 to -50 below is nothing short of miraculous.

A 'norther' swept in bringing snow, wind, and rain, and bemused faces. (photos: B. Betz)

Duruljiin Am

This site, a kilometer closer to Shin Ider than Tsokhiotiin, has six deer stones, only one of which was large and well-carved. The others were smaller, some having face slashes and belts, and deer and mirrors. The settings were poor and damaged by marmots and by humans who enclosed the good stones in a square border. A stone-robbed khirigsuur sat in the middle of the stone placements. We hoped to find a horse mound to date one of the deer stones because of its unusual moose-like carvings. The antlers on this moose-like cervid are more upright and the legs extended, a feature Volkov identified as a 'late' deer stone style. Much of the site has been disturbed, initially by Volkov, but more recently by local people who erected fallen deer stones, perhaps not in their original places.

We set to work around the big khirigsuur with its round fence and its four deer stones and excavated two rock features near the deer stones on the east side of the khirigsuur fence. Both features were empty, and a passing herder told us that they had been disturbed by a local student who also reset two of the small deer stones, facing the wrong way, we noted. DS2—the largest and illustrated by Volkov—has a hat, headband, or hair-do and moose-like 'deer' with more upright antlers and drooping "moose" noses. These images have the same peaked withers of the Mongolian deer, but their legs are straight, and they have 'moose' faces and snouts rather than bird heads and beaks. DS1 has more deer-like animals and a pig and is set properly. DS3 and DS4 are simple stones with only necklaces and belt grooves and earrings. The other unusual feature of these deer stones is that they are set as part of the khirigsuur plan, placed just outside the fence along with associated rock features that may be horse mounds. This pattern—unusual in central Mongolia (although fore-shadowed at Zunii Gol Area 3)—resembles the Altai use of deer stones as part of khirigsuur structures. We also excavated the small Feature 9, a 2 m diameter cobble pavement at the northeast edge of the khirigsuur that included a parallel-sided slab feature–a 15 cm wide trough made of vertical stones running northwest,

but nothing was found. Extensive disturbance makes Duruljiin difficult to interpret and compare with other sites.

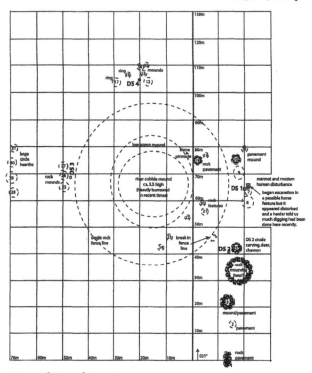

Map of Duruljiin site.

Duruljiin Am khirigsuur and DS 2, and DS1, with DS2 in the distance. (see Bayarsaikhan 2017: Pl. 168, 167 Views north.)

Duruljiin Am Deer Stones. (a, b) DS1; (c, d) DS2. (photos WF; graphics JB)

Deer Stone 1 (N48°54.968', E99°20.929') is white granite with a square cross-section and is found 8 m outside the fence on the southeast side of the khirigsuur. Its south side elements include a spiral earring with a pit at its center, a belt groove with a sword and ax, and three right-facing animals: a running deer with upright moose antlers and a standing deer with moose antlers, above and below a boar. The north side has an earring with a center pit and pendant, a necklace line, a belt groove with a hanging tool, and a leaping Mongolian deer above a boar on its mid-section. The east side face area has pits for eyes, a line for a mouth, and two \\ slashes (perhaps a clue that slashes on deer stones are tattoos?) on the left cheek, a necklace and belt groove with a rein hook. The west side has a pentagonal shield with seven chevron stripes beneath a deer with moose antlers. Three of the four deer have upright deer/moose antlers and are shown running, while the fourth is a standard Mongolian deer. *Deer Stone 2* (N48°54. 981', E99°20.941') is 5 m outside the fence on the east side of the central mound and is presently set facing south. The original south side has a broad head band groove above a pendant earring, a section of 30 necklace pits, five left-facing deer, and a belt groove with a hanging sword. The original east side has two slashes (\\) for a face under the head band, and a chariot rein hook on the belt. This surface is too eroded to see animals. The north side has an earring, a head band groove, necklace pits, and five moose-like deer facing left with extended legs. The west side is eroded but has the headband, necklace pits, and at least one animal with extended legs. Like the iconic Mongolian deer images, the mouths of these 'moose' are open in calling mode but are seen here as having proper moose snouts, not bird beaks. All of these animals stand with straight rather than folded legs, and the upper animal on the north side appears to be running.

Feature 8, one meter northeast of DS2, appeared to be a horse mound. Excavation produced two samples that returned dates of cal. 550-500 BP (sample F8a, charcoal) and cal. 630-600, 560-510 BP (sample F8b, bone). Both dates probably relate to later ritual events or disturbances.

Feature 18 is a small circular mound inside the khirigsuur fence that looked like a horse feature but contained no horse bones and had an unusual parallel set of vertical slabs set into the southwest side of the mound. No cultural finds were recovered.

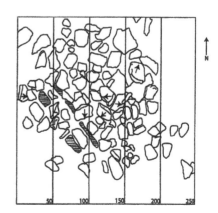

Duruljiin Am Feature 18 with parallel slab insets.

Duruljiin Am DS3; DS4 with DS2 in the distance and the khirigsuur to the right; and DS4. (photo: WF; graphics JB) Deer Stone 3 is granite, small and irregular in shape, set a meter outside the fence on the west side of the central mound, and has three face slashes (\\\) on the east side, a top angling away from the face, a belt groove, and earrings with pendants, but no necklace. *Deer Stone 4* is 10 m outside the fence on the north side of the central mound and is similar to DS3, being irregular and thin and lacking animals and tools, but has two face slashes (\\), pendant earrings, a necklace, a belt groove, and is set improperly facing west. Bayaraa reset this stone facing east.

Volkov initiated the idea that deer figures with legs extended was a later stylistic feature than the iconic Mongolian deer with its legs folded beneath the body as seen widely at northern Mongolian deer stone sites. At Duruljiin and other sites sometimes these figures represent moose rather than deer. The extended leg motif is rare in central Mongolia but is more common in the Mongolian and Russian Altai where this and the depiction of animals and tools 'floating' in the composition is also common, as is the replacement with the MD image by a normal stag or moose/elk usually shown with upright antlers. For this reason, we had hoped to be able to date the Duruljiin 'moose stone' but did not find a suitable sample. Nevertheless, this site exhibits a number of "Altaian" features, including deer stones set within khirigsuur architecture, something rarely found in the central Mongolian DSK heartland. The replacement of the deer stag with a moose must indicate a shift in the identification of the deer goddess concept toward the latter phase of the DSK era, when horses also begin to find

'deer stone' expression.

A large number of khirigsuurs (N48°55.450', E99°21.723') mostly having square fences with standing corner stones, are located around the east and southeast side of the hill north of the Duruljiin deer stone site. As seen at other sites, their fence baselines follow the basal contour of the hill rather than aligning to a fixed azimuth. Two Turkic memorial sites are also present here: Turkic Memorial 1 N48°54.493', E99°20.747'; and Turkic Memorial 2 N48°54.861', E99°20.692'.

Duruljiin Am Turkic Memorial Site-2 khirigsuurs on the southeast slope of the hill north of the DS site.

Urd Khurain

While returning to Ulaanbaatar from Galt on the Millennium Highway, we found a round khirigsuur with a 30 m diameter central mound and a 52 m diameter fence that had been cannibalized for road construction (N48°04.343', E99°10.500'). A single white granite deer stone with a square cross-section and north and south faces oriented 110° and 125° was located three meters outside the east side fence along with 11 or 12 horse mounds. Its west side has a brow band, eight necklace pits, two vertical felines side-by-side with feet to the west, above a moose facing left above a belt groove. The north side has a brow band, a circle groove, seven pits angling down to the left over a horizontal pig facing left, above a belt with a knife and a rectangular whetstone. The east side has a brow band at the top, two slashes \\ above seven necklace pits, above a right-facing ibex (or horse?) crossing onto the north side, above a moose, above a belt groove carrying a double rein hook. The south side has a brow band above a circle groove above six necklace pits, and a belt groove at the bottom with a small sword and an ax. The floating animals are more like the Sayan-Altai deer stone type that we have been trying—not very successfully—to date, and the brow band and standing animals (including deer/moose with upright antlers) resemble the Duruljiin DS1 carvings. There are horse mounds here, but our permit did not allow us to excavate in Arkhangai Aimag, the location of this site.

Ikh Tamir

Near Ikh Tamir, we passed a deer stone standing in the middle of a looted square/slab burial at N47°51.160', E100°45.243'. The deer

The Urd Khurain khirigsuur, cannibalized for road construction, view west; Urd Khurain DS, view south.

stone must have been found when the square burial was dug and was erected after that, 10 m west of a round khirigsuur and bearing 210° from the center of the mound. The broad face of the deer stone orients 008°. The central khirigsuur mound is 11 m in diameter and has a 26 m fence radius. There are ca. 27 external mounds around the east half of the fence, some double tiered, and ca. 22 hearth rings around the west half of the fence. A six-meter diameter rock mound lies ca. 120° from mound center and 14 m southeast of the khirigsuur fence. There is a circular enclosure on the northeast side of the khirigsuur mound.

The west (broad) side of DS1 has a circle groove above four deer ascending to the left, above one deer descending right. There is a second circle (or mirror) groove between the heads of the second and third deer, and then a belt band and a quiver in the lower left between fourth ascending and fifth descending deer. On the north (narrow) side, there is only a belt. The east (broad) side has a circle groove at top over four deer descending right. One 'loose' unconnected antler is seen at top left and an axe above belt band at right. The south (narrow) side has an 11-bar chevron shield above the belt band.

DS1 re-erected from a square burial in the Ikh Tamir region. No drawings were made. (scan: HB et al.;photos: JB)

We found another deer stone at the suum Forest Service Building in Ikh Tamir at N47°51.160', E100°45.243' where it had been moved into town from a site unknown to us in the countryside. It is made of white granite, has many deer images, and a single face slash on its east side. A Turkic figure had also been collected and was erected alongside the deer stone.

Deer Stone and Turkic figure re-set in Ikh Tamir town square near the suum forest service building. There can be little doubt that deer stones were the inspiration for Turkic statuary 2,000 years later.

Tsatsiin Ereg 1, 2, 3

Entering the fertile Ikh Tamir valley, we reached another Volkov deer stone site, Tsatsiin Ereg (N47°45.189', E101°22.230') located in the north side of the valley (Volkov 2002:35, pl 8-12). The large site has been a long-term research target of a team from the Mongolian Institute of Archaeology and the Monaco Museum of History. My notes from our 2009 visit are sketchy because we did not collect data since the site was being researched by Jérôme Magail and his colleagues (Magail 2008; Esin et al. 2014, Magail 2015; Zazzo et al. 2019). Volkov's pits were still open, and some of the deer stones Volkov erected were installed in the wrong orientation.

had a well-defined fence, and beyond that, they estimated ca. 975 external horse mounds—all of which were being mapped. They would also excavate a few horse mounds from the inner and farthest tiers beyond the fence to test our previous ideas about the chronology of khirigsuur ceremonialism suggested by our dates from Urt Bulagiin. The meeting acquainted me for the first time with Magail and his team. We talked about his plans for the khirigsuur study, including ethnoarchaeology, to see what the effect would be of taking 1000 horses out of circulation for a 'single event' burial ceremony. Of course, it would be devastating on a small area, but my idea was that large khirigsuur ceremonies were macro-regional events. We had an interesting discussion and agreed to share publications and data. Our chance meeting was

Volkov's Tsatsiin Ereg-1 DS site east of Ikh Tamir, and our 2009 team meets Jérôme Magail's team from the Monoco Museum of History near one of the horse mounds excavated at the B40 khirigsuur.

Magail's team had just arrived to begin work on the area's Bronze Age sites, especially on its khirigsuurs. Together our combined teams visited the large square B40 khirigsuur they were mapping and whose horse heads they were beginning to excavate (Magail 2008; Zazzo et al. 2019). The mound was around four meters tall,

opportune; Magail has good ideas about deer stones and he and his students have written important reports on Tsatsiin Ereg and other sites, even though they have taken issue with some of my ideas about khirigsuur and deer stone ceremonialism as intense short-term events.

During our brief reconnaissance we noted

three groups of deer stones but did not have time to map and document them carefully. Group 1 at N47°45.189', E101°22,230' has seven deer stones. (See Volkov for more data than we could gather. n.b.: Our numbers do not correspond to Volkov's as we did not have his publication in the field.) DS1 was a 'Galt type' stone with the south side showing a dagger and nine ibex, and on the north side an ax and deer images. DS2 has a pendant circle, a necklace groove above a right ascending deer, and a belt and quiver. Its east side was obscured in shadow during our visit. The north side has a circle without a pendant, a necklace, five deer, a belt, ax, and sharpening stone. The west side was too brightly sun-struck for us to read. DS3 is a tall stone with its south side showing five vertical deer, a circle groove, and a pitted necklace. The east side face area is highly polished, suggesting it once had a painted face. DS4 is a short stone with circles, necklace pits, and a belt band. DS5 was too eroded to read. DS6 is an irregular stone with several deer and an 8-bar chevron. DS7 was found in Volkov's open excavation pit and has two grooves running straight up the DS and several Mongolian deer and a horse.

Leaving the khirisuur area, we found two groups of deer stones along the road at the east end of the site. The first, Tsatsiin Ereg-2 is at N47°45.509'/E101°20.205' and has six deer stones, two of which were lying down in a cluster at the south side of the road. Probably they had been gathered together here from their original settings, perhaps by Volkov. Time did not permit us to document this group.

Tsatsiin Ereg Deer Stone Group 3, and Volkov's massive DS3 found in the center of (a).

Tsatsiin Ereg-1, Deer Stone 2, and (b) DS3, which probably had a painted face. DS7 lies in the open Volkov excavation pit to the right.

Tsatsiin Ereg-3 (47°45.625', E101°20.205') lies north of the road and uphill from Tsatsiin Ereg-2. The site has seven deer stones, three of which are lying on the surface, including a massive, irregular deer stone (Volkov's DS3) with double V-shaped necklace lines with a boar's tusk hanging from it, above three right-descending deer on one side and four deer ascending left on the opposite side. One of its narrow sides has a mirror. The carvings extend close to the base, leaving little ground foundation support for the heavy top portion; no wonder it had fallen on its side! This stone has been illustrated by Volkov 2002: pl.8.3 and by J. Magail (2008, 2015).

Shuvuutiin Am

When we visited this site (N49°58.373',
E99°56.521') in Alag-Erdene suum in late June,
2009, we found it in a farm field enclosed by
a ditch and dirt wall to keep cars and animals
from entering and damaging the crops, which
were just sprouting during our visit. We received permission to inspect the site from the
farm boss. Volkov (2002:27-32) worked here
and noted 31 deer stones, most of which had
been taken from their original settings for use in
square burials. Of all the deer stones, only two
were standing, and they were probably not in
their original settings. We spent one day gathering data on several of the most outstanding
deer stones and making a general map of site
features.

*The operator of the agricultural project on
which the Shuvuutiin Am site is located gave
us permission to document deer stones; The
new face of Mongolia rural economy in the
better-watered valley bottoms.*

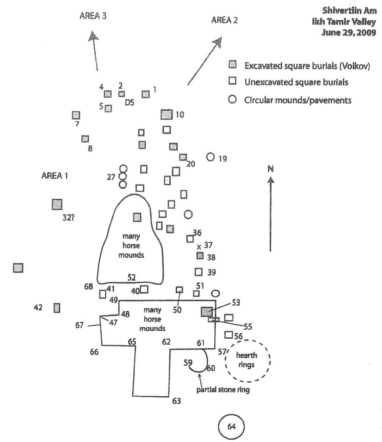

*Sketch map of features
at Shuvuutiin Am.*

Shuvuutiin Am Feature 1 DS original south and north sides, re-erected at the north end of a square burial.
Feature 1 Deer Stone is presently in a square burial, mounted incorrectly, facing north. Volkov drew this stone with a sharply angled top and recorded it as DS24. Its current west (broad) side (originally north) has a large circle with a small 'moon' circle to its right at the top, seven necklace pits, and one double-antlered deer ascending left with a mirror disc between its legs, above a single-antlered deer above a third single-antlered deer head, all ascending left. These figures are above a wide belt band above two left-ascending deer with a sheathed dagger between them. The south (original west) side has four pits over two ascending deer above a complex chevron shield (see illustration, pg. 111), above a right-ascending deer, above a broad belt band, above another right-ascending deer. The east (original south) side top has a large circle with a small circle to its left above 17 necklace pits, above nine deer ascending right above a belt band with a quiver and ax above two horizontal right-facing deer. The north (original east) side has six necklace pits, three deer ascending left above a belt band with a knife, above one left-facing deer.

Shuvuutiin Am Feature 2 DS original south side; original east side with polished face area, presumably once having carried the painted face of its human namesake; Mongolian students tracing Feature 2 art on a plastic sheet. *Feature 2 Deer Stone* also stands in a square burial, has exceptional carving, and has been re-set incorrectly. A large tusk or fang hangs from a necklace groove on the face side. The original north and south sides have earring circle grooves with pendants. The original south side has a partially erased earring circle pendant above nine necklace pits above six right-ascending deer. The original east side has a highly polished (originally painted?) surface at the top where the face would be, above a pitted necklace (indistinct) above four right-ascending deer, above a mirror disc, above another deer with a polished (painted?) surface. The original west (narrow) side has an earring circle groove with pendant above seven pits, above three right-ascending deer, above a belt band, above a right-facing deer with a polished surface.

A Shuvuutiin Am looted Square Burial. At the close of the DSK period about 2600 BP its deer stones, khirigsuurs, and associated boulder features became sources for stone used in building burials and monuments by the Square/Slab Burial culture. One of the few possibly undisturbed square burials at Shuvuutiin Am with some of the hundreds of unexcavated (or looted) features at this site. Mechanized agriculture may soon destroy most of these sites in areas of arable land unless climate warming makes agriculture (once again) untenable in Mongolia.

These are amazing stones, very large and carved with artistic flair. Bayaraa and our students worked on the Feature 2 stone in a square burial that contained six cannibalized deer stones. They also documented the deer stone group in the satellite site in the crop field a couple of hundred meters to the north of Feature 2. Barbara, Julia, and I made a GIS map of the square burials and outlined the deer stone horse mound features which were concentrated in the western and southern area of the main complex. There might be 400-500 small mounds present, with hearth rings south and west of the mounds. The square burials are mostly in the northern and eastern part of the site. We recorded seventy features, at least 50 being square burials.

Following our visit to Shuvuutiin Am the team visited the excavation of a Khitan chiefly burial complex being excavated by the Mongolian National Museum archaeologist, Odbaatar, with Chinese partners. This was excavation at a grand scale—not quite King Tut style, but still very different from our survey work focused on recording deer stones and obtaining dating materials from khirigsuur and deer stone features.

Enroute to UB we stopped for a day to visit Kharkhorum, the imperial city of Chinggis

A chiefly Khitan burial complex being excavated by Ts. Odbaatar and Chinese partners.

Khan's and later khans, which had been under investigation by the German Archaeological Institute for the past decade. The German work concentrated on mapping and excavating the mercantile quarter outside the walls of the Erdenne Zoo monastery that was established soon after the collapse of the Mongol empire. Since the initial investigations by 19th century Russian archaeologists searching for the palace of the khans, most assume that the palace remains lie inside the monastery's walls, directly underneath Erdene Zoo itself. The Japanese financed a wonderful exhibit facility near the public entrance to the monastery, which remains ecclesiastically active today.

A restored stupa at Erdene Zuu Buddhist Monastery in Kharkhorin, the former capital of the Mongol Empire. Turtle sculpture from the time of the Mongol Empire on the high ovoo hill south of Erdene Zuu, one of two described to have rested at the entrances of the imperial city.

2009 Project Summary

En route to Murun we spent a day excavating at the Badrakhin Ovoo deer stone site. Its three small deer stones were poorly carved and lack horse burial features. This region has serious water problems during the summer, and the absence of a flourishing deer stone culture and horse sacrifices may be related to its poor ecology. South of Murun we proceeded to Zunii Gol, a large deer stone site documented by Volkov. Although not as large as Uushigiin Uvör, it is a fascinating site with several large khiriguurs flanking a series of three parallel sets of north-south deer stone alignments. Most stones have large numbers of satellite stone features as well as cobble pavements and other features. These deer stones were made of a chalky greenish stone rather than the usual granite, and they also lacked textured belts, had few belt grooves or beaded necklaces, and few face slashes; their animals were shown with legs more extended than folded, and images of tools were frequently floating in the central panel rather than suspended from a warrior's belt. Strangely, many of the deer stones had been smashed or damaged, apparently purposefully, and we found many small deer stones broken off at the base. Using plastic sheeting, we traced the designs of several of the most important deer stones.

Most surprising was a Zunii Gol deer stone we found almost completely buried below the soil in the third cluster of deer stones. Upon excavation, we found this stone had remarkable carvings of tigers attacking pigs in the central part of the stone usually reserved for iconic Mongolian deer image. At the top of the stone was a frontal view of a large ibis-like bird with outstretched wings. The other side of the stone had a frog in this upper position, a location usually occupied by slashes representing a human face. Horses, cow-like creatures, small carvings of MD, and shield emblems were also present. This stone is unlike any other known in northern Mongolia. Its organization and subject matter are strongly reminiscent of Sayan-Altai stones, while its semi-narrative style involving predatory animal encounters are elements more common in Scythian art than Mongolian deer stone art.

A short distance farther south brought us to Tsokhiotiin Ovoo near the town of Shin Ider, where we excavated new deer stones, traced artwork, and obtained datable horse remains. The nearby site of Duruljiin Am presented us with another unusual deer stone—instead of the iconic MD we found a series of moose-like cervids with broad palmate antlers, drooping muzzles, and extended legs. We suspected this type of stone is later than the classic northern Mongolian deer stones and hoped (in vain, as it happened) that bone samples excavated from a rock mound next to the stone would provide a secure date. Reaching Galt, near the confluence of three major rivers, we spent several days mapping, tracing, and excavating horse features at Khushuugiin Am, the largest and most prominent deer stone site in this region. Here we obtained three horse samples that helped define the chronology of the 'Galt DS type'—use of irregular-shaped stones with unfinished surfaces, usually carved with large upright MD and often lacking face slashes, necklaces, and belt motifs, and tools tend to float unattached. After several days we crossed the Ider Gol and discovered several new deer stone sites at Nukhtiin Am with 2-6 stones in each site, all following the Galt pattern and all toppled and partly buried. This area has a higher concentration of deer stone sites than any other region we've seen in northern Mongolia.

During the next few days we visited sites near Jargalant and made our way south to the central Mongolian valley, documenting small sites along the way. The largest were Tsatsiin Ereg and Shuvuutiin Am, a huge site whose deer stones had mostly been cannibalized to make retaining walls for square burials. Both sites were mapped and drawn by Volkov, and our time allowed only for selective tracing and mapping, without excavation. At Tsatsiin Ereg we met archaeologists from the Mongolian Institute of Archaeology working with Jérôme Magail of the Monaco Museum of Prehistory, mapping and excavating horse burials to test our khirigsuur site formation theory that the horse sacrifices at these sites were single ceremonial events, or at least ones of rapid accumulation, rather than being renewal rituals taking place over decades or centuries. The deer stones in these huge sites are remarkable works of art, but most have never been documented because they have been re-used in antiquity as components of square burials and are inaccessible without excavation. One of the remarkable features of the general area is the relative scarcity of khirigsuurs. Some large ones are present, but the quantity is much reduced from the Khövsgöl-Arkhanghai region to the east. Here khirigsuur burial seems to have been reserved for the powerful leaders, unlike the pattern in Khuvsgul Aimag where medium and small khirigsuurs occur in legions, often in clusters, everywhere across the landscape.

We arrived back in Murun facing the huge task of compiling our data from nine field seasons, two of which included short exploratory forays into the Bayan Ulgii region of the Mongolian Altai. There we explored the western connections of the deer stone culture and its links to Central and Western Pazyryk and Scythian-Saka cultures. In the years that followed—2011-2012 we researched those regions intensively seeking clues to both the origins and relationships of DSK culture as well as the links between archaeology and the spectacular expression of rock art known in the Altai as a result of research by Esther Jacobson and Richard Kortum. The results of our research in these regions will be the subject of a future monograph.

Khyadag West deer stone site.

12. Intersecting Worlds: Eclipse of the Deer Spirit-Master

In the absence of associated human burials, deer stones present a contradiction. The stones appear to represent warriors, chiefs, or heroic persons shown with their personal weapons, belts, and body tattoos. The presence of shamanic elements, celestial images, and iconic deer-bird master spirits, shown, generally, in ascendant flight, suggests individuals whose souls are being sent off to the upper world in organized public ceremonies involving feasting, shamanic ritual, and animal sacrifice. The deer-bird master spirit that protected these individuals in life and assisted their final journey and after-life are charismatic creatures of the northern forests and steppe lands familiar to Late Bronze Age herding societies. On the other hand, the animals that most directly figured in khirigsuur burials and

deer stone settings are not wild forest creatures; they are domesticated horses – the life-blood of the new herding economy and the engines of trade and war that dominated the intensely competitive economic and social life of the Late Bronze Age. It is tempting to view the juxtaposition of the deer-bird master spirit and the horse in LBA ceremonial ritual as either a clash or an intersection of colliding worlds – the unpredictable and uncontrollable world that was the domain of shamanistic ritual and ceremony, from which hunters and warriors protected themselves with deer spirit 'armor,' and the practical world of the herders who must deal with the day-to-day life of rearing and protecting animals, families, and communities. While animal spirits assisted the hunter or warrior, it was the act of offering a horse at a deer stone or khirigsuur ceremony that memorialized one's social position in Bronze Age society. Judging from the adherence to prescribed deer stone and khirigsuur ritual and ceremony, that social world was rigorously hierarchical. The death of a chief called for sacrificing a man's most precious material possession to ensure one's position was maintained in the hereafter.

One can imagine the scene at dawn on the morning of the event: followers and their families gathered at deer stones or khirigsuurs awaiting the rising sun to begin killing their prized horses, stripping them of meat and burying the head, neck, and hooves in precisely-positioned mounds on the east side of the khirigsuur, at locations that must have been determined and regulated according to one's social rank and standing. This was followed by feasts of the sacrificed horses accompanied by other lesser animals at designated oval hearth sites. Khirigsuurs – one hundred times more numerous than deer stones – were the normal form of social departure for the DSK non-elite. By contrast, the creation and setting of deer stones was a rare event commemorating individuals of the highest social position—those who owned chariots and carried chariot rein-hooks on their belts.

After several hundred years of cultural stability and artistic creativity, DSK culture became challenged by a new philosophy that was less keyed to the single unified philosophical worldview reflected in the universal symbolism of the iconic Mongolian Deer and its expression on deer stones. The appearance of horses on deer stones; the breakdown of the rigid, formulaic structure of deer stone composition with its stacked ranks of deer images, the appearance of animals and implements 'floating' on the stone, and especially the introduction of a narrative style emphasizing predator-prey interaction—all portend the arrival of a new societal order. No doubt, DSK culture was being challenged on many fronts as Square Burial, Pazyryk, and perhaps other groups appeared on their borders and eventually replaced DSK culture and its values. The most striking change was the replacement of khirigsuur burials, devoid of burial goods, that required the solidarity of large communities to create huge mounds and sacrificial offerings, by small clan-

based Pazyryk or Square Burial installations filled with mortuary goods and animals, with special attention to horses and horse gear. It would appear that the communal ethic of the DSK was replaced by one honoring conquest, wealth, and material possessions intended to maintain one's standing in the afterlife. The absence of a personal marker such as a deer stone, or any visible way to identify and remember one's leaders, seems indicative of a new social order that was less theocratic and more decentralized. With the passing of the deer stone and khirigsuur, DSK culture and its spiritual world gave way to the Iron Age and its more material, competitive, and horse-based value system.

The passing of the deer-god belief system was a major watershed in Central Asian history, signaling the end of a spiritual world that had been inherited from the Paleolithic, when humans saw themselves as part of the natural world and subject to unpredictable events they sought to influence but could not control. Animal domestication brought DSK people a degree of control over their subsistence needs, but it was horse domestication and the development of horse control technology during the Late Bronze Age that eventually undermined the old belief system. Like the 19th century Alaska Native shamans who converted to Christianity when the old rituals failed to deliver in the new social order, DSK religious and political leaders found in the horse a more effective means of guaranteeing the future of their people.

Much of Deer Stone culture is still a mystery. We still know almost nothing about DSK domestic life and everyday material culture, about the origins of the iconic deer image, the culture's relations with other groups, and why it collapsed and was replaced. No doubt, its people continued to maintain their lives and livelihoods as nomadic herders, traders, warriors, and defenders of their freedom. But by studying deer stones, khirigsuurs, and DSK cultural landscapes, we can learn much about a remarkable people and culture whose legacy has been and continues to be an inspiration to Mongolians today.

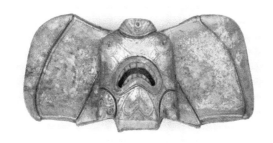

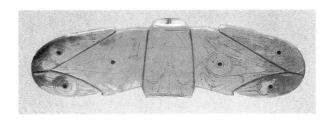

Walrus Ivory harpoon counterweights from the Ekven Old Bering Sea site in Chukotka portraying master spirit images. (credits: Museum of Anthropology and Ethnology, St. Petersburg)

Postscript: A note on Mongolia, Nomadic Art, and Eskimo Connections

In 1963 when I was a student at Dartmouth College I took a course in the art history that considered ancient Chinese bronzes. I was fascinated by the way Shang vessels used for ritual offerings to gods and ancestors changed gradually over centuries. A central motif for many of these vessels was the taotie spirit figure whose 'splayed' dragon-like body wrapped around the sides of the vessel and whose fanged, grinning face must have inspired fear and wonder. Then, suddenly, the ancient continuity was broken, and the ornate style was replaced by elegant, smooth-surfaced vessels with no surface embellishment. Over time, a new stylistic evolution

from simple to complex mythic messaging took place in the Zhou era. I was hooked. I enrolled in anthropology and went off that summer with Prof. Elmer Harp, an Arctic archaeologist, to dig a Dorset Paleoeskimo site in Newfoundland. Paleoeskimo history—and human behavior in general—I discovered, could be studied using similar art historical methods.

When I arrived at the Smithsonian in 1970 I found myself with Henry B. Collins, whose life was dedicated to researching Eskimo origins. By analyzing engraved decoration on Alaskan bone and ivory implements he documented a continuous 1500-year history of Eskimo cultural development in Bering Strait. He also found that the earliest Eskimo cultures—Okvik and Old Bering Sea—already had fully-developed Eskimo features. He noted stylistic similarities with Asian animal style art, while Ipiutak, another 1500 year old Alaska site, also showed Asian influences in elaborate animal carvings and burial masks whose origins could be traced to Zhou China composite jade mortuary masks of the first millennium B.C., several centuries before Ipiutak.

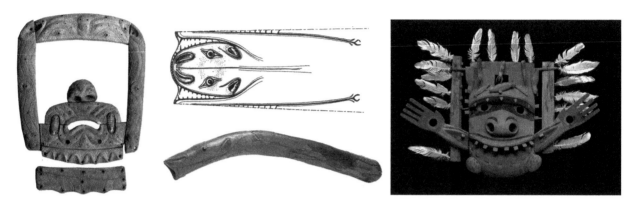

Ipiutak culture funeral mask and shaman sucking tube to extract evil spirits from a sick person; Yup'ik festival mask. (Credits: American Museum of Natural History and Smithsonian NMNH)

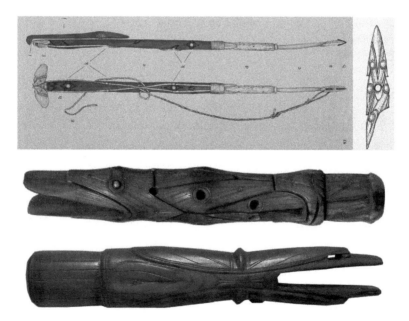

A Shang Dynasty ding ritual bowl with taotei ('the one with insatiable appetite') motif (opposite page, credit: Northwestern University); Bering Sea Eskimo walrus harpoon technology with throwing board, animal-themed counterweight, socketpiece, foreshaft, and harpoon, and Ekven socketpieces. (credits: Princeton University Art Museum, MAE St. Petersburg)

In the decades that followed we learned more about Old Bering Sea culture from excavations at the Ekven and Uelen cemetery sites (Arutiunov and Sergeev 1969, 1975). OBS harpoon and other utensils carried engraved decoration depicting animals and spirit figures whose function was to honor animal spirits and guide weapons with the aid of predator spirit-helpers. Harpoon heads were carved like feathered bird of prey, making them the talons

Chinese ding ritual vessel. (Wikipedia Commons)

of sea-eagle predators; ivory foreshafts took the form of wolf or killer whale predators; and ivory counter-balance weights at the butt ends of the harpoon carried the image of a grinning beast representing the master spirit of animals known in Eskimo mythology as 'the man in the moon'. Other features of OBS and Ipiutak art included representations of spirit transformations from one animal to a sister species (wolf-killer whale), or images showing animal-human-animal transformation. Many of these images combine human and fanged animal features that bear a strong resemblance to *taotie* figures on Shang and Zhou ritual vessels and decorative arts (and to ethnographic arts of historical Northwest Coast Indians–see Fitzhugh 1988).

Since there were no prototypes in Alaska, scholars like Helge Larsen, Henry Collins, Carl Schuster, and Ted Carpenter (see pp. xxx) turned to Asia and found similarities in the Yamal Iron Age, Shang and Zhou China, and the Iron Age of the Central Asia steppe. Shang and Zhou bronze art portrayed master spirits, but the art was highly formalized and static, whereas the Scythian and Saka art of northern nomads was flowing, active, energetic, and stylistically closer to Ipiutak and Old Bering Sea, but was 500-1000 years earlier. Deer stones provided another possibility when they came to light following Russian research after 1950. Volkov, Novgorodova, and Savinov had various theories on deer stone dating (see Bayarsaikhan 2022:17-21) based on typological comparisons of tools and weapons, and argued variously for both pre- or post-Scythian dates. The Deer Stone Project's application of radiocarbon dating to horse remains and hearth feature charcoal associated with khirigsuurs and deer stones settled the issue decisively, establishing the DSK (3400-2700 BP) as solidly pre-Scythian, beginning 4-500 years before Pazyryk and overlapping with it from 2990-2700 BP.

While our work has uncovered substantial data for the ritual complex of the DSK, it has done little to flesh out the broader Deer Stone culture in its economic, subsistence, and settlement forms, as noted by recent reviews (Houle 2016; Wright 2021). Further, as in the case of Eskimo studies, DSK origins and founding influences still remain unknown, as there is scant evidence for prototypes. There is, however, some indication from unusual—and perhaps even aberrant—deer stone carvings seen at Targan Nuur, Khort Uzuur, and Avt Mod in the northern Darkhad, where other sites like Tsatstain have some of the earliest DSK c14 dates (3300-3400 BP). These signals support the notion expressed by Karl Jettmar (1994) that deer stones may have begun in the forested taiga of southern Russia as wooden memorials that began to be produced in stone with the introduction of horse riding and metal tools.

Most deer stones date to the 'middle years' of the DSK complex ca. 3100-2800 BP and conform to Volkov's classic Type I style centered in the well-watered, horse-rich steppe north of the Khangai Mountains. We have demonstrated that Volkov's Types II (Sayan-Altai) and III (European) are not geographically distinct, but rather overlap with Type I in north-central Mongolia, and that Type III stones are found commonly here as miniature deer stones at Khyadag East, Zunii Gol, and other sites. Type II stones are not restricted to the Sayan-Altai Mongolia periphery but are also found also in central Mongolia, mostly in the southern parts of that region.

We also noted changes in deer stone composition in south-central Mongolia that appear to fall toward the late end of the DSK period. Durujiin Ovoo and Khushuugiin Gol display unattached (floating) tools and diverse animals, including horses and moose instead of, or along with, classic Mongolian Deer images, and many of these animals stand with straight legs (rather than shown croched or leaping), and have upright antlers, and realistic heads and snouts. Most illuminating is the Zunii Gol DS10 frog/ibisbill stone with its combination of 'nested' iconic deer along with scenes of felines and wolves confronting bovids and pigs, displaying Scythian/Saka narrative style and content. This stone combines features of transitional late DSK influenced by Pazyryk and Scythic culture.

In addition, there is a pronounced cultural divide in DSK culture between Central and Western (Altaian) Mongolia (including Gorni Altai southern Russia), where khirigsuurs have radials connecting the central mound with the surrounding fence and deer stones are found within khirigsuur precincts or embedded in the central burial mounds. Further, at least in the Mongolian Altai, khirigsuurs (except in a single case at On Khot in Bayan Ulgii) do not have horse mounds that are the crucial features of central Mongolian rites and sites. These regional differences in the treatment of the dead point toward significant cultural variation within the DSK culture sphere. The cause is likely due to geographic and economic realities in the different capacities for horse-rearing, which is much diminished in the mountainous Altai. On Khot represents a rare occurrence of horse mounds in a Mongolian Altai khirigsuur. It remains to be seen if the Altaian DSK dates conform generally to those of central Mongolia, or, perhaps more likely, represents a late DSK persistence after it was displaced in Central Mongolia by Square Burial culture. This question has been difficult to resolve because of the absence of horse remains for dating Altaian sites.

The direct association of deer stones and khirigsuurs in the Altai raises the question: why not also in central Mongolia, where deer stones and khirigsuurs are separated, making individual correlations impossible. What does this reveal about the social values of eastern and western DSK sub-cultures? Clues may be found in chariot symbolism that is more pronounced in western Mongolia. Khirigsuur radials are almost never seen in the east but are common in the west and Russian Gorni Altai. Placing a commemorative deer stone within a khirigsuur unites the individual with one's vehicle for heavenly life and honor. Why was this, and chariot symbolism, not expressed in khirigsuur architecture in the DSK core area?

Another important matter needing research is the impact of DSK culture on the rise of nomadic animal style art. Although we do not know the roots from which DSK art emerged in the Early Bronze Age, the flowing style seen in the Mongolian Deer must have arisen from nomadic societies between 4000-3500 BP. DSK culture must also have included a wide array of figurative art in wood, textiles, and other perishables such as those recovered from the frozen Pazyryk mounds. We know nothing of

DSK artistic products except deer stones. One can only imagine what a full tableau of DSK arts might have included and hope that someday this might be revealed in a frozen or cave site. But it is likely that the spectacular Pazyryk finds grew out of an earlier artistic horizon of which DSK culture was a part, and that this proto-culture also laid the foundation for the explosion of nomadic arts of the Scyths and Saka a millenium later. The appearance of Type III European style deer stones in Western Asia and the fringes of Eastern Europe suggest that a cultural wave borne by horse nomads carried DSK ceremonialism to the Black Sea and the fringes of Europe, much as Turkic and Mongol expansions did in later centuries.

With this review we arrive back at the question that inspired my interest in Mongolia in the first place: the Asian ancestry and influences that contributed to early Eskimo art and cultures surrounding the Bering Strait in the centuries before 2000 BP. After failing to identify specific antecedents among the early cultures of Arctic Russia (Fitzhugh 1998), the maritime corridor in Northeast Asia seemed the likely corridor for cultural transmissions linked to northern China and the eastern Asian steppe. Mongolia's deer stones suggested its nomadic peoples were part of the movement of artistic and ceremonial ideas, facilitated by the spread of metal production, horse culture, and shamanism. Finds of Asian ceramics and iron tools,

ivory imitation of metal chains, bronze open-work ornments, the Asian shamanistic regalia and death masks from Ipiutak, and a bronze horse buckle from an Alaskan Thule site document the continuing stream of Asian culture into Alaska. But we still have yet to identify the specific connections between the nomadic art of Central Asia or the Russian taiga and ancient Eskimo art.

By now it seems unlikely that there is a 'smoking gun' to be found. More likely is a continuing tickle of ideas, rituals, and artistic elements connected with shamanism, ideas and symbols related to mythology, spirit transformation, story-telling, graphic spiritual 'armor' on clothing and body tattoos, and imagery related to hunting and spirit-helpers that found transmssion through cultural pathways via coastal and interior peoples of Northeast Asia. The Sakha and Chukchi northward expansions resulting from 13th century Mongol pressure offers an example of historical processes that must also have operated in earlier times when iron, decorative glass beads, reindeer herding, and Bering Sea ivory trade created connections between northeast Asia and early Alaska Eskimo cultures. Future research in China, Korea, and Northeastern Russia will have much to offer for this longstanding search connecting the peoples, cultures, and arts of northwestern North America with those of the Asian steppe, taiga, and beyond.

Two species that figured prominently in the ancient art of their regions—the Bering Sea walrus (Rosemaris odobenis) *and Asian elk or maral (*Cervus elaphus sibiricus*).*

The deer stones of Bor Khujiriin Gol-1 are more than silent statuary; they include the only example known of silent interaction, of one deer stone speaking to another. DS 4 with its carved human face and bent neck, appears to be speaking to DS 5, only a half meter away and the largest in the series. Is this a shaman chanting, singing, or whispering to his or her warrior-leader?

Acknowledgments

This Deer Stone Diary reports results of nine years of fieldwork (2001-2009) and a decade of research and writing. The Deer Stone Project was supported by grants from the Smithsonian's Robert Bateman and Robert Malott Funds, National Geographic Society, the U.S. Ambassador's Fund, The Ed Nef and Santis Foundations, the American Center for Mongolian Studies, the NMNH Arctic Studies Center, several private donors, and a host of volunteers. American and Mongolian field crew members deserve huge credit for our survey and excavation results and are identified in the team photos accompanying this note.

Ed Nef provided the inspiration and funding for the 2001-2 exploratory projects and the friendship and encouragement in the years following. Dooloonjiin Orgilma mastered our first two years of logistical support, and for years thereafter this crucial task was filled by Adiyah Namkhai, who built on his experience to create his own travel agency. Ochirhuyag Tseveendorj was my co-director for the first two years and was followed subsequently by Jamsranjav Bayarsaikhan who must be credited for making possible almost everything we accomplished. Bayaraa and I were assisted hugely by our intellectual 'god-father' and archaeological elder, T. Sanjmyatav, and by the seasoned ethnologist Tseel Ayush. My other field partners included forensic anthropologist Bruno Frohlich, botanist Paula DePriest, conservator Harriet (Rae) Beaubien, each of whom contributed their own research and publications year after year. Others critical to our success include our drivers, our cook Amraa, our American and Mongolian student field workers, and the many Dukha (Tsaatan) friends like Sanjiin, Bayandalai, Bayaraa, Batsaya, and others who hosted our 2001-2004 visits into the West Taiga and introduced us to their remarkable lives and culture. Similarly, in later years, we were generously hosted by scores of Mongolian families as our caravan paused near their camps.

We are also indebted to the many UB and aimag officials who provided our archaeology permits and allowed us to research in their jurisdictions. Throughout the project we received valuable support from the Mongolia National Museum and its several directors, as well as from the Mongolian Academy of Sciences and its Institute of Archaeology, directed by D. Tseveendorj. The U.S. Embassy in Ulaanbaatar, its several ambassadors, and the U.S. State Department provided support and assistance annually. Office directors at the American Center for Mongolian Studies in UB provided hospitality and 'real work' in helping us get permits, lodging, and meeting arrangements. One of those directors, Peter Marsh, co-edited and arranged the publication of our 2005 monograph.

Back at the Smithsonian, scores of individuals assisted the production of reports and publications. Many were field and laboratory assistants who became co-authors or production managers of our yearly field reports and helped compile maps and illustrations: Matthew Gallon, George Lederer, Christie Leece, Barbara Betz, and Julia Clark, Fiona Steiwer, Marcia Bakry and Dan Cole produced many of our maps and illustrations; librarian Maggie Dittemore provided library support; Paula DePriest and Rae Beaubien marshalled the Museum Conservation Institute's team of laser-scanners who documented deer stones and produced many of the scans used in Bayarsaikhan's 2022 book and this volume and Emily Mansfield assisted as volunteer mss editor..

Although Nancy Shorey was not at the ASC while our fieldwork was taking place, she provided unending administrative support during the research phase, up to and including the production of this book. Peter Mittenthal

of International Polar Institute Press designed
and brought Bayarsaikhan's and this book to
press and distribution. I also thank my ASC
colleagues, Igor Krupnik, Stephen Loring, Aron
Crowell, Dawn Biddison, Bernadette Engelstad,
and John Cloud for years of advice and support.
Included here as master-spirit above all others
is Lynne Fitzhugh who tolerated my disappear-
ances and provided shelter, nourishment, and
emotional support during the covid period
in Vermont when much of the writing of this
book took place.

A warm day at Nukhtiin Am-2 produced an unusual result: the usual small horse mound covered a meter-deep pit containing two doughnut-shaped mace heads.

Annual Field Crew Profiles

Adiyabold Namkhai, our indefatigable project expediter; Ts Ayush, ethnographer; and Sue Lutz, Oi. Sukh-baatar, Paula DePriest, TYs. Sanjmyatav, Steve Young, Baterdene Sanjmyatav, Adiyabold Namkhai; 2001 field team at Ulaan Tolgoi: (back) ?, Saruulbuyan, Sukhbaatar, David Marik, Ed Nef, W. Fitzhugh, Dooloonjiin Orgilma; (front) Steve Young, Sanjmyatav, ?, ?, Stephanie Marik, ?. (photo: Stephanie [Nef] Marik); (left) Kevin Robinson, Scott Stark, Adiyabold, and Tsaatan herders on Kevin's 2003 lake pollen sampling expedition.

2001-2003

I thank colleagues Paula DePriest, Sue Lutz, Bruno Frohlich, Carolyn Thome, Paul Rhymer, Matthew Gallon, and other Smithsonian staff who collaborated in our 2002 field program, and to Steven Young, Director of the Center for Northern Studies, for his assistance in field work and paleo-ecological research. I owe a deep debt of gratitude to Ed Nef of Inlingua Services, Arlington, Virginia, for his inspiration and support throughout the project, and to Dooloonjin Orgilmaa of Santis Corporation, who organized the logistics and served as a gracious local host. I also thank the National Museum of Mongolian History and its directors, Dr. Sanduin Idshinnorov, and A. Ochir, and curators Ochirkhuyag Tseveendorj, Dashdendev Bumaa, and Ts. Ayush who made it possible for us to obtain a cast of Uushigiin Uvör Deer Stone 14; Dr. Enk-tuvshin of the Mongolian Academy of Sciences; Dr. D.Tseveendorj, Director of the Institution of Archaeology; L. Damdinsuren, Governor of Khu-vsgul Aimag, and Vice Governor O. Gunaajav; our

Mongolian research colleagues, Drs. T. Sanjmyatav, O. Sukhbaatar, and Ts. Tsendeekhuu, who participated in our two expeditions in 2001 and 2002, and our student assistants in 2002, Baterdene Sanjmyatav and Ishka. Other members of the 2001 expedition included Saruulbuyan (later to be director of the National Museum), George Proctor, Stephanie and David Marek, and Sorena Griffin. We are deeply grateful to our Tsaatan field hosts, especially Sanjiim, Bayandalai, Bayaraa, and Batsaya, for their support and assistance, and to our interpreters, Sangas Hajidsuren (2001) and Adiya Namkhai (2002), field managers Dooloonhin Orgilmaa (2001), Adiya Namkhai (2002), and Khandaa (2002), Chief Driver Jigjav Zagd (2001-2), and our resourceful cooks, Daksmar (2001) and Amaraa (2002). Funding for the 2001-2 projects came from Ed Nef, the Smithsonian NMNH Robert Bateman Arctic Fund, Robert Malott Foundation, and the National Museum of Natural History.

of Archaeology. Mongolian assistants included L. Manlaibaatar (archaeologist), Oyunbileg, National University, Department of Botany; Undarmaa, Mongolian National University, Department of Botany. Our field project manager/translator was Adiyabold Namkai. Drivers were Nyambayar, Zagdaa, Narangerel, and Khadbaatar, and our cook was Amaraa. Dukha friends Batsaya, Bayandalai, and others graciously welcomed our group to their field camp. American participants included William W. Fitzhugh, Paula DePriest (botanist), David Hunt and Bruno Frohlich (physical anthropologists), Andrea Neighbors, Debbie Bell, Greg McKie, Rae Beaubien, and Carolyn Thome and Paul Rhymer. Funding was provided by the Trust for Mutual Understanding, the Mongolian Ambassador's Fund, National Museum of Mongolian History, Mongolia National University, the Smithsonian National Museum of Natural History and its Center for Materials Research and Conservation, the NMNH Robert

Bruno Frohlich captures GPS data while excavations at Ulaan Tolgoi Deer Stone 4 were underway.

2004

This year our senior Mongolian team members included J. Bayarsaikhan and Ts. Odbaataar, archaeologists from the National Museum of Mongolian History; Oi. Sukhbaatar, geographer and Head of the Reindeer Foundation; O. Sanjmyatav, archaeologist, Center for Chinggis Khaan Studies; and Amgalantugs and Bazargur, archaeologists from Mongolian Academy of Science, Department

Bateman Arctic Fund, Robert Malott Foundation, Alicia Campi, and the American Center for Mongolian Studies. ACMS Mongolia director Peter Marsh, with assistance from J. Bayarsaikhan and Helena Sharp, produced our 2005 monograph reporting 2002-05 research.

2005 field team members at Ulaan Tolgoi and at the end of the season.

2005

The American team included William Fitzhugh, Harriet (Rae) Beaubien (archaeological conservator CMI/SI), Paula DePriest (botanist CMI/SI), Elizabeth Eldredge and Dennis Rydjeski (volunteers), Natalie Firnhaber (UB only, conservator NMNH/SI), Melanie Irvine (NMNH/SI intern), Basiliki Vicky Karas (scanning scientist CMI/SI), Thomas Kelly (photographer), Eric Powell (editor, Archaeology Magazine), Paul Rhymer (UB only, exhibits specialist NMNH/SI), Carolyn Thome (model-maker OEC/SI). Ambassador Pamela Slutz and her husband Ronald Deutsh accompanied the team from Murun to the Darkhat and participated in the visit to the Tsaatan/Dukha. The Mongolian Team included T. Amgalantugs, Ts. Ayush (ethnologist, NMMH), J. Bayarsaikhan (archaeologist, NMMH), Adiabold Namkhai (translator, expediter), Jugii, D. Bazargur, B. Erdene, Odga, and Jugii, Unga (archaeology students), N. Bazarsad (physical anthropologist), Ts. Odbaatar (archaeologist, NMMH), Oyunbileg (botanist), T. Sanjmyatav (archaeologist, MAS), Oi. Sukhbaatar (geographer, Chinghis Khan College), Tunjii (archaeology student), Odga (cook), Ugna (student), and drivers Batbaatar, Khadbaatar, Tserenam, and Tsog.

2006 Field Team at Ulaan Tolgoi. (photo: C. Leece)

2006

This year's project included William Fitzhugh, Paula DePriest, J. Bayarsaikhan, Ts. Ayush, T. Sanjmyatav, D. Amaraa, Adiya Namkhai, Marilyn Walker, Francis Allard, Laura Short, Christy Leece, Khadbaatar, Mendbayar, Tsolman, Onolbaatar, Songuulkhan, J. Oyumaa, Oynubileg, Harriet (Rae) Beaubien, Basiliki Vicki Karass, Leslie Weber, Tsog, Khadbaatar, Narangel, Batbaatar, Tserenam, Funds were provided by the National Geographic Society, Trust for Mutual Understanding, National Museum of Mongolian History, Smithsonian National Museum of Natural History and Center for Materials Analysis and Conservation.

2007

The 2007 Mongolia Deer Stone Project owes its success to organizations and individuals too numerous to name. Funding for the project came primarily from the National Geographic Society and the National Museum of Natural History, Smithsonian Institution. The National Museum of Mongolian History supported the project in many ways, as an institutional partner and through the work of its talented staff: Director Ochir, ethnology curator, Bumaa, and professional staff Bayarsaikhan and Ayush. The American Center for Mongolian Studies (Bryan White and Enkhbaatar) provided assistance and advertising for our scholarly symposium. I especially thank our Mongolian and American field crew for their dedication and hard work. These include Sanjmyatav, Boldbaatar, Chimba, Deegii, Enkhbold, Lkhagva, Onoloo, and Ugna; our drivers Tsog, Tserenam, and Khatbaatar, and in the Altai, Berekhbol; Matthew Rasmussen, Matthew Sagi, Bill Stewart; our cook Amaraa; our Altai field assistant Amra; most especially I thank my assistant Christie Leece and my Smithsonian colleagues Harriet (Rae) Beaubien and Christine, and Paula DePriest. Elaine Ling, Marilyn Walker, and Wayne Paulsen also made important contributions. The project could not have taken place without the hard work of our project manager, Adiya Namkhai and his staff and friends.

2007 Field team at our Darkhad staging location in Murun. (photo: Elaine Ling)

2008

Our team for our early summer work in the Mongolian Altai around Lake Khotan included project leaders Richard Kortum and Bill Fitzhugh, Irina, Natsagaa, J. Bayarsaikhan, driver Janat, student Kyle Strickland, and Tsogoo. The crew in northern Mongolia at Khyadag East included (l-r): Sodoo, Kyle, Amaraa, Sasha, Nasaa, Khadaa, Tseeree, Ayush, Bayaraa, and Mogi. Khadbaatar and Tserenyam were our van drivers.

Mongolian Altai Khotan Lake team in 2008.

2009

2009 field team near Arbulag in some Darkhad 'spring' weather.

As in previous years our permit was arranged by the National Museum of Mongolia directed by J. Saruulbuyan. We had a fine crew of Mongolian and American students and traveled in vans operated by drivers B. Tsogtgerel and B. Tserennyam. B. Doljinsorgodog and Jamsranjav Bayarsaikhan, research director of the National Museum of Mongolia, rounded up student assistants Ts. Sodnombaljir, B. Uuganbayar, and Khangarid. Ethnographer Tseel Ayush gathered data on the Buriat minority living around the town of Tsagaannuur in the northern Darkhad Valley. Our cook was D. Amaraa. American crew members included William Fitzhugh and Richard Kortum and students Barbara Betz and Julia Clark.

Field Camp 2006. (photo: C. Leece)

Dinner preps while camping south of Tsaaganuur.

Ulan Tolgoi camp vista.

Appendix 1. Radiocarbon Date List

site / feature	location/year	sample no.	material	uncorrected	calib (2-sig)	GPS	elevation
Ulaan Tolgoi DS4 S-17	Erkhel / 2003	B-182958 AMS	charcoal	2170 ± 40 BP	BP 2320-2050	N50-00.969' E99-37.678'	6421ft
Ulaan Tolgoi DS4 S-7	Erkhel / 2003	B-182959 AMS	charcoal	2930 ± 40 BP	BP 3220-2950	N50-00.969' E 99-37.678'	6421ft
Ulaan Tolgoi DS4 F1	Erkhel / 2004	B-193738 AMS	bone coll.	2530 ± 40 BP	BP 2750-2470	N50-00.969' E 99-37.678'	6421ft
Ulaan Tolgoi DS4 F2	Erkhel / 2004	B-193739 AMS	bone coll.	2950 ± 40 BP	BP 3240-2970	N50-00.969' E 99-37.678'	6421ft
Ulaan Tolgoi DS4 F3	Erkhel / 2004	B-193740 AMS	bone coll.	2810 ± 40 BP	BP 2990-2800	N50-00.969' E 99-37.678'	6421ft
Ulaan Tolgoi DS4, F5	Erkhel / 2005	B-207205 RAD	bone coll.	2790 ± 70 BP	BP 3220-2800	N50-00.969' E 99-37.678'	6421ft
Ulaan Tolgoi DS4, F6	Erkhel / 2005	B-207206 RAD	bone coll.	2740 ± 70 BP	BP 3150-2780	N50-00.969' E 99-37.678'	6421ft
Ulaan Tolgoi DS5, T1	Erkhel / 2002	B-169296 AMS	charcoal	2090 ± 40 BP	BP 2150-1960	N50-00.969' E 99-37.678'	6421ft
Ulaan Tolgoi DS5, F1	Erkhel / 2005	B-215694 AMS	tooth coll.	2800 ± 40 BP	BP 2980-2790	N50-00.969' E 99-37.678'	6421ft
Ulaan Tolgoi DS5, F2	Erkhel / 2006	B-222535 AMS	tooth coll.	2830 ± 40 BP	BP 3050-2850	N50-00.969' E 99-37.678'	6421ft
Ulaan Tolgoi M1, F1	Erkhel / 2005	B-207209 AMS	bone coll.	1880 ± 40 BP	BP 1900-1720	N50-00.969' E 99-37.678'	6421ft
Ulaan Tolgoi M1, F2	Erkhel / 2005	B-215692 AMS	tooth coll.	2860 ± 40 BP	BP 3080-2870	N50-00.969' E 99-37.678'	6421ft
Ulaan Tolgoi M1, F2	Erkhel / 2005	B-215644 AMS	charcoal	2980 ± 40 BP	BP 3310-3000	N50-00.969' E 99-37.678'	6421ft
Ulaan Tolgoi M1, F3	Erkhel / 2005	B-215693 AMS	tooth coll.	2950 ± 60 BP	BP 3320-2940	N48-49.950' E 99-47.47'	4660ft
Nukhtiin Am DS1/2	F1Galt / 2006	B-222534 AMS	tooth coll.	2830 ± 40 BP	BP 3050-2850	N51-7.402' E99-14.827,	1568m
Evdt 2 DS 2 Circ. feat.	Evdt Valley	B-215643 AMS	charcoal	3030 ± 40 BP	BP 3350-3090	N51-10.142' E99-22.554'	1550m
Tsatstain Kh DS1,F1	Tsaagan / 2005	B-207208 AMS	tooth coll.	2920 ± 40 BP	BP 3160-2920	N51-10.142' E99-22.554'	1550m
Tsatstain Kh DS1,F2	Tsaagan / 2005	B-207207 AMS	tooth coll.	3000 ± 40 BP	BP 3330-3060	N48-05.546' E101-03.504'	5489ft
Urt Bulagyn KYR1-21	Khanuy / 2006	B-222532 AMS	tooth coll.	2780 ± 50 BP	BP 2980-2770	N48-05.546' E101-03.504'	5489ft
Urt Bulagyn KYR1-22	Khanuy / 2006	B-222533 AMS	tooth coll.	2790 ± 40 BP	BP 2970-2780	N48-49.950' E99-47.47' 4	660ft
Nukhtiin Am Md1,F1	Galt / 2006	B-240685 AMS	tooth coll.	2630 ± 40 BP	BP 2790-2730	N51-55.873* E99-23.482*	
Tsagaan Asga K1 F1	Sagsai / 2007	B-240686 AMS	bone coll.	130 ± 40 BP	BP 280-0*	N51-25.125' E99-18.783'	1591m
Khogorgo-3, Md1	Shishged 2007	B-240687 AMS	tooth coll.	3450 ± 40 BP	BP 3830-3620	N49-55.056' E100-03.16'	1720 m
Khushuugiin Devs F1	Erkhel / 2006	B-222536 AMS	tooth coll.	2140 ± 40 BP	BP 2320-1990*	N49-55.056' E100-03.16'	1720m
Khushuugiin Devs. F2	Erkhel / 2007	B-240688 AMS	tooth coll.	2450 ± 40 BP	BP 2720-2350	N49-55.056' E100-03.16'	1720m
Khushuugiin Devs. F3	Erkhel / 2007	B-240689 AMS	tooth coll.	2680 ± 40 BP	BP 2860-2740	N49-55.056' E100-03.16'	1720m
Khushuugiin Devs. F1	Erkhel / 2007	B-243716 AMS	tooth coll.	2410 ± 40 BP	BP 2700-2640%	N49-48.900' E99-53.042'	1589m
Khyadag E. DS pav.7	Erkhel / 2007	B-240690 AMS	bone/tooth	2610 ± 40 BP	BP 2770-2720	N51-25.403' E99-35.547'	5166ft
Hort Uzuur DS3	Hort Azuur/ 2006	B-222537 AMS	charcoal	2230 ± 40 BP	BP 2340-2140*	N51-25.403' E99-35.547'	5166ft
Hort Uzuur DS2,L2, F1	Hort Azuur/ 2007	B-240691 AMS	charcoal	2710 ± 40 BP	BP 2870-2750	N48-59.810' E89-04.403'	6199ft
Tsagaan Gol K2 F1	Tsengel / 2007	B-240692 AMS	tooth coll.	2140 ± 40 BP	BP 2300-2240#	N48-59.810' E89-04.403'	6199ft
Tsagaan Gol K3 F9	Tsengel / 2007	B-240693 AMS	tooth coll.	1740 ± 40 BP	BP 1730-1550	N48-59.810' E89-04.403'	6199ft
Tsagaan Gol K4, F11	Tsengel / 2007	B-243717 AMS	char.mtl	130 ± 40 BP	BP 280-0	N51-28.010' E99-21.906'	1700m
Avtiin Fea.5 Sample 6	Shishged / 2007	B-242730 AMS	charcoal	2670 ± 40 BP	BP 2850-2740		

2008 dates:

site / feature	location/year	sample no.	material	uncorrected	calib (2-sig)	GPS	elevation
Khoton 333 F18	Bayan Ulgii/2008	B-246610 AMS	charcoal	2840 ± 40 BP	BP 3070-2860	N48-38.638' E88-22.60'	2099m
Tsagaan Asga F3	Bayan Ulgii/2008	B-246611 AMS	charcoal	2850 ± 40 BP	BP 3070-2860	N48-30.368; E 88-57.03'	2215m
Tsagaan Asga F4	Bayan Ulgii/2008	B-246612 AMS	charcoal	3000 ± 40 BP	BP 3330-3070	N48-31.181' E88-57.41'	2240m
On Khad Khushuu	Bayan Ulgii/2008	B-246613 AMS	tooth coll.	2930 ± 40 BP	BP 3220-2960		
Bor Hujiriin A1, F2	Tsagaan/2008	B-246614 AMS	tooth coll.	2640 ± 40 BP	BP 2790-2730	N49-44.269' E98-17.826'	2021m
Bor Hujiriin A1, F4	Tsagaan/2008	B-246615 AMS	bone coll.	680 ± 40 BP	BP 680-630†*	N49-44.269' E98-17.826'	2021m
Bor Hujiriin A2, F1	Tsagaan/2008	B-246616 RAD	charcoal	2670 ± 50 BP	BP 2860-2740	N49-44.269' E98-17.826'	2021m
Khuush. Gol F2	Erkhel/2008	B-246617 AMS	tooth coll.	2750 ± 40 BP	BP 2940-2760	N49-42.261' E98-35.708'	1868m
Khushuug. Gol A3, F3	Erkhel/2008	B-246618 AMS	tooth coll.	2910 ± 40 BP	BP 3210-2940	N49-42.190' E98-35.514'	1885m
Khushuug. Gol F6	Erkhel/2008	B-246619 AMS	charcoal	2850 ± 40 BP	BP 3070-2860	N49-42.935' E98-35.077'	1888m
Khyadag E. A3 F32	Erkhel/2008	B-246620 AMS	tooth coll.	2520 ± 40 BP	BP 2740-2470	N49-48.900' E99-54.042'	1598m
Khyadag E. A2	Erkhel/2008	B-246621 RAD	charcoal	2460 ± 50 BP	BP 2730-2350	N49-48.900' E99-54.042'	1598m
Khyadag E. A2	Erkhel/2008	B-246622 RAD	charcoal	2520 ± 50 BP	BP 2750-2440‡	N49-48.900' E99-54.042'	1598m
Khyadag W. F1	Erkhel/2008	B-246623 AMS	bone coll.	2610 ± 40 BP	BP 2870-2750	N49-18.749' E99-51.124'	1678m
Zunii Gol A1, F3	Shin Ider/2009	B-272756 AMS	tooth coll.	2870 ± 40 BP	BP 3140-3090@	N49-18.749' E99-51.124'	1678m
Zunii Gol A2, DS4	Shin Ider/2009	B-272757 AMS	tooth coll.	2710 ±40 BP	BP 2880-2750	N49-18.749' E99-51.124'	1678m
Zunii Gol A3, F1	Shin Ider/2009	B-272758 AMS	tooth coll.	2860 ±40 BP	BP 3080-2870	N49-18.749' E99-51.124'	1678m
Zunii Gol K3, F42	Shin Ider/2009	B-272759 AMS	tooth coll.	2950 ±40 BP	BP 3250-2890	N48-53.353' E99-18.74-'	1876m
TsiokhiotinA1 DS2 F2	Shin Ider/2009	B-272760 AMS	tooth coll.	2790 ±40 BP	BP 2980-2790	N48-54.981' E99-20.411'	9822m
Duruljiin Am F8a	Shin Ider/2009	B-272761 AMS	charred matl	500 ±40 BP	BP 550-500	N48-54.981' E99-20.411'	9822m
Duruljiin Am F8b	Shin Ider/2009	B-272762 AMS	bone coll.	520 ±40 BP	BP 630-600&	N48-42.237' E99-50.070'	1557m
Khooshootiin Am F18	Galt/2009	B-272763 AMS	tooth coll.	2880 ±40 BP	BP 3150-2880		

2013 date

site / feature	location/year	sample no.	material	uncorrected	calib (2-sig)	GPS	elevation
Jargalantiin Am DS F4	Jargalant/2011	B-341484 AMS	tooth coll.	2780 ±30 BP	BP 2950-2790	N48-10.182',E101-50.338'	1638m

ᒣᒣᒣᒣ# B-240692 Tsagaan Gol K2 F1 has a second intercept at BP 2180-2000
% B-243716 Khushuugiin Devseg F1 also has intercepts at BP 2610-2590 and 2540-2340
† B-246615 Bor Hujiriin A1, F4 has a second intercept at BP 600-560
‡ B-246622 Khyadag East A2 has a second intercept at BP 2410-2370
@ B-272756 Zunii Gol A1, F3 has a second intercept at BP 3090-2870
& B-272762 Duruljiin Am F8b has a second intercept at BP 560-510
* Problematic dating result

Deer Stone Project Radiocarbon Dates run by Beta Analytic Laboratory from Deer Stone and Khirigsuur Sites in Khovsgol, Arkhangai, and Bayan Ulgii Aimags, 2003-2013

Appendix 2

Smithsonian Museum Conservation Institute Slag Report for Finds from the 2008 Deer Stone Project Field Season

MCI request number: 6249

Object: objects from an archaeological context near deerstones in Mongolia, mostly copper slag

Material: various (metal slag, geological)

Cultural Area: Khyadag East deerstone site, Khovsgol Aimag, Burentogtokh sum, Mongolia (49° 48,900' N, 99° 53,042' E, elevation 1589 m)

Date: 2500 BP

Accession Number/Identification: n/a

Requested by: Dr. William Fitzhugh
Department: Arctic Studies Center, Department of Anthropology
Unit: NMNH

Report Author: Judy Watson, Physical Scientist, MCI

Further Contributions to the report by: Martha Goodway, Jeffrey Speakman
Date of request: February 20th, 2009

Report dates: September 4th, 2009

Requested analysis

Photography; analysis and imaging using SEM-EDS; analysis using XRF, DTA, metallography as appropriate.

Purpose of analysis

To gain an understanding of the fragments in order to determine if local iron smelting was taking place around 500 BC. The site is being investigated as part of the American-Mongolian Deer Stone Project, directed by Dr. William Fitzhugh and co-directed by Jamsranjav Bayarsaikhan (head of Research Department/Archaeologist, National Museum of Mongolia, Ulaanbaatar, Mongolia).

Executive Summary

33 samples from an archaeological context at the Khyadag East deerstone site in Mongolia were analyzed using SEM-EDS and XRF in order to determine whether they presented evidence of local iron smelting around 500 BC. Results indicate no evidence of iron smelting, but most of the objects are consistent with copper smelting slag.

SEM background

Scanning electron microscopy with energy dispersive spectrometry (SEM-EDS) works by sending a focused beam of electrons at a sample and measuring the energy of the x-rays emitted by the excited area of the sample. The emitted x-rays provide information about the elements present, and in some cases about elemental abundance. Previously this type of analysis has required destructive sampling, embedding, polishing, carbon coating, and analysis under high vacuum. The development of low vacuum (environmental (ESEM) or variable pressure (VP-SEM)) SEM, specially adapted detectors, and larger sample chambers has allowed the introduction of whole objects (up to 30 cm. in diameter and 8 cm high) into the chamber of the SEM for imaging and analysis without being altered.

For imaging, SEM provides two options. The first makes use of secondary electrons, which are generated near the surface of a sample when it is excited by the electron beam. Secondary electron imaging therefore provides good topographic information. The other type of imaging uses backscattered electrons, which come from deeper within a sample and provide information about the elemental composition of a sample, as heavier elements appear brighter than lighter ones. Backscatter imaging therefore offers not only morphological information about a sample, but also information about compositional differences within a sample.

Instrumental parameters for SEM analysis

The samples were imaged and analyzed using a Hitachi S3700-N scanning electron microscope and a Bruker XFlash energy dispersive spectrometer with Quantax 400 software. Samples were placed onto an aluminum sample holder and analyzed at either full vacuum (< 1 Pa) or at 40 Pa, between 8 and 16 mm working distance, and 15–20 kV accelerating voltage.

Instrumental parameters for XRF analysis

The samples were analyzed using a handheld x-ray fluorescence spectrometer (Bruker Tracer III-V ED-XRF) at 12 kV and 15 µA for 60 seconds.

Results and discussion

Thirty-three samples were analyzed, the majority of which did seem to be metal slag. The presence of copper in these samples is inconsistent with an identification of iron slag, but is consistent with copper slag. The variation between the slag samples indicates that they are the product of more than one smelting event.

The remaining samples include one that is likely to be rock (sample 3), and a possible fragment of furnace lining or crucible (sample 2) (see Tables 1 and 2).

Attached as an appendix to this report are some results and images for each of the samples. Each sample summary contains photographs of the sample, sample mass, an XRF spectrum, and a table with rough SEM-EDS results. Some sample summaries also contain one or more SEM images and one or more elemental maps.

The SEM results are qualitative only and should be taken as approximations. This is due to the fact that sample topography has an effect on the analysis (and analytical totals were low). The results were normalized, but in the tables presented in the sample summaries, only the most commonly abundant elements were presented for comparative purposes (as well as S, Cl, and P).

The raw data from the analyses conducted on these samples will be deposited and archived in the project folder in the R drive at MCI.

Group	Samples in Group	Supporting Factors
non-slag	2, 3, 4, 27	chemistry, morphology, density
copper slag	1, 5, 6, 7, 8, 9, 10, 11, 12, 13, 14, 15, 16, 17, 18, 19, 20, 21, 22, 23, 24, 25, 26, 28, 29, 30, 31, 32, 33	chemistry, morphology

Table 1. Possible groups found and the samples that fall into them.

Sample no.	Group
1	Cu slag
2	non-slag
3	non-slag
4	non-slag
5	Cu slag
6	Cu slag
7	Cu slag
8	Cu slag
9	Cu slag
10	Cu slag
11	Cu slag
12	Cu slag
13	Cu slag
14	Cu slag
15	Cu slag
16	Cu slag
17	Cu slag
18	Cu slag
19	Cu slag
20	Cu slag
21	Cu slag
22	Cu slag
23	Cu slag
24	Cu slag
25	Cu slag
26	Cu slag
27	non-slag
28	Cu slag
29	Cu slag
30	Cu slag
31	Cu slag
32	Cu slag
33	Cu slag

Table 2. Samples assigned to groups. (Page 214)

Addendum to Investigation of Mongolian Slag by Jeffrey Speakman

Copper rarely occurs in native form but instead is primarily found in nature in other forms, such as chalcopyrite ($CuFeS_2$) which accounts for about 50% of modern copper production. Copper in these ores typically averages 0.6 %. In Mongolia most copper is derived from Porphyry copper deposits. These are copper ore bodies that are associated with porphyritic intrusive rocks and the fluids that accompany them during the transition and cooling from magma to rock. Porphyry orebodies typically contain between 0.4 and 1 % copper. In order to concentrate the copper in chalcopyrite and porphyritic ores, it is necessary to employ an extractive process such as smelting. At this end of this process one is left with copper that can then be used for making tools, etc. and a slag that contains the unwanted materials. Copper slag is typically enriched in iron, silica, and aluminum, and other elements. Depending on the efficiency of the smelting technology, copper will be present in weight percent quantities.

Below is a comparison of data published by Maldonado and Rehren (2009) and data generated by Watson for the Khyadag slags. As can be seen from the table and accompanying figures, the Khyadag slag quite similar to that from Mexico. Based on the presence of copper in the Khyadag ores there is little doubt that these samples are slag resulting from copper production.

Sample	SiO_2 (%)	Al_2O_3 (%)	FeO (%)	CaO (%)	MgO (%)	Na_2O (%)	K_2O (%)	P_2O_5 (%)	SO_3 (%)	CuO (%)
1-1c	34.1	7.20	49.7	0.63	1.88	0.36	0.92	0.05	0.13	2.41
1-2b	32.4	10.86	46.9	1.46	2.06	0.56	0.82	0.11	0.27	1.29
1-4a	35.0	9.65	43.7	1.72	2.30	0.61	1.11	0.07	0.26	1.48
1-4c	35.2	6.40	50.3	2.44	1.62	0.58	0.82	0.09	0.59	0.73
2-1b	40.0	3.44	46.2	4.29	0.61	0.56	0.50	0.01	0.24	1.44

Sample	SiO_2 (%)	Al_2O_3 (%)	Fe2O3 (%)	CaO (%)	MgO (%)	Na_2O (%)	K_2O (%)	P_2O_5 (%)	SO_3 (%)	CuO (%)
Khyadag1_1_1	22.7	10.3	51.7	4.3	2.1		1.2	0.7	0.6	6.0
Khyadag1_2_1	27.9	13.5	40.8	4.5	2.6	1.4	1.8	0.9	1.1	4.6
Khyadag1_3	20.5	10.6	49.7	4.4	2.3	1.6	1.6	0.7	1.0	6.3
Khyadag1_4_1	18.2	9.6	54.1	3.9	2.3	1.3	1.2	1.0	1.4	6.2
Khyadag1_5	20.8	9.9	56.5	3.5	1.9	0.9	1.1	0.7	0.7	3.6

Table 3. Bulk element composition of "Platy" Copper slag from Mexico (XRF data reported in Maldonado and Rehren 2009) compared to 5 SEM-EDS analyses of Khyadag sample 1. Note that Maldonado and Rehren report iron as FeO, whereas Watson reported values for the Khyadag slag as Fe2O3. To convert FeO to Fe2O3 multiply the FeO values by 1.1114. (Page 215

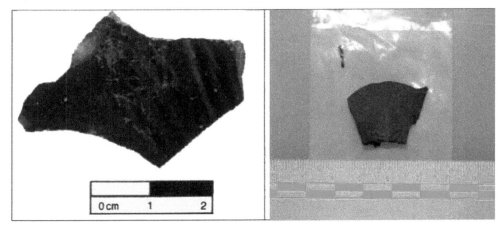

Figure 1. Left: Example of a platy slag fragment from Mexico (Maldonado and Rehren 2009). Right: Khyadag sample 1.

MCI6249   Khyadag slag   Sample 2

Mass 4.0 g

Spectrum	Na2O	MgO	Al2O3	SiO2	P2O5	SO3	ClO	K2O	CaO	Fe2O3	CuO
khyadag2n_1_1	2.7	2.5	20.8	53.4	0.6	0.6	0.2	2.1	6.4	9.8	0.0
khyadag2n_2_1	2.4	2.8	22.6	50.5	0.5	0.6	0.2	2.2	6.6	10.7	0.0
khyadag2n_3_1	2.8	2.9	23.2	50.6	0.6	0.6	0.3	2.2	6.2	9.6	0.1
khyadag2n_4_1	2.5	2.9	22.3	52.0	0.7	0.6	0.2	2.4	5.8	9.6	0.0
khyadag2n_5_1	1.3	3.6	23.6	47.2	0.8	0.6	0.0	1.9	8.0	11.6	0.3

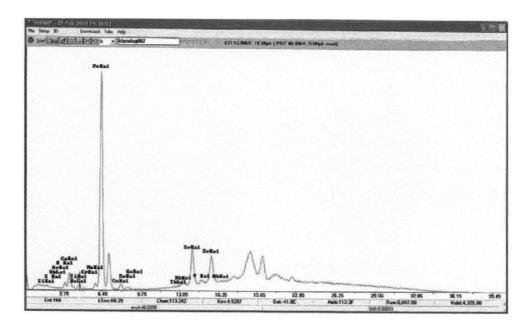

Mass 7.8 g

Spectrum	Na2O	MgO	Al2O3	SiO2	P2O5	SO3	ClO	K2O	CaO	Fe2O3	CuO
khyadag3_1_1	0.6	1.1	6.0	83.4	0.6	0.5	0.2	1.0	2.0	4.2	0.2
khyadag3_2_1	0.9	1.5	8.3	78.7	0.7	0.4	0.2	1.3	2.4	4.4	0.7
khyadag3_3_1	1.2	1.4	7.3	73.9	2.6	0.5	0.4	1.4	5.1	5.8	0.2
khyadag3_4_1	0.8	1.6	8.8	75.0	1.0	0.4	0.3	1.4	3.2	7.0	0.1
khyadag3_5_1	0.7	1.7	8.2	73.6	2.3	0.4	0.2	1.3	4.8	6.0	0.4

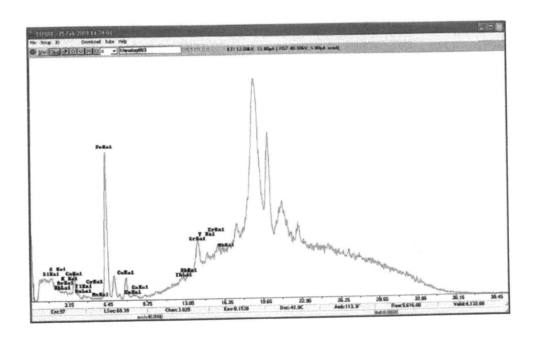

Deer Stone Project Radiocarbon Dates from Deer Stone and Khirigsuur Sites in Khovsgol, Arkhangai, and Bayan Ulgii Aimags, 2003-2009

site / feature	location/year	sample no.	material	uncorrected	calib (2-sig)
Ulaan Tolgoi DS4 S-17	Erkhel / 2003	B-182958 AMS	charcoal	2170 ± 40 BP	BP 2320-2050
Ulaan Tolgoi DS4 S-7	Erkhel / 2003	B-182959 AMS	charcoal	2930 ± 40 BP	BP 3220-2950
Ulaan Tolgoi DS4 F1	Erkhel / 2004	B-193738 AMS	bone coll.	2530 ± 40 BP	BP 2750-2470
Ulaan Tolgoi DS4 F2	Erkhel / 2004	B-193739 AMS	bone coll.	2950 ± 40 BP	BP 3240-2970
Ulaan Tolgoi DS4 F3	Erkhel / 2004	B-193740 AMS	bone coll.	2810 ± 40 BP	BP 2990-2800
Ulaan Tolgoi DS4, F5	Erkhel / 2005	B-207205 RAD	bone coll.	2790 ± 70 BP	BP 3220-2800
Ulaan Tolgoi DS4, F6	Erkhel / 2005	B-207206 RAD	bone coll.	2740 ± 70 BP	BP 3150-2780
Ulaan Tolgoi DS5, T1	Erkhel / 2002	B-169296 AMS	charcoal	2090 ± 40 BP	BP 2150-1960
Ulaan Tolgoi DS5, F1	Erkhel / 2005	B-215694 AMS	tooth coll.	2800 ± 40 BP	BP 2980-2790
Ulaan Tolgoi DS5, F2	Erkhel / 2006	B-222535 AMS	tooth coll.	2830 ± 40 BP	BP 3050-2850
Ulaan Tolgoi M1, F1	Erkhel / 2005	B-207209 AMS	bone coll.	1880 ± 40 BP	BP 1900-1720
Ulaan Tolgoi M1, F2	Erkhel / 2005	B-215692 AMS	tooth coll.	2860 ± 40 BP	BP 3080-2870
Ulaan Tolgoi M1, F2	Erkhel / 2005	B-215644 AMS	charcoal	2980 ± 40 BP	BP 3310-3000
Ulaan Tolgoi M1, F3	Erkhel / 2005	B-215693 AMS	tooth coll.	2950 ± 60 BP	BP 3320-2940
Nukhtiin Am DS1/2, F1	Galt / 2006	B-222534 AMS	tooth coll.	2830 ± 40 BP	BP 3050-2850
Evdt 2 DS 2 Circ. feat.	Evdt Valley	B-215643 AMS	charcoal	3030 ± 40 BP	BP 3350-3090
Tsatstain Kh DS1,F1	Tsaagan / 2005	B-207208 AMS	tooth coll.	2920 ± 40 BP	BP 3160-2920
Tsatstain Kh DS1,F2	Tsaagan / 2005	B-207207 AMS	tooth coll.	3000 ± 40 BP	BP 3330-3060
Urt Bulagyn KYR1-21	Khanuy / 2006	B-222532 AMS	tooth coll.	2780 ± 50 BP	BP 2980-2770
Urt Bulagyn KYR1-22	Khanuy / 2006	B-222533 AMS	tooth coll.	2790 ± 40 BP	BP 2970-2780
2006-2007 dates:					
Nukhtiin Am Md1,F1	Galt / 2006	B-240685 AMS	tooth coll.	2630 ± 40 BP	BP 2790-2730
Tsagaan Asga K1 F1	Sagsai / 2007	B-240686 AMS	bone coll.	130 ± 40 BP	BP 280-0*
Khogorgo-3, Md1	Shishged 2007	B-240687 AMS	tooth coll.	3450 ± 40 BP	BP 3830-3620
Khushuugiin Devs F1	Erkhel / 2006	B-222536 AMS	tooth coll.	2140 ± 40 BP	BP 2320-1990*
Khushuugiin Devs. F2	Erkhel / 2007	B-240688 AMS	tooth coll.	2450 ± 40 BP	BP 2720-2350
Khushuugiin Devs. F3	Erkhel / 2007	B-240689 AMS	tooth coll.	2680 ± 40 BP	BP 2860-2740
Khushuugiin Devs. F1	Erkhel / 2007	B-243716 AMS	tooth coll.	2410 ± 40 BP	BP 2700-2640%
Khyadag E. DS pav.7	Erkhel / 2007	B-240690 AMS	bone/tooth	2610 ± 40 BP	BP 2770-2720
Hort Uzuur DS3	Hort Azuur/ 2006	B-222537 AMS	charcoal	2230 ± 40 BP	BP 2340-2140*
Hort Uzuur DS2,L2, F1	Hort Azuur/ 2007	B-240691 AMS	charcoal	2710 ± 40 BP	BP 2870-2750
Tsagaan Gol K2 F1	Tsengel / 2007	B-240692 AMS	tooth coll.	2140 ± 40 BP	BP 2300-2240#
Tsagaan Gol K3 F9	Tsengel / 2007	B-240693 AMS	tooth coll.	1740 ± 40 BP	BP 1730-1550
Tsagaan Gol K4, F11	Tsengel / 2007	B-243717 AMS	char.mtl	130 ± 40 BP	BP 280-0
Avtiin Fea.5 Sample 6	Shishged / 2007	B-242730 AMS	charcoal	2670 ± 40 BP	BP 2850-2740
2008 dates:					
Khoton 333 F18	Bayan Ulgii/2008	B-246610 AMS	charcoal	2840 ± 40 BP	BP 3070-2860
Tsagaan Asga F3	Bayan Ulgii/2008	B-246611 AMS	charcoal	2850 ± 40 BP	BP 3070-2860
Tsagaan Asga F4	Bayan Ulgii/2008	B-246612 AMS	charcoal	3000 ± 40 BP	BP 3330-3070
On Khad Khushuu	Bayan Ulgii/2008	B-246613 AMS	tooth coll.	2930 ± 40 BP	BP 3220-2960
Bor Hujiriin A1, F2	Tsagaan/2008	B-246614 AMS	tooth coll.	2640 ± 40 BP	BP 2790-2730
Bor Hujiriin A1, F4	Tsagaan/2008	B-246615 AMS	bone coll.	680 ± 40 BP	BP 680-630†*
Bor Hujiriin A2, F1	Tsagaan/2008	B-246616 RAD	charcoal	2670 ± 50 BP	BP 2860-2740
Khuush. Gol F2	Erkhel/2008	B-246617 AMS	tooth coll.	2750 ± 40 BP	BP 2940-2760
Khushuug. Gol A3, F3	Erkhel/2008	B-246618 AMS	tooth coll.	2910 ± 40 BP	BP 3210-2940
Khushuug. Gol F6	Erkhel/2008	B-246619 AMS	charcoal	2850 ± 40 BP	BP 3070-2860

References

Allard, F., and Erdenebaatar, D. 2005. Khirigsuurs, ritual and mobility in the Bronze Age of Mongolia. *Antiquity* 79: 547–63. https://doi.org/10.1017/S0003598X00114498

____, D. Erdenebaatar, S. Olsen, A. Caralla, and E. Maggiore. 2007. Ritual and horses in Bronze Age and present-day Mongolia: Some preliminary observations from the Khanuy Valley. In *Social orders and social landscapes,* edited by Laura Popova, Charles Hartley, and Adam Smith, pp. 151–167. Newcastle upon Tyne: Cambridge Scholars Press.

Arutiunov, S.A., and Dorian Sergeev. 1969. *Ancient Cultures of the Asiatic Eskimos: The Uelen Cemetery.* Institute of Ethnography. Moscow: Nauk.

____. 1975. *Problems of the Ethnic History of the Bering Sea.* The Ekven Cemetery. Institute of Ethnography. Moscow: Nauk.

____, and William W. Fitzhugh. 1988. Prehistory of Siberia and the Bering Sea. In *Crossroads of Continents: Cultures of Siberia and Alaska*, edited by William W. Fitzhugh and Aron L. Crowell, pp. 117-139. Washington: Smithsonian Institution Press.

Баярсайхан Ж. 2009. Буган чулуун хөшөө, хиригсүүрийн тахилгын байгууламжийн судалгааны асуудалд. Nomadic Heritage Studies. Museum Natonale Mongoli. Tomus IX, Fasc 6. УБ.,2009. т. 41-62.

____. 2017. Монголын умард нутгийн буган хөшөөд [Mongolyn umard nutgijn bugan hushuud]. Ulaanbaatar.

Beaubien, Harriet F., and Basiliki Vicky Karass. 2005. Conservation Report SCMRE 5974, 2005 Field Season, Joint Mongolian-Smithsonian Deer Stone Project, Hovsgol Aimag, Mongolia. In *Mongolia Deer Stone Project: Field Report* 2005, pp. 57-66. Arctic Studies Center, Smithsonian Museum and National Museum of Mongolian History. Washington and Ulaanbaatar.

____, B.V. Karas, and W. Fitzhugh. 2007. Documenting Mongolia's Deer Stones: Application of Three-Dimensional Digital Imaging Technology to Preservation. In *Scientific Research on the Sculptural Arts of Asia,* edited by J.G. Douglas, P. Jett, and J. Winter. Pp. 133-142. Archetype Publications and Freer Gallery of Art, Smithsonian Institution.

Bokovenko, Nikolai. 2006. Th Emergence of the Tagar Culture. *Antiquity* 80: 860-879.

Broderick, L.G., J.L. Houle, O. Seitsonen, and J. Bayarsaikhan. 2014a. The Mystery of the Missing Caprines: Stone Circles at the Great Khirigsuur in the Khanuy Valley. *Studia Archaeologica* 34(13): 164-171. Ulaanbaatar.

____, O. Seitsonen, Bayarsaikhan, J., and J-L. Houle. 2014b. Lambs to the slaughter: a zooarchaeological investigation of stone circles in Mongolia. *International Journal of Osteoarchaeology* 26 (3): 537-543. https://doi.org/10.1002/oa.2425

Bunker, Emma C., Bruce Chatwin, and Ann E. Farkas. 1970. *Animal Style Art from East to West.* The Asia Society. New York.

____, James C.Y. Watt, and Zhixin Sun. 1997. *Nomadic Art of the Eastern Eurasian Steppes: the Eugene V. Thaw and Other New York Collections.* The Metropolitan Museum of Art and Yale University Press. New York and London.

Chard, Chester. 1958. The Western Roots of Eskimo Culture. In *Actas del XXXII Congresso Internacional de Americanistas*, San Jose, Costa Riva, 2. Costa Rica.

____. 1974. *Northeast Asia in Prehistory.* Madison: University of Wisconsin Press.

Chernetsov, V.N. 1935. Drevnyaya Primorskaya Kul'tura na Poloustrove Yamal {An Ancient Maritime Culture of the Yaman Peninsula]. *Sovetskaya Etnografiya* 4-5:109-133.

____, and W. Mozhinskaya. 1974. *Prehistory of Western Siberia. In Anthropology of the North. Translations from Russian Sources.* Henry N. Michael, ed. Montreal and London: Arctic Institute of North America and Queen's McGill University Press.

Childs-Johnson, Elizabeth. 1998. The Metamorphic Image: A Predominant Theme in the Ritual Art of Shang China. *Bulletin of the Museum of Far Eastern Antiquities* 70:5-171.

Chinese Archaeology. 2017. The Excavation of the Huahaizi No.3 Site in Qinghe County, Xinjiang. *Chinese Archaeology* 17(1): 151-162. https://doi.org/10.1515/char-20170012; http://www.china-embassy.org/eng/zt/Xinjiang/t1068732.htm

Chlenova, Nataliia. 1984. *Olennye kamni kak istoricheskii istochnik (na primere olennykh kamnei Severnogo Kavkaza)* [Deer stones as an historical source (based on examples from the deer stones of the Northern Caucasus)]. Novosibirsk: Nauka, 1984.

Chugunov, Konstantin, Hermann Parzinger, and Anatoli Nagler. 2003. *Der skythische Fürstengrabhügel von Aržan 2 in Tuva. Vorbericht der russisch-deutschen Ausgrabungen 2000-2002.* Eurasia Antiqua 9:113-162.

Clark, J. K. (2014). *Modeling Late Prehistoric and Early Historic pastoral adaptation in Northern Mongolia's Darkhad Depression.* Unpublished Ph.D. dissertation. University of Pittsburgh.

Collins, Henry B. 1937. *Archaeology of St. Lawrence Island, Alaska.* Smithsonian Miscellaneous Collections 96(1). Washington: Smithsonian Institution.

_____. 1951. Origins and Antiquity of the Eskimo. *Annual Report of the Smithsonian Institution for 1950.* Pp. 423-467. Washington: Smithsonian Institution.

_____. 1959. Eskimo Culture. *In Enciclopedia Universale del'Arte,* Instituto per la Collaborazione Culturale. Venezia, Rome.

_____. 1971. Composite masks: Chinese and Eskimo. *Anthropologica n.s.* 13(102):271-278.

_____. 1973. Eskimo Art. *In The Far North. 2,000 years of American Eskimo and Indian Art,* ed by Henry B. Collins, Frederica de Laguna, Edmund Carpenter, and Peter Stone. Washington, DC: National Gallery of Art.

Cunliffe, Barry. 2019. *The Scythians: Nomad Warriors of the Steppe.* Oxford University Press.

De Priest, Paula. 2003. Traditional knowledge of lichens by Mongolia's Dukha reindeer herders. In *Mongolia's Arctic connections: the Hovsgol deer stone project 2001-2002 field report,* pp. 33-36. Arctic Studies Center, Smithsonian Institution.

_____. 2005. Tsaabug, tsaahag, tsaatan: an ethno-ecology of Mongolia's Dukha reindeer herders. In *The Deer Stone Project: Anthropological Studies in Mongolia 2002-2004,* edited by W. Ftizhugh, pp. 99-106.

Dikov, Nikolai. 1958. *Bronzovyi vek Zabaikal'ya.* Ulan-Ude.

_____. 1979. *Ancient Cultures of Northeastern Asia.* Moscow: Nauk. (in Russian)

Dumond, Don, and Richard Bland. 1996. Holocene Prehistory in the *Northernmost North Pacific.*

Journal of World Prehistory 9(4): 401-451.

Esin Yu.N., J. Magail, H. Rousseliere, and Ph. Walter. 2014. Les peintures dans l'art pariéetal de la culture Okuniev. *Bulletin du Musée d'Anthropologie préhistorique de Monaco,* No. 54: 163–183.

Farkas, Ann. 1975. *From the Lands of the Scythians: Ancient Treasures from the Museums of the U.S.S.R., 3000 B.C.-100 B.C.* Metropolitan Museum of Art, the Los Angeles County Museum of Art.

Fedorova, Nataliya, Pavel A. Kosintsev, and W. Fitzhugh. 1998. *"Gone into the Hills": Culture of the Northwestern Yamal Coast Population in the Iron Age.* Russian Academy of Sciences, Ural Division, Institute of History and Archaeology; Institute of Plant an Animal Ecology; Arctic Studies Center, Smithsonian Institution. Ekaterinburg Publishers. (In Russian)

Fitzhugh, William W. 1974. Ground Slates in the Scandinavian Younger Stone Age with reference to circumpolar Maritime adaptations. *Proceedings of the Prehistoric Society* 40:45 58.

_____. 1975. A comparative approach to northern maritime adaptations. In: W. Fitzhugh (ed.): *Prehistoric maritime adaptations of the circumpolar zone,* pp. 339 386. International Congress of Anthropological and Ethnological Sciences, Symposium volume. The Hague: Mouton.

_____. 1988. Comparative Art of the North Pacific Rim. In *Crossroads of Continents: Cultures of Siberia and Alaska,* edited by William W. Fitzhugh and Aron Crowell, pp. 294-312. Washington: Smithsonian Institution Press.

_____. 1998. Searching for the Grail: Virtual Archeology in Yamal and Circumpolar Theory. *Publications of the National Museum, Ethnographic Series,* 18:99-118. Copenhagen: Danish National Museum.

_____. 2002. Yamal to Greenland: Global Connections in Circumpolar Archaeology. In *Archaeology: the Widening Debate,* edited by Barry Cunliffe, Wendy Davies, and Coliin Renfrew, pp. 91-144. Oxford University Press.

_____. 2009a. Pre-Scythian Khirigsuurs, Deer Stone Art, and Bronze Age Cultural Intensification in Northern Mongolia. In *New Directions in Steppe Archaeology: the Emergence of Complex Societies in the Third to First Millennium BCE,* edited by B. Hanks and K. Linduff, pp. 378-411. Cambridge: Cambridge University Press.

_____. 2009b. Stone Shamans and Flying Deer of Northern Mongolia: Deer Goddess of Siberia or Chimera of the Steppe? *Arctic Anthropology* 46(1-2):72-88.

_____. 2009c. The Mongolian Deer Stone-Khirigsuur Complex: Dating and Organization of a Late Bronze Age Menagerie. In *Current Archaeological Research in Mongolia*, edited by Jan Bemmann, Hermann Parzinger, Ernst Pohl, and Damdinsuren Tseveendorzh. Pp. 183-199. Bonn: Vor- und Fruhgeschichtliche Archeologie , Rheinische Friedrich-Wilhelms-Universitat.

_____. 2014a. Mongolian Deer Stones, European Menhirs, and Canadian Arctic Inuksuit: Collective Memory and the Function of Northern Monument Traditions. *Journal of Archaeological Method and Theory* 24(1):149-187. doi:10.1007/s10816-017-9328-0

_____. 2014b. The Ipiutak spirit-scape: an archaeological phenomenon. In *The Foragers of Point Hope. The biology and archaeology of humans on the edge of the Alaskan Arctic*. Edited by C.E. Hilton, B.M. Auerbach, and L.W. Cowgill, pp. 266-290. Cambridge University Press.

_____, J. Bayarsaikhan, and Marsh, P. (eds.). 2005. *The Deer Stone Project: Anthropological Studies in Mongolia 2002-2004*. Smithsonian Arctic Studies Center and National Museum of Mongolian History.

_____, _____. 2011. Mapping Ritual Landscapes in Bronze Age Mongolia and Beyond: Interpreting the Ideoscape of the Deer Stone-Khirigsuur Complex. In *Mapping Mongolia: Situating Mongolia in the World from Geologic Time to the Present*, edited by P. Sabloff and F. Hebert, pp. 166-192. Philadelphia: University of Pennsylvania Museum of Archaeology and Anthropology.

_____, _____. 2021. *Khyadag and Zunii Gol: Animal Art and the Bronze to Iron Age Transition in Mongolia*. Vestnik 66(3):908-933. St. Petersburg. (W. Fitzhugh and J. Bayarsaikhan)

_____, Julie Hollowell, and Aron Crowell (eds.). 2009. *Gifts from the Ancestors: Ancient Ivories from Bering Strait*. 328 pp. Princeton: Princeton University Art Museum. Distributed by Yale University Press.

_____, Richard Kortum, and J. Bayarsaikhan. 2013. *Rock Art and Archaeology: Investigating Ritual Landscape in the Mongolian Altai 2012*. Arctic Studies Center: National Museum of Natural History, Smithsonian Institution. http://www.mnh.si.edu/arctic/html/pdf/MongoliaFieldReport2012_FINAL%20April%2023.pdf

Flegontov, P., Altınışık, N.E., Changmai, P. et al. 2019. Palaeo-Eskimo genetic ancestry and the peopling of Chukotka and North America. *Nature* 570, 236–240 (2019). https://doi.org/10.1038/s41586-019-1251-y

Frohlich, Bruno, and N. Bazarsad. 2005. Burial Mounds in Hovsgol Aimag, Northern Mongolia: Preliminary Results from 2003 and 2004. In: Fitzhugh et al. *The Deer Stone Project: Anthropological Studies in Mongolian 2002-2004*, pp. 57-88. Washington and Ulaanbaatar.

_____, T. Amgalantugs, J. Littleton, D. Hunt, J. Hinton, E. Batchatar, M. Dickson, T. Frohlich, and K. Goler. 2008. Bronze Age burial mounds (Khirigsuurs) in the Hovsgol Aimag, Mongolia: A reconstruction of biological and social histories. *Studia Archaeologica Instituti Archaeologici Academiae Scientarum Mongolicae* VI, XXVI, Fasc. 6. Ulaanbaatar, Mongolia.

_____, T. Amgalantugs, J. Littleton, D. Hunt, J. Hinton, and K. Goler. 2009. Bronze Age burial mounds in Khovsgol Aimag, Mongolia. In *Current archaeological research in Mongolia*, edited by J. Bemmann, H. Parzinger, E. Pohl, and D. Tseveendorj, pp. 99–115. Bonn: Rheinische Friedrich-Wilhelms-Universität.

_____. Frohlich, B., et. al. 2010. Theories and Hypotheses Pertaining to Bronze Age Khirigsuurs in Hovsgol Aimag, Mongolia In *American-Mongolian Deer Stone Project: Field Report 2009*, pp.196-210. Arctic Studies Center, Smithsonian.

Goulden, C. E., T. Sitnikova, B. Boldgiv, and J. Gelhaus (Editors). (2006). *The Geology, Biodiversity and Ecology of Lake Hövsgöl (Mongolia)*. 526 pp. Backhuys Publ., Amsterdam.

Gryazhnov, M. P. 1950. *Pervyi Pazyrykskii kurgan*. Leningrad: Iskusstvo.

_____. 1978. Cayan-Altai Olenni Kamni. *Problemi Arkheologii* vol?: 222–231. Leningrad: University of Leningrad.

_____. 1980. *Arzhan-Tarskii Kurgan Ranneskivskogo Vremeni*. Leningrad: Nauka.

_____. 1981. Монументальное искусство

273

на заре скифо-сибирских культур в степной Евразии Контакты и взаимодействия древних культур (тез. докл. научн. конф.). Ленинград.

_____. 1984. *Der Großkurgan von Arzan in Tuva, Südsibirien.* Materialien zur Allgemeinen und Vergleichenden Archäologie 23 (München, 1984).

Haas, Randall, Todd A. Surovell, and Matthew J. O'Brien (2019) Dukha mobility in a constructed environment: Past camp use predicts future use in the Mongolian Taiga. *American Antiquity* 84:215-233.

Hanks, Brian K. 2010. Archaeology of the Eurasian steppes and Mongolia. *Annual Review of Anthropology* 39: 469–486.

Hatakeyama, Tei. 2002. The Tumulus and Stag Stones at Shiebar-kul in Xinjiang, China. *Newsletter of Steppe Archaeology*, 13: 1–8.

Macaulay, George Campbell. 1904. *The History of Herodotus.* Book IV. Translated by George Rawlinson. http://classics.mit.edu//Herodotus/history.html

Honeychurch, W. 2015. *Inner Asia and the spatial politics of empire: archaeology, mobility, and culture contact.* New York: Springer. http://dx.doi.org/10.1007/978-1-4939-1815-7

Houle, Jean-Luc. 2016. Bronze Age Mongolia. *Oxford Handbook Archaeology of East Asia.* DOI: 10.1093/oxfordhb/9780199935413.013.20

Jacobson, Esther. 1993. *The Deer Goddess of Ancient Siberia: A Study in the Ecology of Belief.* Leiden, New York, Kuhn: E. J. Brill

_____. 1995. *The Art of the Scythians: the Interpenetration of Cultures at the Edge of the Hellenic World.* Leiden: E. J. Brill.

_____. 2002. Petroglyphs and the Qualification of Bronze Age Mortuary Archaeology. *Archaeology, Ethnology, and Anthropology of Eurasia* 3(11): 32-47.

_____. 2001. Cultural Riddles: Stylized Deer and Deer Stones of the Mongolian Altai. *Bulletin of the Asian Institute*, New Series 15:31-56.

_____. 2015. *The Hunter, the Stag, and the Mother of Animals: Image, Monument, and Landscape in Ancient North Asia.* Oxford: Oxford University Press.

Jettmar, Karl. 1994. Body-Painting and the Roots of the Scytho-Siberian Animal Style. In: B. Genito (ed.), *The Archaeology of the Steppes: Methods and Strategies.* Papers from an international sympo-

sium held in Naples 9–12, November 1992. Istituto Universitario Orientale, Dipartimento di Studi Asiatici, Series minor 44 (Napoli 1994:3–15).

Khudiakov, Iulii Sergeevich. 1987. Khereksury i olennye kamni [Khirigsuurs and deer stones]. In: *Arkheologiia, etnografiia i antropologiia Mongolii*, pp. 136–62. Novosibirsk: Nauka.

Kovalev, A.A., D. Erdenebaatar, and I.V. Rukavishnikova. 2016. A Ritual Complex with Deer Stones at Uushigiin Uvur/Ulaan Uushig, Mongolia: Composition and Construction Stages Based on 2013 Excavations. *Archaeology, Ethnology, and Anthropology of Eurasia* 44(1): 82–92. (in Russian) DOI: 10.17746/1563-0110.2016.44.1.082-092

Kubarev, V.D. 2009. Two Bronze Age Steles in Gorny Altai [Deer Stones in the Culture of Eurasian Nomads]. *Archaeology, Ethnology and Anthropology of Eurasia* 37(1): 34.

Larsen, Helge, and Frohlich Rainey. 1948. *Ipiutak and the Arctic Whale Hunting Culture. Anthropological Papers of the American Museum of Natural History* 42. New York: American Museum of Natural History.

Lazzerini, Nicholas, Antoine Zazzo, Aurélie Coulon, Charlotte Marchina, Vincent Bernard, Mathilde Cervel, Denis Fiorillo, Dominique Joly, Camille Noûs, Tsagaan Turbat, and Sébastien Lepetz. 2020 Season of death of domestic horses deposited in a ritual complex from Bronze Age Mongolia: Insights from oxygen isotope time-series in tooth enamel. *Journal of Archaeological Science: Reports 32.* https://doi.org/10.1016/j.jasrep.2020.102387

Lebedintsev, A. E. 1990. *Early Coastal Cultures of Northwestern Priokhot'ye.* Moscow: Nauk. (in Russian)

LeGrand, Sophie. 2006. The Emergence of the Karasuk Culture. *Antiquity 80*: 843-879.

Lepetz S., A. Zazzo, V. Bernard, S. de Larminat, J. Magail, and J.-O. Gantulga. 2019. Customs, rites, and sacrifices relating to a mortuary complex in Late Bronze Age Mongolia (Tsatsyn Ereg, Arkhangai). *Anthropozoologica* 54 (15):151-177. https://doi.org/10.5252/anthropozoologica2019v54a15. http://anthropozoologica.com/54/15

Littleton, J., B. Floyd, B. Frohlich, M. Dickson, T. Amgalantogs, S. Karstens, and K. Pearlstein (2012). Taphonomic analysis of Bronze Age burials in Mongolian khirigsuurs. *Journal of Archaeological*

Science 39: 3361–3370.

Magail, J. 2008. Tsatsiin Ereg, site majeur du début du Ier millénaire en Mongolie. *Bulletin d'anthropologie préhistorique de Monaco* 48: 107–21.

———. 2015. Les stèles ornées de Mongolie dites 'pierres à cerfs', de la fin de l'âge du Bronze, in Rodriguez, G. & Marchesi, H. (ed.) *Statues-menhirs et pierres levées du Néolithique à aujourd'hui*: 89–101. Saint-Pons-de-Thomières: Direction régionale des affaires culturelles Languedoc-Roussillon Groupe Archéologique du Saint-Ponais.

Makarewicz, C.A., C. Winter-Schuh, H. Byerly, and J.-L. Houle. 2018. Isotopic evidence for ceremonial provisioning of Late Bronze Agekhirigsuurs with horses from diverse geographiclocales. *Quaternary International* 476:70- 81. https://doi.org/10.1016/j.quaint.2018.02.030

Miniaev, Sergei. 2013. On the Interpretation of Certain Images on Deer Stones. *Silk Road* 11:54-59.

Naiden, F.S. 2013. *Smoke Signals for the Gods: Ancient Greek Sacrifice from the Archaic through Roman Periods*. Oxford; New York: Oxford University Press.

Nef, Ed. 2020. *Life Out Loud. A Memoir of Countless Adventures and No Regrets*. Ed Nef Foundation. Arlington Va.

Novgorodova, E. A. 1989. *Drevnaya Mongoliya. Nekotoriye Problemi Khronologii e Ethnokulturnoi Estorii [Ancient Mongolia. Some Problems in Chronology and Ethnocultural History]*. Moscow: Nauka

Okladnikov, Alexei P. 1954. Olennyi kamen b reki Ivolgi [A deer stone from the Ivolga River]. *Sovetskaia arkheologiia* 19:207–20.

———. 1981. *Ancient Art of the Amur Region*. Leningrad: Aurora.

Ольховский.В.С. 2005. Монументальная скульптура населения западной части евразийских степей эпохи раннего железа. Москва.

Olson, Sandra L. 2006. *Early Horse Domestication: Weighing the Evidence*. BAR International 1560: 81.

Orekhov, A.A. 1987 *An Early Culture of the Northwest Bering Sea*. Moscow: Nauk. (in Russian; English edition translated by Richard Bland)

Pitulko, Vladimir V. 1991. Archaeological Data on the Maritime Cultures of the West Arctic. *Fennoscandia Archaeologica* 8:23-34.

———. 2003. An Early Holocene sitge in the Siberian High Arctic. *Arctic Anthropology* 30(1):13-21.

———, P.A. Nikolsky, E.Y. Girya, A.E. Basilyan, V.E. Tumskoy, S.A. Koulakov, S.N. Astakhov, E.Y. Pavlpova, and M.A. Anisimov. 2004. The Yana RHS site: humans in the Arctic before the Last Glaciation. *Science* 303: 52–56.

———, E.Y. Pavlova, P. Nikolskiy, and V.V. Ivanova. 2012. The oldest art of the Eurasian Arctic: personal ornaments and symbolic objects from Yana RHS, Arctic Siberia. *Antiquity* 86(333):642–659.

Polosmak, N. V. 2000. Tattoos in the Pazyryk World. *Archaeology, Ethnology, and Anthropology of Eurasia* 4(4): 95–102.

Powers, Roger, and Richard H. Jordan. 1990. Human Biogeography and Climate Change in Siberia and Arctic North America in the Fourth and Fifth Millennia B.P. *Transactions of the Royal Society of London* A330: 665-670.

Qu, Feng. 2013. Qu, F. (2013). *The Legacy of Shamans? Structural and Cognitive Perspectives of Prehistoric Symbolism in the Bering Strait region*. Doctor's Dissertation, Department of Anthropology, University of Alaska Fairbanks.

———. 2014. Eskimo Art Prototypes in the Chinese Neolithic: a Comparison of Okvik/Old Bering Sea and Liangzhu Ritual Art. *Sibirica* 13(3): 45-78. DOI: https://doi.org/10.3167/sib.2014.130303

———. 2015. Body Metaphor or Second Body: Learning from Ancestral Cosmologists. *Coreopsis: Journal of Myth and Theatre*. Winter/Spring 2014/2015. C:\Users\fitzhugh\Documents\my files\papers\Feng Qu 2015 - Body Metaphor or Second Body Coreopsis.mht

———. 2017. Ivory versus Antler: A Reassessment of Binary Structuralism in the Study of Prehistoric Eskimo Cultures. *Arctic Anthropology* 54(1): 90–109.

———. 2021. *An exploration of prehistoric ontologies in the Bering Strait region*. Cambridge: Cambridge Scholars Publishing.

Rogers, J. Daniel. 2019. The complexity of nomadic empires." *Social Evolution & History*, 18, (2) 145–162. https://doi.org/10.30884/seh/2019.02.08.

Rudenko, Sergei I. 1970. *Frozen Tombs of Siberia: the Pazyryk Burials of Iron Age Horsemen*. Berkeley: University of California Press.

Savinov, D. G. 1994. *Deer Stone Cultures of Central Eurasia.* St. Petersburg.

Schuster, Carl. 1951. Survival of the Eurasiatic Animal Style in Modern Alaskan Eskimo Art. *Selected papers of the 29th Congress of Americanists.* New York, 1949. Edited by Sol Tax, pp. 35-45. Chicago: University of Chicago Press.

Schuster, Carl, and Edmund Carpenter. 1986. *Materials for the Study of Social Symbolism in Ancient and Tribal Art: a Record of Tradition and Continuity.* 12 vols., edited and written by Edmund Carpenter, assisted by Lorraine Spiess, vol. 1(4). New York: Rock Foundation.

Sher, Yakov A. 1988. On the Sources of the Scythic Animal Style. *Artic Anthropology* Vol. 25, No. 2 (1988), pp. 47-60.

Sikora et. al. 2019. The population history of northeastern Siberia since the Pleistocene. *Nature,* 570, 182-188. https://doi.org/10.1038/s41586-019-1279-z

Song, Yaoliang. 1992. *The Deified Human Face Petroglyphs of Prehistoric China.* Hong Kong: Joint Publishing Company, Ltd.

_____. 1998. Prehistoric Human Face Petroglyphs of the North Pacific Region. *Arctic Studies Center Newsletter 6* (Supplement). National Museum of Natural History, Smithsonian Institution.

Takahama, S., T. Hayashi, K. Masanori, R. Matsubara, and D. Erdenebaatar. (2006). Preliminary Report of the Archaeological Investigations at Ulaan Uushig (Uushigiin Övör) in Mongolia. Kanazawa University (Japan). *Archaeological Bulletin* 28, 61–102.

Taylor, W.T. 2017a. Horse Demography and Use in Bronze Age Mongolia. *Quaternary International* 436(A): 270–82.

_____, T. Jargalan, B., Lowry, K., Clark, J., Tuvshinjargal, T. & Bayarsaikhan, J. 2017b. A Bayesian chronology for early domestic horse use in the Eastern Steppe. *Journal of Archaeological Science* 81: 49–58.

_____, S. Wilkin, J. Wright, M. Dee, M. Erdene, J. Clark, T. Tuvshinjargal, J. Bayarsaikhan, W. Fitzhugh, and N. Boivin. 2019. Radiocarbon Dating and Cultural Dynamics Across Mongolia's Early Pastoral Transition. *PLOS ONE* 14(11): Article-e0224241

_____, Julia Clark, Jamsranjav Bayarsaikhan, Tumurbaatar Tuvshinjargal, Jessica Thompson Jobe, William Fitzhugh, Richard Kortum, Robert N. Spengler III, Svetlana Shnaider, Frederik Valeur Seersholm, Isaac Hart, Nicholas Case, Shevan Wilkin, Jessica Hendy, Ulrike Thuering, Bryan Miller, Alicia R. Ventresca Miller, Andrea Picin, Nils Vanwezer, Franziska Irmer, Samantha Brown, Aida Abdykanova, Daniel R. Shultz, Victoria Pham, Michael Bunce, Katerina Douka, Emily Lena Jones, and Nicole Boivin. 2020a. Early Pastoral Economies and Herding Transitions in Eastern Eurasia. *Nature Scientific Reports 2020*, 10:1001. https://doi.org/10.1038/s41598-020-57735-y

_____, Marcello Fantoni, Charlotte Marchina, Sébastien Lepetz, Jamsranjav Bayarsaikhan, Jean-Luc Houle. Victoria Pham, and William Fitzhugh. 2020b. Horse Sacrifice and Butchery in Bronze Age Mongolia. *Journal of Archaeological Science: Reports* 31. 102313. https://doi.org/10.1016/j.jasrep.2020.102313

Tisskkin, Alexei A. 2020. Advancing Archaeological Research of the Mongolioan Altai through the Scientific Study of Deer Stones: New Discoveries from Buyant Valley. *Asian Perspectives* 59(2): 453-478.

Tishkin, A.A. and E.B. Shelenova. 2014. *The Use of «Deer» Stones in the Construction of Turkic Fencings of the Mongolian Altai.* Bernaul: Alai State University DOI 10.14258/izvasu(2014)4.1-37.

Tseveendorj, D., N. Urtnasan, A. Ochir, and G. Gongorjav (eds.). (1999). *Historical and cultural monuments of Mongolia.* Ulaanbaatar: Mongolian Academy of Humanities (in Mongolian).

Tsybiktarov, A. 2003: Central Asia in the Bronze and Early Iron Ages: Problems of Ethno-Cultural History of Mongolia and the Southern Trans-Baikal Region in the middle 2nd – early 1st Millennia BC. *Archaeology, Ethnology and Anthropology of Eurasia* 13, 2003, 80–97.

Turbat T., J. Bayarsaikhan, D. Batsukh, and N. Bayarkhuu. 2011. *Jargalantyn amny bugan khushuud [Deer Stones of Jargalant Am].* Ulaanbaatar: NOMKHUR.

Vainshtein, Sevyan I. 1972. *Ethnographic History of the Dukha.* Moscow: Nauka. (in Russian)

_____. 1980. *Nomads of South Siberia: The Pastoral Economies of Tuva.* Cambridge: Cambridge University Press.

_____. 1981 On the Distribution of the Reindeer Economy Among the Samoyed Peoples. *Congressus Quintus Internationalis Finno-Ugristarum* 8:118–123.

Van Straten, Folkert T. 1995. *Hierà Kalá: Images of Animal Sacrifice in Archaic and Classical Greece*. E. J. Brill. Leiden.

Varenov, Andrei V. 1998. Olennye kamni iz Vostochnogo Turkestana [Deer stones of Eastern Turkestan]. In: *Konferentsiia po pervobytnomu iskusstvu: Tezisy dokladov*. pp. 91–92. Kemerovo: Izd. Sibirskoi assotsiatsii issledovatelei pervobytnogo iskusstva pri KemGU.

Volkov, V. V. 1981 Olennye kamni Mongolii. Academy of Sciences, Moscow and Ulaanbaatar. Nauka (reprinted, Moscow 2002).

_____. 1995. Early Nomads of Mongolia. In: J. Davis-Kimball / V. A. Bashilov / L. T. Yablonski (eds.), *Nomads of the Eurasian Steppes in the Early Iron Age*, pp. 319-332. Berkeley: University of California Press.

Volkov, V. V., and A. E. Novgorodova. 1975 Olennye Kamni Uushgiin Overa (Mongolia). *Pervobytnaia arkheologiia Sibiri*. Pp. 78–84. Leningrad: Nauka.

Watson, J., M. Goodman, and J. Speakman. 2009. Smithsonian Museum Conservation Institute Slag Report for Finds from 2008 Deer Stone Project Field Season. Project no. 6249. Appendix 1 in *2009 Mongolia Field Report*. Arctic Studies Center. National Museum of Natural History, Smithsonian Institution.

Wright J. 2007. — Organizational principles of Khirigsuur monuments in the lower Egiin Gol valley, Mongolia. *Journal of Anthropological Archaeology* 26 (3): 350-365. https://doi.org/10.1016/j.jaa.2007.04.001

_____. 2014. Landscapes of inequality? A critique of monumental hierarchy in the Mongolian Bronze Age. *Asian Perspectives* 51 (2): 139-163.

_____. 2015. Inequality on the surface: horses, power, and practice in the Eurasian Bronze Age. In B. Arbuckle and S. McCarty (eds), *Animals and Inequality in the Ancient World*. Pp. 277-295. University Press of Colorado, Boulder.

_____. 2017. The honest labour of stone mounds: monuments of Bronze and Iron Age Mongolia as costly signals. *World Archaeology* 49(4): 547-567. https://doi.org/10.1080/00438243.2017.1360791

Zazzo A., S. Lepetz, S.J.O Gantulg, and J. MaGail. 2019. High precision dating of ceremonial activity around a large ritual complex in Late Bronze Age Mongolia. *Antiquity* 93 (367): 80-98. https://doi.org/10.15184/aqy.2018.175